The Entertainment Industry

The Entertainment Industry

Michael J. Haupert

Emerging Industries in the United States

Larry L. Duetsch, Series Editor

GREENWOOD PRESS
Westport, Connecticut • London

Library of Congress Cataloging-in-Publication Data

Haupert, Michael.
    The entertainment industry / Michael Haupert.
        p.   cm. — (Emerging industries in the United States, ISSN 1539–7289)
    Includes bibliographical references and index.
    ISBN 0–313–32173–6 (alk. paper)
    1. Performing arts—United States—History—20th century.   I. Title.
PN2266.H38   2006
338.4′779020973–dc22   2006020535

British Library Cataloguing in Publication Data is available

Copyright © 2006 by Michael Haupert

All rights reserved. No portion of this book may be
reproduced, by any process or technique, without the
express written consent of the publisher.

Library of Congress Catalog Card Number: 2006020535
ISBN: 0–313–32173–6
ISSN: 1539–7289

First published in 2006

Greenwood Press, 88 Post Road West, Westport, CT 06881
An imprint of Greenwood Publishing Group, Inc.
www.greenwood.com

Printed in the United States of America

The paper used in this book complies with the
Permanent Paper Standard issued by the National
Information Standards Organization (Z39.48–1984).

10 9 8 7 6 5 4 3 2 1

Contents

Preface

Entertainment is amusement. Its purpose is to create a relaxing, enjoyable environment in which to escape the stresses of daily life for a while. It has taken countless forms over the centuries, ranging from recreational amusement, such as jogging or painting, to passive entertainment, like watching television or listening to music. Entertainment can also take the form of everyday activities—gardening or cooking, for example. In fact, the list of activities that could be considered entertainment is virtually endless and differs from person to person. The realm of possibilities is so grand as to make it impossible to cover the subject thoroughly in one volume.

In order to better approach the topic of entertainment, I have taken the liberty of narrowing the definition and selecting a few representative examples. For the purposes of this book, my definition of entertainment is spectator entertainment. I have substituted breadth of coverage with depth in a small number of areas.

Since the varieties of spectator entertainment are also vast, I was selective about which types of entertainment to cover. I tried to choose a variety that represents the broad landscape of spectator entertainment but at the same time is connected by a theme. In so doing, I established some criteria for what I would include.

The criteria I used were simple: it had to be a form of entertainment accessible to and pursued by Americans in large numbers, across cultural and income categories; in other words, it had to be mass entertainment. In addition, I sought those entertainment venues that not only entertained masses of people, but also did so while withstanding the test of time. This left out fads, regional favorites, and forms of entertainment pursued with great interest and skill but by only a small number of people.

A few examples of entertainment not included illustrate this point—opera, for example. While opera is certainly an ancient, well-regarded, and well-established form of entertainment, I did not include it because it is not generally accessible to a wide range of Americans and consequently has not had broad appeal at any time in the twentieth century. During the past century, opera has been available primarily only in the largest cities and attended, for the most part, only by well-educated, upper-income Americans.

Books are on the other end of the scale. As a part of the broader entertainment sector of reading, they are enjoyed more widely than many other leisure activities. But a leisure activity is not necessarily entertainment, and when considering mass entertainment, reading does not really apply since it is almost always a private pursuit.

Hobbies are an example of entertainment pursued by devotees and accessible to a wide variety of people. Hobby-specific clubs, periodicals, and television programs devoted to topics as diverse as cooking, antiques, and motorcycles exist. However, specific hobbies are usually pursued by small numbers of people. In addition, the general category of hobbies could include hundreds of individual topics with little or no relation to one another.

Having set the criteria, I then selected six representative types of entertainment. I doubt there is anyone who has not participated in at least one of these and, with the possible exception of vaudeville, most are familiar with all of them. Only vaudeville no longer exists. It is included both for its historical importance and because it represents a number of types of entertainment. Although it has disappeared from the entertainment landscape, there are vestiges of vaudeville to be found in many areas of entertainment today. Television, especially in its early days, is a stepchild of vaudeville. Vaudeville's stage relatives, such as opera, ballet, and symphony, still exist, but to this day, they do not enjoy widespread mass appeal. Opposed to vaudeville, they are expensive, somewhat elite, and not found in cities of every size.

The six specific forms of entertainment I cover in this book are vaudeville, recorded sound, movies, radio, television, and spectator sports. They all share some aspects in common. They were, or are, all consumed by large numbers of Americans. All are, or were, accessible to a wide variety of income classes, in virtually any community, and they are all easily recognizable as entertainment. Television, radio, and recorded sound are all primary forms of entertainment available widely and cheaply in most homes and which appeal to all ages and income levels in every geographic area of the country. While they may be consumed alone or in small groups in the home, the fact that the same program is entertaining millions at the same time makes them eligible for inclusion as mass entertainment.

Technology is another common thread in each of these forms of entertainment. It defines some of them (radio, television, movies, and recorded sound) and has had a profound impact on all of them. While vaudeville and spectator sports existed before the dramatic technological advances of the twentieth century, these advances redefined both industries when they did come along. Spectator sports thrived by strategically exploiting radio and television. Vaudeville, on the other hand, was displaced by the technological advances that produced radio, television, and the movies.

As this volume is one of a series focusing on American industries in the twentieth century, I have confined my coverage of entertainment to that century. There are a few instances where my story strays beyond the confines of the twentieth century when it is necessary for clarity. It was easy to stay within this time frame for industries like radio and television, which did not debut until well into the 1900s. However, for vaudeville and sports, which have ancient roots, the reader should expect some cursory coverage of these topics before the twentieth century.

The chapters are arranged in a somewhat chronological order, and within chapters the topics are pursued, again, somewhat chronologically. Because of the nature of each subject, it is not always best to tell the story in a linear timeline. In some cases, topics are best covered in their entirety within chapters even though this disrupts the timeline. The book begins with a brief look at the entertainment market and ends with an historical review of the industry over the course of the century. In between are individual chapters on each of the six types of entertainment. I begin with the vaudeville industry even though spectator sports may actually predate it. It provides a reasonable springboard, however, for the following chapters, all of which have close ties to vaudeville. The recorded sound, radio, movie, and television industries, for example, all drew heavily from vaudeville for their early talent sources both on and off the stage. Directors, booking agents, and technicians all crossed from one venue to the next. Even today some of that crossover in talent regularly occurs. Actors still frequently move between television and the movies, and singers record their music for sale and perform it on television and radio.

While the sports industry is certainly older than all but perhaps vaudeville (or its stage antecedents, such as Greek theater), it is placed last among the chapters because it bears less similarity to the others. The other formats are clearly derivations of one another, while sports is less so, even though spectator sports do share a lot in common with the other means of entertainment, and there certainly is crossover. Sports owe their explosion in popularity and profitability to television and radio broadcasts and the hefty fees that come with them. Vaudeville regularly featured prominent sports heroes on their bills, and the first highlights of sporting events debuted on the weekly newsreels at the movies in the pretelevision days.

Within chapters, the organization typically begins with a discussion of the origin of the method of entertainment. In the case of recorded sound, radio, television, and motion pictures this is a technological review of the inventive period that led to the dawning of the medium. In the case of sports and vaudeville, there is a brief look at the distant mists of their origins, but these chapters quickly move to a focus on the twentieth century evolution of the American market.

The aim of this book is to serve as an introduction to the topic of entertainment as an economic entity. It is not meant to be an exhaustive treatise or to boldly break new ground in the analysis of the industry, but rather to serve as a starting point for anyone with an interest in the topic. The chapters are for the most part self-contained. Though there is overlap between the industry segments, they each have a story that stands on its own. Entertainment is a fascinating industry, with colorful personalities, intriguing origins, and, at the bottom line, a straightforward business model. Despite the glitz and glamour often associated with the various types of entertainment, they are businesses designed to make a profit.

I use economics as a lens through which to view the historical evolution of these six segments of the entertainment industry. However, this book does not presume a prior level of expertise in economics. Economic jargon is kept to a minimum, and where I felt it necessary to use economic terms and concepts I have taken care to define them. Therefore, while the book is written in such a manner that any chapter could arguably stand alone, terms defined in earlier chapters are not redefined later. Similarly, related innovations among two or more entertainment venues are discussed in greater detail in the chapter in which they are first introduced and only briefly summarized in later chapters.

The foundation for the growth of the entertainment industry is to be found in the focus that is laid out in the first and last chapters of the narrative: that the growth of the American economy has been the primary factor in the growth of the American entertainment industry. The growth of the economy, which decreased work hours and increased income, and its concomitant technological improvements, which both decreased the cost of providing entertainment as well as increased the amount of leisure time available to consume that entertainment, was the catalyst. Technological improvements contributed to increased labor productivity, shorter workweeks, and increased wages. At home, that technological revolution decreased the amount of time needed to finish household chores, thus freeing up time for entertainment. It is the increased wealth measured by both income and free time that has allowed for the explosion in demand for entertainment.

Over the course of the twentieth century, the average American saw a 33 percent decrease in the number of hours on the job, enjoyed an inflation-adjusted income increase by a factor of 25 (after taxes no less), and responded by nearly tripling expenditures on entertainment. Add to this the decreased amount of time needed to accomplish household chores such as cooking, cleaning, and yard work, the impact of the automobile on personal mobility, and the increased ability to be entertained at home made possible by radio, television, and recorded music, and the elements are all in place for the consumption of entertainment on a mass scale. The result, as you will see, was a century of spectacular growth and innovation.

The final chapter of the book takes a look at 15 persons who had a profound impact on the entertainment industry. No attempt was made to pick the 15 most important people, however that might be defined, but rather to single out a small number who through their actions had a major impact. This list includes executives like David Sarnoff, who rose to power at RCA and had a profound influence on the way in which radio and television evolved; Jackie Robinson, the first African-American to play in the major leagues after a half century of segregation; and Mary Pickford, actress and entrepreneur, who captured the hearts of American moviegoers on the big screen and helped revolutionize the movie industry with her business acumen.

Finally, I have included in the bibliography a list of those works that I found especially helpful in writing this book. The list should be useful to anyone who wishes to delve more deeply into the fascinating world of entertainment.

There is no absolute demarcation between these various types of entertainment. It is not always clear where one ends and another begins, nor even where they might be separated. As a result, the coverage of the entertainment industry requires some knowledge of one medium in order to understand the other. Entertainment is an industry that brings joy to millions. It continues to be a growing sector of our economy, generating billions of dollars in revenue and employing millions of workers. Let's take a look at how and why it has changed over the century.

Timeline

1834 Tony Pastor, credited with elevating entertainment to a family level by removing it from its more traditional saloon setting, is born.

1846 Benjamin Franklin Keith, "father of vaudeville," is born in Hillsboro Bridge, New Hampshire on January 26.

1867 Inventor Eldridge Johnson is born on February 18. He and Thomas Edison are credited with the invention of the phonograph.

1869 The first all-professional baseball team, the Cincinnati Red Stockings, is founded.

In November, Rutgers faces off against Princeton in the first college football game.

1873 Radio pioneer Lee de Forest is born in Council Bluffs, Iowa.

1878 On April 24 the Edison Speaking Phonograph Company is organized in Connecticut.

1881 Tony Pastor opens Tony Pastor's New Fourteenth Street Theater in October. What makes this theater stand out from other entertainment venues is its lack of a saloon. It is recognized as the first "family" stage entertainment in America, ushering in what will eventually become vaudeville.

1883 Benjamin Franklin Keith opens his first vaudeville theater in Boston. Keith, along with partner Edward Albee, will go on to dominate the industry in the early part of the next century.

1885 Benjamin Franklin Keith and Edward Albee go into business together, offering a combination light-opera-vaudeville show.

1889   Louis Glass invents the "jukebox," though it would not be known by that name for another generation.

1891   Dr. James Naismith introduces the game of basketball in Springfield, Massachusetts.

1894   The first kinetoscope parlor, the precursor to the modern movie theater, opens in New York on April 14.

1896   The theater syndicate is formed by six theater owners, Marc Klaw and A. L. Erlanger the most prominent. They establish a booking monopoly and by 1904 control the booking in over 500 theaters, including all but a few of the first-class theaters in New York City.

On April 23 Thomas Edison makes the first public display of his motion picture projector, which he calls the Vitascope.

The modern Olympic Games open in Athens, Greece.

1897   Transmission rights for a sports event are sold for the first time when the National League sells Western Union the rights to transmit the results of its baseball games over its telegraph wires. Each team receives $300 in free telegrams as compensation.

1899   Guglielmo Marconi immigrates to the United States from Italy. Later that year he is granted the first patent related to wireless communication.

1900   The Association of Vaudeville Managers of the United States is organized. It unites theater owners across the country in what the association went out of its way to point out was not a trust. Of course, this is exactly what it was—a blatant attempt to corner the market on vaudeville talent and exploit that monopoly for profit.

The first vaudeville actors' union, the White Rats of America, is established by George Fuller Gordon in June.

Nipper the dog first appears as a trademark for the Victor Talking Machine company. He will go on to become one of America's most enduring and recognizable trademarks.

1901   On February 22 the White Rats of America, the vaudeville actors' union, stages a successful protest against the new booking system established by theater owners, walking out of theaters on the East Coast and in the Midwest. Within two weeks theater owners cave in to their demands to end the system.

Eldridge Johnson founds the Victor Talking Machine Company.

1902   Enrico Caruso makes his first recording for Victor on their prestigious Red Seal label.

Harry and Herbert Miles establish the first distribution company for motion pictures.

1903 *The Great Train Robbery* is released. It is the first motion picture that truly resembled what we would recognize today as a movie.

European nations sign the first international treaty governing the use of airwaves for wireless transmissions. The United States refuses to sign.

1904 On July 11 Mabel Whitman, manager of the Whitman Sisters vaudeville act, insists that the Jefferson Theater in Birmingham, Alabama, allow black patrons to sit in the "whites only" section, or her act will not go on. The theater manager acquiesces, marking the first time that Birmingham segregation ordinances were successfully challenged.

1905 Harry and John Davis open the first permanent movie theater in Pittsburgh.

1906 Benjamin Franklin Keith and Edward Albee incorporate the United Booking Office.

The Victor Talking Machine Company introduces the Victrola model, which will go on to become the industry standard.

On Christmas Eve inventor Reginald Fessenden broadcasts the first recognized radio signal.

Lee de Forest is granted a patent for the audion tube, the invention on which the radio industry would eventually be founded.

1907 Enrico Caruso records "On with the Motley," which becomes the first million-selling recording.

1908 The Motion Picture Patents Corporation is formed by merging the ten major companies holding the important motion picture industry patents, including Edison, Vitagraph, and Biograph, the three largest holders of patents for cameras, film, and projectors.

The term television is coined by *Scientific American* in an article speculating about future technological innovations.

1909 The Copyright Act is revised, creating new protection for music publishers, authors, composers, and songwriters.

1910 The General Film Company, a cartel of distribution and production companies in the movie industry, is formed.

On June 24 the United States passes the Wireless Ship Act, requiring that any ship carrying more than 50 passengers or sailing more than 200 miles between ports be equipped with radio communication equipment.

1912 TOBY (Theater Owners' Booking Association), an African-American vaudeville circuit, is established by Sherman Dudley.

The federal government nationalizes the broadcast spectrum with passage of the Radio Act, requiring all operators of radio equipment be licensed and allocated a wavelength on which to broadcast.

Swimming becomes the first sanctioned event for women in the Olympic Games.

The Titanic sinks on April 11. David Sarnoff relays the tragedy to a spellbound America from his post in a New York City wireless station. Sarnoff will go on to become CEO of Radio Corporation of America, one of the largest corporations in the United States.

1913　Construction on the Palace Theater, the grandest of the vaudeville stages, is completed and it opens for business in Times Square.

1914　Benjamin Franklin Keith, father of vaudeville, dies of heart failure.

Lee de Forest and Howard Armstrong meet in court for the first time in what will become a lifelong battle between the two inventors over radio patents.

"Doc" Herrold begins the first regular radio broadcast by illegally tapping into the Santa Fe Railway streetcar lines to broadcast to an audience in San Jose, California.

1916　The White Rats strike vaudeville theaters in December for more than a month. Both sides lose money, but management breaks the union.

The Harvard-Yale football game becomes the first sporting event broadcast over the radio waves.

In November Lee de Forest earns the dubious distinction of being the first person to incorrectly predict the outcome of a presidential election over the airwaves when he signs off at 11 p.m. on election night by declaring Charles Evans Hughes the winner over Woodrow Wilson.

1918　U.S. antitrust legislation dissolves the General Film Company and Motion Picture Patent Corporation trusts, changing the landscape of the motion picture industry.

1919　Paramount merges with Famous Players and Lasky, becoming the first fully integrated movie company, producing, distributing, and exhibiting motion pictures.

United Artists is created by Charlie Chaplin, Mary Pickford, Douglas Fairbanks, Sr., D. W. Griffith, and William Hart.

On October 17 the Radio Corporation of America (RCA) is incorporated. Born out of the merger of General Electric and Marconi Wireless, it would go on to dominate the radio and the television industries for the next half century.

Jackie Robinson is born on January 31 in Cairo, Georgia.

1920   In July *Variety* begins a best-seller chart for phonograph recordings. This would ultimately become the "Top 40."

On November 2 the first licensed commercial radio broadcasting station, KDKA, begins operation in Pittsburgh.

1922   On August 28 the first commercial airs on a licensed radio station. The Queensboro Corporation pays station WEAF in New York $50 to advertise a new apartment complex they are leasing.

The Supreme Court rules that Major League Baseball does not constitute interstate commerce, thus legalizing what has become one of the most effective monopolies in American history.

1924   Will Hays establishes the Production Code Administration, essentially a censorship board for the movie industry.

1925   Charles Jenkins is granted the first patent for a television system. His mechanical system will prove to be unworkable, however.

The Chicago Cubs become the first professional sports team to regularly broadcast their games—giving the rights away for free to local radio stations.

1926   AT&T sells its radio assets to RCA, abandoning the radio business to concentrate on telephones.

1927   Edward Albee merges Keith-Albee with the Orpheum circuit, giving him nationwide control of vaudeville theaters.

Columbia Record Company purchases United Independent Broadcasters and renames the company the Columbia Phonograph Broadcasting System, later changed to Columbia Broadcasting System, or CBS.

On October 6 *The Jazz Singer*, the first talking picture, is released. Within five years silent films will disappear from the market.

Philo T. Farnsworth receives the first patent for electronic television. He will go on to be recognized as the father of television.

1928   Edward Albee sells the Palace Theater to Joseph P. Kennedy and David Sarnoff who rename it Radio-Keith-Orpheum Circuit.

The first Academy Awards are presented. *Wings* is named best picture, Emil Jennings wins the best actor award, and Janet Gaynor the best actress award.

Mickey Mouse stars in his first film under the nom de plume Steamboat Willie.

Philo Farnsworth makes the first successful public demonstration of television on September 1, showing a clip of a Mary Pickford movie.

Timeline

1930   The National Association of Performing Artists (NAPA) is formed for
       the purpose of eliminating the free use of recordings by radio
       stations. Ironically, the recording industry will be sued in years to
       come for paying radio stations to play their music.

       The government initiates its first antitrust legislation against RCA,
       forcing it to unravel its monopoly agreements with GE and
       Westinghouse.

1931   *Cimmaron* becomes the first Western to win the Academy Award for
       best picture. It would be sixty years before another Western won the
       honor.

1932   The Palace closes to vaudeville with its last show on November 16.

1933   In June the National Industrial Recovery Act is signed into law,
       legalizing the oligopolistic structure of the movie industry and
       solidifying the "studio era" of production in which a small number of
       companies would control the industry from production through
       exhibition.

       The Screen Actors Guild is formed as a union for movie actors.

       Mary Pickford makes her last screen appearance, starring in
       Secrets, distributed by United Artists.

1935   Philo Farnsworth scores a legal victory over RCA in a patent
       infringement suit. The victory will ultimately lead to RCA licensing
       patent rights from Farnsworth—the first time the corporation was
       ever on the buying end of a licensing agreement.

1937   Baron Pierre de Coubertin, founder of the modern Olympic Games,
       dies in Geneva, Switzerland on September 2.

1938   RCA Victor debuts the record club.

       Howard Armstrong begins experimental FM broadcasts. FM
       would not become commercially successful until long after his
       death.

1939   The first commercial television broadcast is made at the Worlds Fair
       in New York City.

1941   The American Broadcasting Corporation is born when the FCC
       forces RCA to divest itself of one of its two broadcast networks. RCA
       keeps NBC. The network would actually assume the ABC moniker
       two years later.

1942   In August the American Federation of Musicians (AFM) goes on
       strike for nearly a year, winning wage and working condition
       concessions for artists from the recording industry.

1943   Olivia de Havilland challenges the movie industry "renewal clause" of
       her contract in court. She would eventually win, bringing about the
       end of the studio era.

1945   The DuMont television network is born, joining CBS and NBC as one of the three major networks.

1946   The New York Yankees become the first professional sports team with a local television contract, selling the rights to their games for $75,000 for the season. By the end of the century they would receive four times that amount per game.

1947   On December 23 the last true vaudeville show closes on the stage of the State Theater in New York, which had been running vaudeville shows continuously since 1919.

Columbia purchases time on 537 radio stations to introduce its new songs, ushering in an era of publishers paying stations to air their music; this was quite a change from a decade earlier when publishers were suing radio stations to keep them from playing their music without paying for it.

Jackie Robinson breaks Major League Baseball's color barrier when he takes the field for the Brooklyn Dodgers. He becomes the first African American to play professional baseball in more than half a century.

1948   Columbia introduces the $33\frac{1}{3}$ rpm LP (long playing) record.

For the second time the movie industry is found to be in violation of antitrust laws, and studios are forced to divest. This marked the formal end of the studio system.

The LPGA (Ladies Professional Golf Association) is founded with the help of Babe Didrikson Zaharias.

1949   Victor introduces the 45 rpm rapid changer, which allows a record player to play a series of records, automatically dropping one at a time onto the turntable.

The sitcom (situation comedy) is born. *Mama* airs for the first time in what will become an eight-year run.

The first regular newscast is aired. *The Camel News Caravan*, anchored by John Cameron Swayze, broadcasts 15 minutes of news each night from New York City.

The National Basketball Association is formed through the merger of two struggling professional leagues, the NBL and the BAA.

1951   American Bandstand, hosted by Dick Clark, debuts, marrying television and the recorded music industries.

The first live coverage of a Congressional hearing takes place. Senator Estes Kefauver chairs the committee investigating organized crime.

1953   Bill Haley releases "Shake, Rattle and Roll," regarded by many as the first true rock and roll hit, on independent label Essex.

Elvis Presley records his first two songs as a birthday present for his mother.

Howard Armstrong makes his final contribution to radio with his discovery of the concept of multiplexing, which would eventually lead to stereo broadcasting. Armstrong would not live to see his concept carried to its conclusion.

The FCC chooses the RCA system of color television broadcasting as the industry standard.

1954 Howard Armstrong commits suicide on January 31, distraught over his legal difficulties.

1955 RKO becomes the first studio to sell one of its movies to a television network. General Teleradio uses the films to fill time on its television schedule.

The DuMont television network ceases to operate, leaving in place the three networks (ABC, CBS, and NBC) that will dominate the television landscape for the next generation.

1956 President Eisenhower holds the first live presidential press conference, originating from San Francisco.

1964 *The Beatles* invade America for the first time.

The cassette tape is introduced by the Phillips Company.

The FCC mandates that all television sets constructed must be able to receive both UHF and VHF signals.

1968 Wimbledon becomes the first major tennis tournament to allow professionals to compete.

1970 The first cable superstation is born when Ted Turner launches station WTBS in Atlanta (originally called WTCG).

A new Monday night tradition is born when the NFL begins its Monday night broadcasts on September 21. The Cleveland Browns defeat the New York Jets 31-21.

The Women's professional tennis tour debuts under the sponsorship of Virginia Slims.

1971 On March 11, Philo Farnsworth, age 64, acknowledged inventor of television, dies. On December 12 David Sarnoff, longtime executive of RCA and a bitter rival of Farnsworth in the race to commercialize television, dies at the age of 80.

1975 The first satellite transmission of a cable television signal takes place on September 30 when the Muhammad Ali vs. Joe Frazier heavyweight boxing championship is broadcast from Manilla.

1976 The Copyright Act's First Sale Doctrine is passed. The doctrine states that the first purchaser of any copyrighted work can use it anyway they see fit as long as it is not duplicated and sold for commercial gain. This paves the way for the home video and audio recording markets.

The sale of satellite receivers to private households is allowed, opening up the market for satellite television.

1977 The Supreme Court rules that the FCC does not have the authority to bar pay channels from cable systems.

1979 Screen legend Mary Pickford dies a virtual recluse on May 27.

1980 The Sony Walkman, the original personal audio headset device, debuts.

Cable News Network makes its first broadcast. It will revolutionize television news.

1981 MTV broadcasts for the first time, launching the music video industry.

The International Olympic Committee votes to allow openly professional athletes to compete in the games for the first time beginning with the 1984 games.

1982 The first compact disc hits the market. CDs will virtually wipe out records and tapes in the music industry.

1984 The Cable Communications Policy Act is passed, deregulating the cable industry.

College football teams break loose from NCAA control of television rights when they successfully sue the NCAA for antitrust violations.

1985 RCA comes full circle when it is sold to GE, the company from which it was spawned half a century earlier.

1992 Cable television is once again regulated by the FCC. The reregulation of the industry is mostly in the area of pricing.

1994 The Home Audio Recording Act is passed, putting a surcharge of 2 percent on the price of audio tape recorders and 3 percent on blank cassette tapes to be placed in a fund for distribution to record companies, artists, music publishers, and songwriters.

1995 The FCC repeals its ban on network ownership of television programs.

1996 The Telecommunications Act is passed, loosening the restrictions on ownership of television and radio stations.

Tiger Woods earns his first professional golf paycheck.

— 1 —

The American Entertainment Industry in the Twentieth Century

Entertainment is very much a social activity. Even if the actual event takes place in isolation, such as watching a television show or listening to a compact disc alone, the social interaction that takes place afterward is often an important component of the entertainment. Talking about the big game at work or a lunch chat about the previous night's latest episode of *Survivor* are examples of a social activity resulting from entertainment that may not have originally been consumed in a social setting. Very often the entertainment takes place in a direct social context. Live performance, for example, is consumed in the presence of hundreds or even thousands of others. Very often watching television or enjoying recorded music is also done in the company of others. In fact, the social interaction is one of the parts of entertainment itself—enjoying it with others.

Being part of the crowd sometimes is a reasonable explanation for the demand for some entertainment. Wanting to experience what so many others have experienced, and wanting to be able to discuss it with them afterward in social settings at work or at home, is valued in and of itself. Even if I did not enjoy the movie or performance that everyone else saw, I can talk about what I did not like. I can be the critic. So whether I share the enjoyment of the actual entertainment or not, it is still possible for me to enjoy the discussion of it afterward.

In many ways the entertainment industry is indistinguishable from any other industry. Like the automobile, prepared food, or paperclip industries, goods are produced. Like the accounting, hairstyling, and travel industries, services are provided. In each case the market for these goods responds to the basic principles of economics—primarily supply and demand. The market then operates to allocate the goods, whether they be automobiles or videocassettes, haircuts, or theater performances, from sellers to buyers. In many ways, however, these industries are quite different from the provision of paperclips or completed tax returns. This book seeks to highlight the evolution of the entertainment industry over the twentieth century and explore some of its unique economic principles.

Americans, like any people throughout time and across cultures, seek entertainment for a variety of reasons, most of which are in some way related to the desire for relaxation. Entertainment is a way of relaxing, recharging, rejuvenating, and unwinding. In an increasingly stressful world, entertainment and relaxation have become even more important than ever before. Stress is cited as one of the leading killers in the United States. Leisure, as opposed to stress, is what entertainment is all about. As our society changed and our economy grew over the twentieth century, the entertainment industry has grown and changed with it.

WHAT DETERMINES THE DEMAND FOR ENTERTAINMENT?

The standard economic explanations for demand are equally applicable to the entertainment industry. People usually demand more of a good when their incomes increase or the price of the good decreases. A change in the price of related goods can also affect demand. For example, if the cost of going to the theater goes down, more people are likely to attend.

Demand for goods is also affected by the number of potential buyers and their tastes and preferences. In larger cities more televisions are likely to be sold than in smaller cities. While tastes and preferences are difficult to explain, their impact on demand is straightforward. When a hit song is recorded, buyers clamor for it. What *makes* it a hit song, however, is difficult if not impossible to explain.

INCOME AND LEISURE TIME

Americans saw an increase in their after-tax income over the twentieth century from $287 billion to $7.1 trillion real dollars (that is, adjusted to account for the impact of inflation). The average manufacturing worker saw his real wage rise by a factor of five. This increase in income also allowed Americans to purchase more entertainment. The percentage of personal consumption expenditures by Americans devoted to recreation and entertainment rose from 3 percent at the beginning of the century to almost 9 percent by the end.

The decrease in the length of the workweek also contributed to an increase in leisure consumption. The average workweek decreased by one-third over the century from 59 hours to 39 hours, freeing up a tremendous amount of time for leisure pursuits. Additional time for leisure has also been made available by inventions, which led to the reduction of the amount of time needed for household chores such as laundry, cleaning, and cooking.

CHANGES IN POPULATION

The population of the United States increased from 76 million in 1900 to 280 million in 2000. By itself this increase in population made for a larger market, thus leading to an increase in demand for entertainment. It is not just the growth of the population, however, but how it grew that is significant. The dramatic shift of population from the country to the city is also an important factor in explaining the growth of the entertainment industry. Urbanization aided the growth of the entertainment industry in two ways. Farmers have always worked more hours than nonfarm workers. In addition, nonagricultural employees have earned higher wages than agricultural workers throughout the century. The move of the population from the farm to the city in the twentieth century decreased the number of hours worked and increased the income of the average American. Agricultural wages have ranged between one-third and two-thirds of manufacturing wages since 1900. During the twentieth century, the percentage of Americans living in urban areas increased from 39 percent to 79 percent, and the number of cities with population in excess of 50,000 increased from 78 to 601. Both of these factors contributed to an increase in the demand for entertainment.

In addition to the higher incomes and lower work hours brought about by urbanization, the cost of pursuing entertainment is also lower for city dwellers because of the closer proximity of venues such as theaters and stadiums. There is also a greater supply of entertainment opportunities in the city. Thus, urban dwellers have access to more entertainment options, and it doesn't cost them as much to get to them.

THE CHANGING AMERICAN HOUSEHOLD

While tastes and preferences are hard to explain, some reasons for their change can be surmised by looking at how American households have evolved over the past century. To say that America has changed over the past century is an understatement indeed. One way to get a true appreciation of how different America is today is to look at the use of time. Americans have more leisure time and they spend more money entertaining themselves than they ever have. Both the quantity and the quality of entertainment have been dramatically redefined over the course of the twentieth century. According to the 1900 census, the average American worked nearly 60 hours per week and spent $9 per person on recreation, most of which was spent on books and toys. The typical use of leisure time was reading or playing music or games together in the parlor. Many things considered leisure activities today would not have been considered as such at the end of the nineteenth century. Jogging, for example, while a popular form of recreational entertainment today, was unknown a century ago when there was little, if any, focus on physical fitness. Other popular pastimes, such as television and the movies, were still pipe dreams in the minds of inventors.

The changing demographic pattern and increase in income have altered the way in which Americans spend their leisure hours. In 1900 the typical worker was a man. Only 18 percent of women were in the workforce, and almost none of them were married. Indeed, it was common for a woman to exit the workforce at marriage to devote her time to managing the household and raising the children. These tasks took the lion's share of every day before modern conveniences such as washing machines, dishwashers, and microwave ovens became commonplace.

Move forward to the dawn of the twenty-first century. The average American household has two working parents, yet more leisure time. Despite working a fulltime job outside the home, the average woman today has more leisure time than a century earlier. The amount of time spent on domestic chores has been reduced thanks to technology, and many households hire outside workers to do the bulk of these chores, ranging from childcare to housecleaning. Electricity has been the primary time saver for women, though indoor plumbing is close behind.

Consider laundry to get an idea of how dramatically household chores have changed over the twentieth century. In 1900, water had to be hauled indoors—perhaps up several flights of stairs for the urban apartment dweller—and boiled, usually over a wood-burning stove (the wood for which had to be cut, split, and hauled). The clothing was then scrubbed on a washboard by hand. After scrubbing and wringing the laundry by hand, it had to be dried. It could either be hung outside to dry in the air or inside by the fireplace (which also required wood that had to be cut, split, and hauled)—if one existed. If you could afford it, a wringer was available to help squeeze water out of the clothing to speed the eventual drying process. A load of laundry for a typical family was an all-day affair and one that required constant attention, since the clothing was washed and wrung by hand. It was not possible to multitask. The laundry could not simply be put in a machine and forgotten for the next hour while other chores were completed.

TECHNOLOGY

Technology has had an impact on the leisure industry both at home and at work. It has freed up household time that previously went into chores. It has reduced the amount of labor needed in the workplace, meaning workers have shorter workweeks and are less likely to be physically exhausted, thus making it more likely for them to seek entertainment. Computers, robots, sophisticated tools, and machinery have all made workers more productive. It takes fewer hours today to make just about everything than it did a century ago. As a result, workers can produce more in less time. This increase in worker productivity means Americans earn more and work less than they used to. This creates more time for entertainment and more money to spend on it.

Technology also created more and newer ways to enjoy this new found leisure time. The first big innovation of the century was the recorded sound industry, followed closely by the motion picture industry and then the radio. These latter two industries ruled until the 1950s, when television exploded upon a postwar America ready to spend money and anxious to escape the drudgery of the Depression and the war years. Not until the personal computer became a household fixture at the end of the century would anything come along to rival the television for the leisure time of Americans.

Automobiles also made their mark on the entertainment industry. They created a more mobile society, increasing the scope of possible entertainment venues and lowering the cost of reaching them. This has broadened the horizon of potential forms of entertainment for Americans. It is one of the most important reasons for the increase in out-of-home types of entertainment. The car itself has even become entertainment in some areas: NASCAR is the ultimate example, in which people are entertained by watching automobiles race around a track. Drive-in movies, while not inherently unique from their theater brethren, were made possible by the automobile.

UNIQUE PROPERTIES OF ENTERTAINMENT

There are also some properties of the entertainment industry that don't necessarily apply to other markets. These include uncertain demand, producers who have an unusually high personal attachment to their product (think *art* as opposed to *commerce*), and goods that cannot readily be inventoried.

The quality of entertainment goods is seldom known in advance. What is more, no two are alike, so it is hard to predict exactly what the quality will be the next time they are produced. If I have never eaten a banana, I must experience it to know what it is like. However, having eaten one, I know what to expect the next time I eat one, since all bananas taste the same. But not all movies are the same. Not even all horror movies or all Steven Spielberg movies or even all the *Star Wars* movies are the same. As a result, more so in entertainment than in other industries, consumers rely on signals for quality indicators. In the movie industry, for example, the quality of a movie cannot be determined until the movie has been seen. In order to try and avoid buying tickets to bad movies, consumers rely on the opinion of critics and word-of-mouth reviews from friends who have already seen the movie to give them an indication of its quality.

Live performances such as operas, symphonies, plays, musicals, concerts, and vaudevilles all share certain characteristics. In particular, they cannot be inventoried—that is produced now and then stored for sale at a later time. The consumption of their product takes place at the same time as their final production, and customers must come to them, as the product cannot be shipped to the customers or to an intermediary middleman for resale. Over time technology has blurred these lines of distinction, since a live performance can be recorded and sold like any other commodity. However, while a taped version of a concert or a play is a substitute for the live performance, the degree of substitution is highly debatable. Listening to a high-quality digital recording of a concert may, for example, be a closer substitute for the concert than would be a similarly high-quality video recording of last night's big championship football game. But the fact that tickets to live events can be sold for exorbitant prices suggests that the substitutability is far from perfect.

THE SUPPLY OF ENTERTAINMENT

Technology also changed the supply of entertainment for public consumption, progressing from live theater to the movies and adding home entertainment in the form of recorded music, radio, television, and ultimately the Internet. The American entertainment industry responded to the demands of the public and adapted the latest technologies in an effort to capitalize on the growing demand for entertainment services.

The unknown quality of many forms of entertainment not only causes problems for consumers, but can be a challenge for the producers as well. Consider the movie industry as an example. The success of a movie is almost impossible to predict. Even after a movie smashes box office records, it may not be clear as to why it was so much more popular than other films. Even knowing what made one movie, play, television show, or recording popular usually adds nothing to the predictive ability of what makes the next one popular. No actor is a guaranteed box office hit every time, no recording artist has produced an unending string of hit songs, and no genre of play, film, or television series has proven to be eternally popular. Without really knowing what factors influence the quality of the final product, producers are at an extreme disadvantage, and the final result is the volatile movie industry that exists. Some movies are box office bonanzas, and others are bombs. There is no clear pattern to explain the difference. Neither the presence of star actors and directors, glitzy special effects, copious advertising, or storylines that were successful in previous movies or that are based on best-selling books have proven to be sure-fire recipes for a successful movie.

The fact that the costs of producing entertainment are almost all borne before the product can be marketed means that the entire investment must be made before the producers know if it will be a success. These costs, known as "sunk costs," cannot be recovered if the show is a bomb. A test market for a movie is not feasible because the entire cost of the movie must be undertaken before it can be shown anywhere. It isn't similar to a potential new sandwich at McDonalds, which can be tested in select markets to see if it is a viable option.

The skills of those producing entertainment goods are highly variable, and in many cases are not identifiable before hiring. For example, not all athletes are of the same quality. In fact, there is a huge discrepancy in talent (defined here only as ability to generate revenue, usually through ticket sales). This leads to a market with high salaries for the few who are most easily identifiable as high-quality workers (i.e., superstars). However, that still does not guarantee high quality. Even an award-winning actor can make a bad film or a star athlete can have a bad season. This leads to a division of the marketplace into "superstar" employees and "secondary" employees. The difference is not in the known outcome of the quality of their product, but rather the likelihood of the quality being high. A superstar actor (a recent Tony Award winner, for example) is more likely to produce a high-quality acting job (and high box office revenues) than is a "secondary" actor.

The time value of money is an issue in the entertainment industry as it is in many industries. For example, when a studio produces a movie costing $100 million, the money is entirely spent before any income can be earned on ticket sales. That means the $100 million cannot be used by the studio for anything else—another movie, paying off debts, or simply earning interest in a savings account. The longer the time lag between spending the money and earning any income to pay it back, the more expensive the investment becomes in terms of foregone income. Besides these time value of money issues, entertainment suffers because some of its goods either do not inventory at all or do so poorly. For example, while a movie can be inventoried, some movies do not hold up well because of their topical nature or their dated technology. Silent movies, for example, are physically deteriorating because the film they were recorded on is unstable. In addition, they were all filmed in black and white, and, of course, have no soundtrack, both of which limit their marketability. As a result, there is very little opportunity to earn income on many previously produced films.

The existing stock of previously created entertainment sometimes can compete with what is newly produced. Television is perhaps the best example, although this is also true of radio and recorded sound. Old movies seldom compete head-on in theaters, but newly released films may go up against films released several weeks earlier. In television, entire cable networks are devoted to old material. TVLand, Turner Classic Movies, and American Movie Classics are all cable channels devoted to rerunning previously aired television shows or movies. There is even an ESPN Classic channel that airs old sporting events. Radio stations that concentrate on playing songs from previous decades are another good example.

—2—

Vaudeville: The Original Variety Show

INTRODUCTION

In 1913, Martin Beck finished construction of the Palace Theater in Times Square in Manhattan. It was one of the grand theaters of its day and would quickly become a status symbol of vaudeville entertainers everywhere: to play the Palace was to have made it to the top—the top of the preeminent form of entertainment in the United States in the first quarter of the twentieth century. At the time of its construction, the Palace was the best of the best. Vaudeville was entering its glory years, roughly a decade, where it was without equal at the top of a growing entertainment market. More people, more entertainers, more money, more shows, and more interest were lavished on vaudeville than on any other form of entertainment in America. It was the king of entertainment in a wealthy kingdom of leisure. Within a generation, it would disappear virtually without a trace, leaving behind a legacy that would serve as a foundation for a new medium of entertainment: television. Its grand theaters would be converted for yet another entertainment successor, the motion picture, and its entertainers would take very different paths. Some would go on to even greater fame and riches in the movies, radio, and television, while others would fade from sight. Vaudeville's light blazed brightly but briefly as it fell from the prince of entertainment to a forgotten pauper.

The first real mass entertainment medium of the twentieth century was vaudeville. Before technology made entertainment a packaged and stored commodity, live entertainment ruled the industry. This took the form of staged shows: opera, symphony, theater, burlesque, and vaudeville. The former were attended primarily by the well-educated and upper class. Burlesque was mainly a saloon-based form of entertainment, appealing to the male working class and featuring scantily clad women singing and dancing. Only vaudeville appealed to the mass audience.

Simply defined, vaudeville was a live variety show. While it usually contained acting and music, it differed from theater or opera or symphony performances because it contained so much more. Vaudeville was more like a talent show; it contained a little bit of everything—basically, anything that might entertain an audience. Do not be fooled into thinking that the talent was amateurish, however. Big-time vaudeville was the top of the entertainment pyramid and featured the greatest entertainers in the world.

Vaudeville flourished in America for the first two decades of the twentieth century and spawned many of the early actors who went on to propel the movie and television industries to their current dominant positions in the entertainment industry. Like theater and opera, vaudeville was performed live. Unlike theater and opera however, it was neither as formal nor as exclusive. Vaudeville also contained elements of the circus and appealed to a much broader customer base than did the theater, opera, or symphony.

A typical vaudeville show lasted about two hours and featured as many as ten different acts, ranging from the stars of opera and Broadway to acrobats and animal acts with the occasional appearance of the famous and bizarre. Prices were low compared to more formal stage shows, and the acts traveled from city to city, usually on a weekly basis. Thus, the local theater provided great variety, and the vaudeville acts performed before a wide range of audiences.

Vaudeville flourished in America in response to the growth of the economy. As Americans became wealthier, spending on entertainment increased and subsequently, on venues for entertainment. While related to burlesque shows that had long been playing in saloons, vaudeville provided a family version in a family-friendly setting. It became the primary mode of entertainment for a generation of Americans, beginning in the late nineteenth century and peaking in the 1920s, before it gave way to the movies. During that brief but active period, thousands of theaters were built, some among the grandest ever seen, millions of customers were entertained, and tens of thousands of entertainers were employed. While the vast majority of them faded from the spotlight when the final curtain came down, a few went on to become even more famous in radio, the movies, and television. Names like Jack Benny, George Burns, Gracie Allen, and the Marx Brothers are better known for their postvaudeville careers, but they all started the same way—on the small-time circuit, traveling between one-night stands in small towns, perfecting their craft, and entertaining Americans from New York to New Albin, in theaters from the grand Palace in Manhattan to storefronts in Spokane and everywhere in between. This is a brief history of that mostly forgotten but very important form of entertainment. Vaudeville was the foundation for the electronic media that would follow, yet it is a distant memory today. Few Americans have actually seen a true vaudeville show, as the last one played some seventy years ago.

ORIGIN OF THE WORD VAUDEVILLE

The exact source of the word "vaudeville" is unknown. It is fairly certain, however, that it is French in origin. One possibility is the French phrase *vaux-de-Vire*, meaning popular satirical song. These songs were performed by minstrels in the valley (vaux) near the town of Vire in Normandy during the fifteenth century. A second possibility is the workers in Paris who gave evening entertainment known as *vire-vaudeville* or *vaudevire*. In either case, the reference is to a variety of entertainment, which is what vaudeville became by the nineteenth century.

Vaudeville descended from European entertainment known as "variety," in which traveling entertainers would convene in a town for a night or perhaps a week, perform, and move on. The performance consisted of a variety of acts, depending on the particular gathering of talent. The fare ranged from singers and dancers to comedians, contortionists, and the occasional dramatic actor. This form of entertainment arrived in America with the earliest European settlers but really began to flourish in the 1880s.

The first known use of the word vaudeville in the United States was in 1840 when a Boston "Vaudeville Saloon" advertised a variety program. Exactly what this variety program included is unknown. But it is clear that the nineteenth century saw a proliferation of establishments that billed themselves variously as vaudeville, variety, burlesque, advanced vaudeville, refined vaudeville, progressive vaudeville, and glorified vaudeville. Eventually, "variety" came to be the term used for rougher forms of entertainment, like stag shows and burlesque, while vaudeville referred to a more refined family version.

TONY PASTOR AND THE BIRTH
OF AMERICAN VAUDEVILLE

The predecessor to vaudeville was the concert saloon, or burlesque hall. In 1872, there were approximately 80 of them in New York City alone. The difference between this and vaudeville was the intended audience, and hence the character of the show. Burlesque was a form of entertainment prominently featuring a chorus of busty women, decidedly not family entertainment, but a common training ground for new talent. The chorus girls were the main entertainment, but other acts were featured. Al Jolson, Will Rogers, Fannie Brice, and Sophie Tucker, all of whom went on to become major stars in vaudeville, stage, radio, and the movies, honed their skills on the burlesque stage.

While vaudeville in America had its roots in the burlesque and variety shows performed in saloons, it differed in its targeted audience and hence the type of acts it featured. Vaudeville was family entertainment. Burlesque and variety were aimed at working men. The fare was cruder, often vulgar, and likely to be accompanied by loud cheering and jeering from the audience. Double entendres, suggestive lines and clothing, and dancing girls were not allowed on the vaudeville stage as they were in the saloons. The atmosphere was not a smoke-filled bar with sawdust-covered wooden floors and spittoons, but a well-appointed theater with comfortable, even elegant seats.

Variety performances were initially used as bait for customers to draw them into beer halls in the decades of the 1870s and 1880s. The first true American vaudeville hall was built by Tony Pastor, a saloon owner who opened a separate theater for entertainment in New York in 1881. That marked a clear demarcation from the beer hall environment. Pastor's theater provided entertainment that was appropriate for women and children as well as appealing to men, offering a so-called "double audience" fare. By 1885, the concept had spread to other cities along the eastern seaboard.

Tony Pastor was an entertainer. Born in New York City in 1834, he began singing for money at the age of twelve in P. T. Barnum's museum. He fashioned a successful career as a songwriter and singer, appearing regularly on the stage in local saloon theaters by his early twenties. In 1865, he began staging and starring in his own shows. He soon recognized the potential profit to be earned from an audience that would include women if the shows could be tamed down. By the early 1870s, he instituted "ladies night," when women would be granted free admission to see an entertainment program without the raciness usually seen in the saloon. No alcohol was served in the theater; it was confined to the adjoining saloon hall. This was Pastor's first move out of the saloon concerts into what could truly be called vaudeville. In October of 1881, he made the break that marks the watershed between American variety entertainment and vaudeville. He physically removed his theater from the saloon to a separate building, Tony Pastor's New Fourteenth Street Theater, where it remained until his death in 1908. His shows caught on with the public, because he provided a variety of good family entertainment that was free of alcohol, profanity, and lewd behavior. This was the same concept he pioneered in his saloon, but the theater presented the package in a nicer environment. He advertised new shows every week, twice weekly matinees, and reserved seats for 50 cents (about $10 today).

Pastor's theater was not opulent like its followers would be. Rather, it was important for what it did not have—a saloon. The physical removal of his theater from the saloon sent a message to the marketplace. He was offering entertainment for its own sake, not as a hook to sell more beer. It was the first serious attempt to earn a profit specifically on a variety show. His shows were the first to separate the image of drunken male entertainment and variety. The shows he sponsored were forbears of vaudeville, although they lacked their polish. The evolution of vaudeville would improve upon Pastor's offering but continue to follow his recipe: a venue for family-oriented entertainment, free from alcohol, vulgarity, and raucous behavior. Vaudeville was born, and for the next forty years, it would only get better.

KEITH, ALBEE, AND THE BUSINESS OF VAUDEVILLE

After Tony Pastor, the vaudeville mantle was picked up by Benjamin Franklin Keith and Edward F. Albee. Like Pastor, they were pivotal in the rise of the vaudeville industry. However, unlike Pastor, they were not showmen. Rather, they were businessmen. Keith is often referred to as the father of American vaudeville. Along with Albee, he assembled the most impressive string of theaters and monopolized the booking of vaudeville talent, ultimately establishing nearly total control over the industry before his death in 1914.

Keith was not far behind Pastor. He staged his first variety show in a Boston storefront in 1883. Others followed, and soon his variety shows became a regular, rotating offering. Each week a different group of acts, all catering to families, was offered. This humble beginning grew into an empire consisting of thousands of theaters, featuring the most famous performers, working the Keith circuit, which dominated the East Coast. A parallel network, the Orpheum circuit, evolved in the West, with Chicago as the dividing line. This duopoly existed for awhile until the two circuits merged their theaters to create a nationwide monopoly of first class theaters. This type of market takeover would later be repeated by movie moguls, who also recognized the value of controlling the points of consumption of their product.

Keith was born in New Hampshire in 1846 and spent most of his twenties working and traveling with circuses. Albee was born in Maine in 1857 and ran away with Barnum's circus at the age of eighteen to become a tent boy. It was at the Barnum circus that the two first met.

In 1885, Keith and Albee teamed up to offer a combination light opera/vaudeville show, which proved to be a success. By 1887, they determined that continuously playing vaudeville acts was the best formula for profit. It allowed them to open additional theaters, and within five years, they had theaters in Boston, New York, Providence, and Philadelphia.

While Tony Pastor pioneered the family atmosphere by bringing decorum to the stage and freeing the theater of smoke and drink, it was Keith and Albee who brought decorum to the audience. Prior to them, the audience at a vaudeville show resembled the crowd at a sports stadium more than a theater. Customers did not hesitate to voice their displeasure at the acts with booing, raucous behavior, and a well-aimed piece of ripe fruit. If an act did not interest a patron, he or she saw nothing wrong with starting up a conversation with a companion or wandering outside of the theater for a break. Keith made several personal entreaties to the crowd in his day, informing them that this was not acceptable behavior in that setting. He handed cards to patrons as they entered the theater, imploring them not to misbehave during the show, with entreaties such as "gentlemen will kindly avoid the stamping of feet and pounding of canes on the floor," and "all applause is best shown by the clapping of hands." These pleas for the "gallery gods," the cheap-ticket patrons sitting in the upper balcony, to be decorous in their behavior worked for the most part in the big-time theaters but not the small-time venues. In small venues the crowd hooted and booed bad acts, heckling the worst. In big theaters the crowd was more likely to give a bad act the silent treatment, as opposed to the clapping and cheering that greeted a good one. A particularly bad act might result in the audience walking out, especially if it was the closing act, but only rarely would booing result.

Keith and Albee built up the premier theater chain in the nation, monopolizing the biggest and best theaters in the biggest cities along the East Coast. More important to their financial success than their monopoly of the eastern theaters was their near total control of the vaudeville labor supply. Audience behavior was one thing, but Keith and Albee's real goal was the economic reorganization of the industry, which ultimately gave them wealth and power. Their organization was based on the theater syndicate of the late nineteenth century. This was a centralized booking agency that controlled the booking of talent for the "legitimate" theater, as it came to be known in contrast to vaudeville. The legitimate theater was the place for dramatic shows, akin to today's Broadway. Keith and Albee did for the vaudeville stage what the Syndicate did for the legitimate theater—bring an economic structure that monopolized the booking of talent for the industry and scheduled virtually all performance circuits.

Circuits were the schedules that performers followed—which theaters they would perform in on what dates. Circuits existed before Keith and Albee but were not as prominent or extensive. The first circuit of any sort was set up in the late 1880s by F. F. Proctor. It wasn't until the formation of the Association of Vaudeville Managers of the United States in 1900 that they became a significant factor. The organization united theater owners across the country in what the association went out of its way to point out was not a trust. Of course, this is exactly what it was—a blatant attempt to corner the market on vaudeville talent and exploit that monopoly for profit.

In 1896, the Syndicate was formed by six "legitimate" theater entrepreneurs, theater owners Marc Klaw and A. L. Erlanger being its most prominent. The so-called "legitimate" theater was different from vaudeville because it offered full-length plays. Klaw and Erlanger established a monopoly over booking, compelling producers to stage shows in Syndicate theaters and pooling the profits from the theaters owned or leased by the Syndicate. In 1904, the Syndicate controlled more than 500 theaters, including all but a few of the first-class theaters in New York City, dominating the American legitimate theater as a powerful player until the Great Depression.

In the spring of 1900, they persuaded a group of promoters representing the top major vaudeville houses around the country to merge into the Vaudeville Managers' Association. The stated purpose of this joint venture was to protect the interests of both the theaters and the actors and to coordinate performance dates and locations in an economical manner for the benefit of all. Instead, the result was what economists call a monopsony—a stranglehold on the labor market by a single employer. By uniting all the top theater managers under one umbrella, they served as the de facto single buyer of talent for the top-level vaudeville theaters. Any performer wishing to perform in the big time would have to go through what would eventually come to be called the United Booking Office (UBO). Theater owners paid annual dues and in turn were allowed access to all the top acts, whose agents booked through UBO since it was the only access to the top theaters. The performers also paid dues, through their agents, and in turn had access to work in the biggest and best theaters in addition to scheduled routes that minimized downtime and distances traveled between performances.

THE UNITED BOOKING OFFICE

The UBO was incorporated in 1906 by Keith and Albee. It booked acts into its theaters, which included the big-time circuit and many small-time theaters as well. Agents were granted franchises allowing them to book their clients into theaters doing business with the UBO, which included virtually any theater worth playing in. While the franchises were free, they did serve to control the behavior of the agents holding them, since they could be revoked at anytime by the UBO. Agents without the ability to book through the UBO were unlikely to survive, since their clients would be shut out of the best theaters. They still battled with well-heeled independents like Oscar Hammerstein and competing agents like William Morris, but the UBO pretty much had a stranglehold on the industry. The Orpheum circuit had a similar hold on theaters west of Chicago.

Theaters used the UBO because it was a regular source of the best talent in the industry. Of course, the Keith-Albee-owned theaters worked exclusively through UBO. Agents could book a circuit for their clients, thus assuring them of regular work for an entire season, which usually lasted about forty weeks. The bookings were arranged in a pattern which minimized downtime due to travel. Over time, the certainty of a circuit scheduled through the UBO established a sterling reputation, making the promised income bankable for the actors. The circuit was a valuable commodity, allowing actors to use it as collateral for a loan.

By 1915, Keith-Albee controlled about 1,500 theaters in North America, either through ownership or control of talent through the UBO. Since all the best acts booked through the UBO, any theater owner earning Keith's wrath could find himself out of talent. Most of Keith's influence was originally east of Chicago. West of Chicago the Western Vaudeville Association, containing Martin Beck's Orpheum Circuit, was in control. Though the two were bitter competitors, they both contracted acts through the UBO because of its stranglehold on the talent. The ability of acts to be scheduled coast to coast through one service was a boon to the performers, who could embark on a tour that was prearranged for the entire season or even over two seasons.

Keith and Albee used their dominant booking position to their advantage in negotiations with the talent. Acts who turned down offers deemed reasonable by Keith-Albee might suddenly find themselves blacklisted, and shut out of their circuit. Acts that proved to be recalcitrant, late, uncooperative, or demanding were likely to be disciplined by Keith and Albee. Having to deal with the management of the Keith-Albee circuit was enough to turn off some actors. If they could earn almost as much money, they sometimes chose the less prestigious, smaller circuit, though not often. Despite the tough negotiating stance taken by Keith-Albee, the prestige associated with the big time was more often than not too strong a lure. This makes sense if the long-term benefits of playing on the major circuit are considered. The major circuit was more likely to be populated by booking agents of other big-time theaters and hence more likely to lead to future employment in the big time. It was also the stomping ground of the bigger critics and reporters and better audiences, all of whom were more likely to generate positive buzz that would improve the demand for the act and its fortunes.

On the other hand, Keith-Albee used access to its stable of stars to squeeze theaters and discourage or encourage the opening of new theaters in certain places. A theater owner who balked at a Keith-Albee suggestion might find that he no longer had access to the premier lineup of stars they represented. In the same way, a theater owner who threatened to open a competing venue in the neighborhood of one of the Keith-Albee strongholds would be unable to gain access to the top talent for that theater. In contrast, the competing Keith-Albee theater would suddenly be filled with all-star lineups, drawing the customers away from the competition.

Keith died of heart failure in 1914 and was succeeded by his son, A. Paul Keith, who died of influenza in 1918, leaving E. F. Albee in charge. Albee proceeded to increase the size of his empire, purchasing independent theaters and smaller chains alike, as well as building huge new palaces in some of the largest cities. He was roundly despised as a tyrannical hard-line negotiator for the remainder of his life. In 1927, Albee merged Keith-Albee with the Orpheum circuit, giving him control of vaudeville across the entire nation. It would not last long, however, as the entire industry soon fell victim to the motion pictures.

THE BOOKING PROCESS

Before Keith and Albee established a monopoly on booking, actors arranged their own tours, contacting theaters they were interested in playing and contracting for dates. However, self-booking was a difficult and time-consuming practice, and it took the actors away from what they did best—perform. Agents, who specialized in negotiation and scheduling logical circuit routes, eventually arose and came to be the standard method of booking. On the smallest circuits, however, performers still did their own booking. This often took the form of responding to ads in the industry trade papers, such as *Billboard* and *Variety*.

There were two primary methods of booking an act. Blind booking occurred when a theater manager booked an act without ever seeing it. This was most commonly done for well-known acts. Most acts were booked by theater managers through agents, who negotiated with booking managers. Most often, theater managers would see an act at a small-time theater or at an audition in a major theater. If they saw something they liked, they contacted an agent who went to the sixth floor of the Palace Theater, headquarters of the UBO. About twenty bookers, each representing a different group of theaters, were there to draw up contracts between acts and theaters. The bookers were responsible for putting together the show for each theater. In doing so, they had to juggle acts, salary demands, and travel schedules while balancing each show so that it had the right combination of acts and fitted within the prescribed budget for the theater. The bookers tried to get the best combination of talent for the least amount of money, while the agents tried to get the highest salary for their client with the least amount of travel. Agents had to be careful of the threat of being blacklisted by Keith-Albee if they turned down a "reasonable" salary offer or were caught booking with another circuit (more real in 1910–1911 and 1916–1917, when the managers were union busting).

There were many benefits to theater managers from this arrangement. The theaters gained the drawing power provided by the Keith-Albee circuit. The acts were virtually guaranteed to appear, as cancellation of one booking meant cancellation of the rest of the tour. This was no small problem for independent theaters that routinely lost acts at the last minute when a better offer came along for the actor. Since the UBO dominated the bookings, the theater could be assured the acts they were getting would not have appeared locally elsewhere. Territorial exclusivity was guaranteed for theaters booking through UBO. The likelihood of an act violating the territorial exclusivity agreement was minimized by the threat of blacklisting any theater that violated it. Another benefit of the UBO was the collection of and access to records regarding each act's popularity and content. This was valuable information for theater managers.

On the downside, having a booking agent book your acts meant loss of control of your own theater. The agent did not necessarily have an individual theater's best interests in mind, did not know its clientele like the theater manager did, and might not book the combination of budget and talent preferred by the manager. Despite the drawbacks associated with the UBO, it did provide an element of stability to the system.

Most theaters worked on what was called a play-or-pay contract. This meant that once booked, an act had to be paid whether the theater manager wanted it or not. A manager could not fire an act just to save money, or because he found a better act to replace it, without paying the act its full salary. Ultimately, it protected the actor from managers who changed a program at the last minute and left an actor hung out to dry. The arrangement also protected the theater from an actor who tried to skip out on an engagement in lieu of a better offer. If an actor broke the contract, then he or she had to pay the booking office the amount of its salary for the number of weeks cancelled.

A booking agent was a skilled person. By the end of the 1920s, bookers averaged salaries of about $1,500 per year, slightly higher than the average U.S. salary. They had to juggle several factors as they booked acts for a theater. The entire show had to be affordable, feasible, and entertaining to the audience, which preferred a variety of acts. A good booker had to be familiar with a lot of different acts so they could judge their fit in a particular program. Whether booking for a big-time or small-time theater, the show was built around the headliner, the most famous name on the program, akin to the star of a movie today. Top-notch places, like the Palace, would use four or five big names on one bill, any one of whom would have been the headliner in another venue. The biggest problem with this arrangement was the fragile egos of some stars. An actor used to being the center of attention was not often happy to share such billing.

Managers had to balance a show—would this singer go with this dramatic performance and that comic? How would Houdini the magician balance a bill with a top Broadway star and a dog act? How much could the manager afford to spend for the female vocalist spot? Not only the combination of talent, but also the order in which it was offered was an important responsibility of the theater manager. Even if a booking agent was used to determine the makeup of the bill, the theater manager was responsible for setting the order and timing of the act, as well as enforcing decency standards and finding a substitute should an act cancel or be dismissed for some reason.

There was a symbiotic yet somewhat strained relationship between theater managers and the talent. Stars, even small stars, earned much more than theater managers, though they had to endure a grueling travel schedule to earn it. This created a tension between some managers and acts. Stars couldn't afford to be too demanding, however, because managers filed regular reports to the central booking office on the acts appearing in their theaters. These reports commented on the quality of the act and the appropriateness of the material for a general audience and were used by booking agents when determining contracts. Bad reports from theater managers could severely damage an act's ability to get a good circuit—or any circuit at all for that matter. The threat of a bad report could be enough for any actor to yield

19

to the demands of a theater owner. Fines were another way to keep actors in line. If an actor was particularly obnoxious or out of line, he could be fined by the theater management.

Just as in show business today, talent could only take one so far. An active, aggressive agent was also important. Competition between agents could get fierce as they fought to obtain the highest salaries (and the greatest fee, since they earned a percentage of the salary) and best circuits for their clients. They also stole clients from one another when possible. Talent routinely shopped around for a better agent—especially if they were not getting the bookings they felt they deserved.

The biggest stars on the big-time circuit had fewer cares. The agents of the Keith and Orpheum booking circuits had agents in the big cities to help arrange for the purchase of tickets, sleeper cars, lodging, and the handling of luggage and props for the acts. The actor only had to make sure to be at the theater on time. On the small circuit, not only did the talent have to take care of all these details themselves, but they were paid less money to do it, and in the smaller towns they played, the rail connections were fewer and farther between, the hotels smaller, and the network of specialized theater help was spartan at best.

THEATER ARCHITECTURE

The best theaters were built to exacting standards, with the comfort of the audience and the quality of the presentation in mind. The acoustics, lighting, coloring, and size and pitch of the stage were carefully calculated to provide the best setting for the acts. The size, shape, and arrangement of the seating was designed with an interest in maximizing not just the number of seats but the comfort and sightlines of the patrons. The actors were considered in the construction of the dressing rooms. In the best theaters, they were luxurious, rivaling a top hotel room in size and comfort. They were well ventilated and heated, featured private baths, and were accessible by elevator. Of course, older theaters in smaller towns were less luxurious.

Big-time theaters, such as the Palace, were often lavish, with marble staircases, richly carpeted hallways, sculpted plaster ornamentation, and luxurious box seats. Great attention was given to providing for the comfort of the patrons in the form of comfortable seats, spacious lobbies, and large comfortable lounges and restrooms. First class theaters were not necessarily the largest theaters. Many were intimate, offering every audience member a seat close enough to the stage to feel a personal interaction with the show. The Palace, for example, seated only 1,736. In contrast, the Hippodrome in New York held more than

6,000 and the Loew's Paradise Movie Theater in the Bronx, considered the quintessential movie palace of the 1930s, accommodated nearly 4,000.

The ideal location of a theater was near convenient public transportation and other businesses. Walk-up traffic was an important source of attendance for vaudeville shows. Therefore it was in a theater owner's best interest to locate near shopping and business districts, where a lot of foot traffic was generated. In addition, public transportation was important, as it was the preferred method of transportation for many of the patrons who frequented vaudeville houses. It was also important to be located in a neighborhood that was considered safe. A sure way to discourage attendance was to locate your building in a questionable neighborhood.

The 1910s saw the construction of some of the grandest theaters in the nation. The first of these luxury theaters was the State Lake in Chicago, the pride of the Orpheum Circuit. When it opened in 1919, it was the largest vaudeville house in the country, seating over 3,000 patrons. It was only the first, however, as several grand theaters would soon open, such as the Roxy, Paramount, and Strand, all in New York City. These theaters were opulent, in the fashion of the Palace. In addition to physical comforts, the theaters featured a well-trained, smartly uniformed staff ready to pamper the audience in whatever way possible. The attitude of the theater owner was to provide a setting that allowed every patron to feel like they were special. A night at the theater was the only opportunity many of the audience members had to enjoy such luxury. To help pay for such grandiose accoutrements, many of these theaters increased the standard bill to three or four shows a day. Thus, some of the grandest vaudeville houses were actually on the small-time circuit.

The glitzy theaters met with a humbling end with the passing of vaudeville. Many were shuttered and torn down, victims of urban renewal or the changing economy, which made their real estate more valuable as a high-rise office building than a theater. Others were converted for alternate uses—most often as a movie theater. Few remain standing today, and if they are, they are largely unrecognizable. For the most part, we must rely on old photographs to give us a glimpse of the majesty of vaudeville palaces.

THE CIRCUITS

Vaudeville was divided into two distinct categories: big time and small time. Among small-time theaters there were various stratifications ranging from the Loew theaters, considered the best of the small time, to the dime museums, the lowest rung on the vaudeville ladder.

Big-time theaters on the other hand, were more homogenous in nature. Big time meant full weeks on the same stage, fewer performances per program, higher salaries, and higher admission fees and production costs. Small time was characterized by a split week (two different shows a week, usually in two different towns), three to six performances every day, only occasional headliners, lower salaries, lower admission fees, and much cheaper production costs.

At the top of the heap was the big-time circuit, comprising about a hundred theaters in the largest cities across the country. The performers would do two shows a day. The theaters were large, grand, and comfortable, offering a host of amenities for both customers and performers. At the biggest and best theaters, the performers enjoyed comfortable dressing rooms, bathrooms, and well-lit stages in acoustically superior halls. The orchestra providing musical accompaniment for the acts was professional and capable of sight-reading music well enough to accompany acts which changed every week.

The standard show on the big-time circuit featured eight to ten acts. Smaller chains, like Morris or Loew might run as many as twenty-two acts, or as few as two acts, which served as fillers for movies during the late 1920s when vaudeville was in its decline. Whatever the number of acts, it was generally accepted that a successful theater had to have an inviting and friendly atmosphere and provide clean, wholesome, and entertaining fare.

Most vaudeville was not big time. The majority of theaters, patrons, and performers were involved with small-time vaudeville. There were an estimated 10,000 performers who attempted to make a living in vaudeville. Of those, only about 800 could be accommodated on the big-time circuit. If one traveled far enough off the beaten track, one could end up in the small-small-time, which was a training ground for up and coming acts. Acts cut their teeth on small circuits, honing their craft and waiting for the break that would vault them to the big time—the goal of every performer. On the small-time circuit the two-a-day acts gave way to four- or even five-a-day acts, or "continuous" performance. This pattern would eventually reappear even on the big time as a last ditch, unsuccessful effort to save vaudeville in the 1930s.

In addition to more shows per day, the weekly pay was lower, the accommodations and facilities not as grand, the travel grind a bit harder, and the support staff not quite as talented. Everything about the small time was smaller. Instead of an orchestra, music would be provided by a pianist and a drummer, who, while talented enough to play the needed music, certainly could not compete with an entire orchestra.

At the bottom of the pecking order was the one-night stand show or dime museum. These were in small towns, often without a regular theater. The show might be performed in a warehouse, storefront, or school. In the best of situations, an actual theater existed, spartan though it may be, with poor lighting and acoustics and without dressing rooms or bathroom facilities. In these towns, shows would be performed as many as six times a day. Occasionally a "name" act would be booked for a special two-performance day en route between towns as a means of earning some money on an otherwise off-day. For the most part however, the performers were new acts looking to break into the business, has-beens on the way out, or eternal optimists who loved the life but didn't have the talent to match their desire.

Most famous vaudeville headliners did time on the one-night stand and small-time circuits as part of their apprenticeship to break into the big time. They perfected their delivery, timing, and audience repartee as they worked their way to the top with a well-polished act. These circuits saw some of the greatest names in vaudeville, and even some of the best actors on the stage and screen, pass through as they worked their way up the ladder. Vaudeville stars such as Fannie Brice, Eddie Cantor, and Al Jolson, and screen legends Charlie Chaplin, Cary Grant, and Jimmy Cagney all came through the system in this way.

The small time was not an easy lifestyle. Work was seldom guaranteed—and if it was, it wasn't under the same conditions existing on the big-time circuit. On the small time, even if a worker could get a multiweek commitment, it was a series of engagements, ranging from one night to a week, requiring a grueling travel schedule, accompanied by endless nights in cheap lodging, eating cheap food, searching for cheap rail fares, often involving multiple station changes from one small town to the next. In the big cities the situation was even worse. Instead of playing at the premier theaters in New York or Chicago, small-time performers played at second-rate theaters on the edge of town or in marginal neighborhoods, but faced the big-city prices and settled for the same lower quality of food and lodging. All of this was financed by the performers out of their earnings. On occasion, a booking was cancelled, stranding a performer in a foreign town with neither work nor money.

Among small-time circuits, not all were equal. At the top of the heap was the Loew circuit. Marcus Loew, known as the "king of small-time vaudeville" was able to attract top acts to his tours because of his people skills. He believed that a contented employee was a happy employee. By offering nonpecuniary perks like clean, comfortable dressing rooms, professional treatment, and logical travel circuits designed to minimize the travel grind to his small-time theaters, he appealed to many actors. This attitude allowed him to compete with bigger theaters even without being able to match their salaries.

Loew's small-time theaters charged 5–25 cents admission and did three turns or more a day. By 1918, his empire had grown to 118 theaters throughout the United States and Canada, including 32 in New York City alone, where he had theaters in several neighborhoods in Manhattan, the Bronx, and Brooklyn. He could book acts on his New York circuit, moving them from one theater to the next. The circuit was low paying but involved no travel. It was decent work without the expense or grind of travel, but it still had three or four performances per day and nobody set a career goal of surviving on the small-time circuit.

The small-time theaters catered primarily to neighborhood crowds. The show changed regularly, so the patrons could come over and over again and see a different entertainment bill. While they may have been nicely decorated, they tended to have smaller seating capacities and featured a slightly rowdier crowd. These theaters were more likely than big time to feature material more on the fringe of family entertainment. They were closer to the variety hall mode of entertainment—especially on amateur night.

The entry point for many acts was amateur night at the local theater. Fanny Brice was discovered this way. Like many actors on the circuit, she grew up in New York. She made her initial amateur appearance before she was fifteen at the *Keeney Theater* in Brooklyn, collecting $5 plus "tips" (coins thrown onstage while she sang) for winning the show. As so many other "discoveries" occurred, she was spotted by an agent in the audience, went on to perform at other local theaters, winning several other amateur competitions, dropped out of high school to pursue a full-time career, and joined the circuit, ultimately rising to the level of star act and becoming one of the most famous female performers in the business.

In 1907, Klaw and Erlanger and the Schuberts, scions of the legitimate theater, jumped into the lucrative vaudeville business, challenging the Keith-Albee theaters with "advanced vaudeville," as they called it. They worked through the William Morris agency to book talent, forming the United States Amusement Company (USAC) to go head-to-head with the UBO. The brief competition for talent caused salaries to increase. Keith-Albee met the salary increases and then fought back with a blacklist, declaring that any act that left the Keith-Albee circuit to appear with a competitor would be prohibited from appearing on a Keith-Albee circuit in the future. This threatened blacklist was enough to keep many acts from switching over despite the lure of higher salaries. This domination of the labor market allowed the UBO to withstand the challenge and resume control of the market in a matter of months. A settlement was eventually reached whereby Keith-Albee paid the USAC $250,000 to cease vaudeville productions for a period of fifteen years. Schubert resurrected his attempts to compete in the early 1920s but failed again at the hands of an even more entrenched Keith-Albee circuit.

The two major circuits, Keith-Albee in the East and Beck in the West, battled one another for supremacy using the stars as the battleground. Whoever could attract the best talent could attract the biggest crowds. These battlegrounds took place in only a few major cities where both circuits had theaters. Otherwise, Chicago served as the dividing line between the Keith-Albee dominance in the East and the Orpheum control of the West. While the big circuits usually paid higher salaries, they needed to charge much higher admission prices as well. When Keith-Albee theaters were charging $2 in the 1920s (approximately $20 today) for the best seats, Loew's theaters were only getting 50 cents.

The second city of vaudeville was Chicago. Not only was it the second largest population center in the country, but both major circuits and many minor ones booked talent there. The biggest player in town was the Western Vaudeville Managers Association. It had agreements with both the Keith-Albee and the Orpheum chains, forming a partnership that booked acts from coast-to-coast. Only New York boasted more theaters than Chicago. Both cities had enough so that an act could stay busy an entire season without ever leaving town or playing the same theater twice.

A standard circuit was usually forty weeks per year. If booked on one of the circuits through a booking agent, the entire run was booked in a logical order, minimizing travel time. Performers could fill in the remaining weeks with individually booked appearances in independent theaters or alternate venues, working year-round if they so desired. The more popular the act, the easier it was to fill any vacant weeks on the schedule and cut down on idle travel time.

The price for the service of having the circuit book a tour was a 5 percent commission. This was deducted from a performer's check before the house manager paid the actor. The performer's agent also got a cut, usually another 5 percent. This was also deducted from the gross check, and paid to a clearing house, either the Vaudeville Collection Agency (Keith) or the Excelsior Collection Agency (Orpheum) for payment to the agents. The collection services not only facilitated the payment of agents but also served to regulate the 5 percent commission. The charge for operating the collection services was 50 percent of the agent's fee. Thus, for every act booked through the circuit, the circuit collected 7.5 percent of the salary, the agent received

2.5 percent, and the performer 90 percent. Out of this, the performer had to pay transportation, lodging, and meals and any maintenance of props. In addition, in order to avoid the maximum 5 percent cut, some agents charged flat fees for additional "services" rendered. These fees might amount to another $25–50 per week. Agents had to be careful how they collected this, however, because if it did not pass muster with the booking office, the agent could be expelled.

Smaller towns could not afford to book an act for an entire week and instead booked a split week for fewer nights at a reduced salary. This was better than no work at all, but less profitable for the actor since it required transportation to and from the town for a shorter engagement and made it hard to book the rest of the week, unless a matching split in a nearby town could be booked to complete the week.

The salary for a split week was not necessarily proportional to the number of shows short of a full week. Rather, it was a matter of supply and demand. The more the demand for the act, the less the reduction in salary, and the healthier the theater, the less they needed to trim the salary. Top theaters seldom needed to play short weeks, but if they did, say as a replacement for an act, they could pay a lower salary than a smaller theater might offer on the strength of their higher profile. The higher profile of the theater was often enough to draw acts willing to work for a steep cut in exchange for greater exposure. Top acts, on the other hand, seldom played to split weeks, and when they did, they usually earned fully proportional salaries.

The western vaudeville swing in the early twentieth century centered on San Francisco. A typical route included three weeks in San Francisco in various houses. This made up for the long jumps between cities on the route West, and the accompanying lost days on trains, or small towns with small houses and tiny paydays. Since there really was no major theater between Omaha and San Francisco, western circuits often found actors in small theaters for one-night stands. This brought the famous acts to the hinterlands and allowed the actors a chance to avoid a week without income.

THE PALACE THEATER

In vaudeville, the Palace was at the top, attainable only by the most famous and talented after years of honing their act and toiling on the road. An actor could tour the same cities and play in the same theaters he or she had on the way up, but now as a headliner, perhaps with fewer appearances and sometimes an increase in pay. However, once at the Palace, there was nowhere else to go. Though it was the Holy Grail for actors, it was also precarious, because from the Palace, the only way to go was down. Unless he or she could stay in top form and continue touring, life didn't necessarily get any easier. It was a desperate scramble to get to the top, and a desperate scramble to stay there. It was hard for even the biggest stars, because there was always a large supply of hopefuls looking for the break that would make them the next big star.

Besides housing the premier theater, the Palace also held the offices of the UBO and Edward F. Albee, czar of the Keith-Albee circuit after Keith passed away. His offices were on the sixth floor, and it was here that the fate of many an aspiring star was determined. With a mere nod of his head, Albee could either agree to book an act on his big-time circuit, even allow it on the stage of the Palace, or relegate it to another season on the small-time circuits, whose booking agents were located on the floor below.

Prior to the opening of the Palace in 1913, the top theater in town was Oscar Hammerstein's Victoria Theater. Performers liked it for the clientele it attracted—more sophisticated and "show wise" than most others. The theater opened on February 8, 1904, and featured a small glass-walled rooftop theater with a partial retractable roof. Hammerstein routinely turned weekly profits of $4,000 from the Victoria. Oscar's son, Willie, was the booking agent for the theater and was regarded as the most eccentric in the business. He had a fondness for booking topical acts, bringing to the stage anyone with a sensational story to tell. Willie once signed a woman named Evelyn Nesbitt Thaw to an eight-week contract at $3,500 per week. She played to sold-out crowds who were eager to hear her personal account of the grisly murder she witnessed her husband commit. Willie also liked prominent athletes. Boxing champion Jim Corbett, wrestling champion Frank Gotch, and baseball star Adrian "Cap" Anson were among the many sports headliners booked at the Victoria.

The construction of the Palace in 1912 was the opening salvo in a bitter war between the two dominant theater chains in the United States. Martin Beck and the Orpheum circuit controlled the western half of the country and Keith the eastern half. Beck, however, had designs on making inroads into the eastern market, so he bought a site in Times Square and built what would become the preeminent theater in all of vaudeville.

Beck opened the Palace, located at 47th and Broadway in New York, in 1913. New York was the center of vaudeville at the time, just as the industry was approaching its apex. The Palace took off when Beck booked Broadway star Sarah Bernhardt for a staggering $7,000 one-week appearance. This salary was more than double the top-paid vaudeville act of the day and more than the entire weekly payroll of smaller theaters. Every show was a sellout, with tickets being scalped for as much as $5—more than twice their face value. The Palace duly impressed patrons and performers with its grace, beauty, and clientele, and a legend was born. Within a year it became the top theater in the country, a status it retained until it closed in 1932.

Keith was furious, and when Beck's main financial supporter backed out of the deal shortly after it opened, he gained revenge by acquiring a 75 percent interest in the Palace. Thus the Palace was known as Keith's Palace and became the crown jewel of the Keith-Albee circuit. Keith did not settle for just this coup, however. He showed Beck what happened to men who crossed him. He bought the Majestic Theater in Chicago, putting him in direct competition with Beck, whom he eventually drove out of the city. It was a harbinger of things to come, as Keith-Albee ultimately acquired control of the entire Orpheum chain in 1927.

Not everyone jumped at the chance to play the Palace. Some big names refused invitations because they were afraid of not being able to live up to the buildup. The most famous example was the radio star team of Amos and Andy, who were repeatedly offered a spot on the bill but were never confident their material would play to the Palace crowd. Consequently, they never appeared.

The opening day matinee audience each week at the Palace was filled with top agents, talent scouts, and booking agents looking for new acts for their own circuits, theaters, and talent pools. There were also plenty of actors looking for ideas to improve upon, build on, or outright steal for their own acts.

During its first decade, the glory years of the Palace, Albee employed a sidewalk patrol to discourage scalping. Patrons identified by the patrol as having purchased scalped tickets were denied entrance. By the late 1920s, when the Palace began to fade along with the rest of vaudeville, the patrol was eliminated for economic reasons. Albee could no longer afford either to pay them or to turn anyone away. In fact, in order to bolster crowds, large blocks of tickets were sold at reduced prices to lodges, societies, and clubs.

The Palace seated just under 1,800. Prices were 25–50 cents for balcony seats and $1.50 on the main floor. A typical show cost about $7,000 a week to stage, plus overhead expenses of about $4,000 to cover utilities and staff. With a typical week generating over $20,000 in revenues, the Palace was a virtual money machine and the envy of all its competitors. Ultimately even the Palace proved it was no match for the same fate suffered by all vaudeville theaters. They disappeared in favor of the movies, which siphoned off their audiences and eventually took over their theaters as well. By the time the Palace featured its last vaudeville show on November 16, 1932, it was losing money.

In 1928, the Palace was sold to Joseph P. Kennedy and David Sarnoff of Radio Corporation of America (RCA), who renamed it the Radio-Keith-Orpheum Circuit. In May of 1932 the last two-a-day played at the Palace. On May 17, the new policy of ten acts doing four and five shows a day began. With it went the glory of the Palace. It was no longer any different than any other grand stage, whether in New York or New Berlin. It had become just another stage. Within the next six months the Palace would add movies to its bill, increasing their prominence until they were the main feature with live acts as merely fillers. This indignity did not last long, however. On February 7, 1933, the Palace played its last live/picture combo. The next day it switched to a straight movie house. In 1935, the Palace made a final attempt to resurrect vaudeville, adding live acts to its movie lineup. The experiment lasted only a few weeks, and except for a 1950 revival tribute, the last vaudeville act appeared on the Palace stage on September 25, 1935.

LIFE ON THE ROAD

The lifestyle of a performer was not luxurious. The grind was tough for all but the very biggest stars. Constant travel, dingy hotel rooms, and mediocre food were the norm. Theaters featuring drafty dressing rooms—or none at all—with limited access to toilets were not uncommon. Not all theater managers were honest, and it was a rare performer who had no story of short or missing paychecks to share. If a performer reached the big time, things improved. The travel was still arduous, but it meant more one-week bookings than broken weeks, and the cities were at least able to be found on a decent map. But even for the best, travel was an occupational hazard that had to be regularly endured.

Bert Lahr, a top vaudeville comedian who would later go on to fame as the Cowardly Lion in the motion picture version of the *Wizard of Oz*, spent the 1926–1927 season on the following tour, a good example of a big-time circuit. Beginning in late August of 1926, he started in St. Louis and continued on in order to Chicago, Minneapolis, Winnipeg, Vancouver, Seattle, Portland, San Francisco, Los Angeles, San Jose, Oakland, back to San Francisco, back to Los Angeles, Denver, Kansas City, St. Louis again, back to Chicago, Des Moines, Davenport, Chicago for a third time, Cleveland, Toledo, Detroit, Indianapolis, Cincinnati, Dayton, Louisville, Columbus, Canton, Akron, Youngstown, Erie, Syracuse, Rochester, Ottawa, Montreal, Providence, Boston, New York City, Philadelphia, Baltimore, Washington, D.C., New York City again, Brooklyn, Newark, Mt. Vernon, Paterson, and finally, ending in early July 1927, once again in

New York City. Except for his third trip to Chicago, he never played in the same theater twice during the tour. This tour covered forty-eight cities in less than forty-eight weeks over an 11,000-mile route—and Lahr was a major star at this time, meaning he had a much easier travel log than did a small-timer, who likely would have played half again as many cities, on split weeks and in smaller towns with more difficult rail connections, making for longer and more onerous hauls, playing in smaller theaters and enjoying lesser accommodations for much less money. And for every star, there were hundreds of small-timers hoping to become a star.

Actors decided where to work based on a number of factors, most of them directly or indirectly measurable by the pocketbook. Although the most important, salary was not the only consideration. The typical touring act was required to pay its own transportation and living expenses on the road. Therefore, the highest salary did not necessarily mean the best net paycheck. That depended on the route one had to travel to earn that check. Two weeks in New York at $2,000 per week was going to go farther than two weeks spread out among New York, Boston, Portland, and Providence for $2,200—not to mention the wear and tear on the body from traveling. While four cities in two weeks does not sound so bad, consider that the typical touring star might hit forty cities in a year on a major circuit—sixty or more on a minor circuit.

THE CASEY LETTERS

Besides the access to the big-time circuit, another advantage to acts of using the UBO was its function as arbitrator and copyright enforcer. Since the material used by an actor was his or her lifeblood, it was protected with great care. Actors could register a description of their act by sending a registered letter to the trade papers. If a dispute arose over ownership of material, the letter was opened to verify the registration. Letters could also be filed with Pat Casey, head of the Vaudeville Managers Protective Association, who followed the same procedure. The association would send a letter informing an actor of infringement of another actor's material. Because it was an arm of the UBO, which controlled the fate of most vaudevillian careers, such a letter was not regarded lightly. In case of a dispute, Casey acted as the arbiter, and his decision carried the weight of law.

A twenty-minute act was literally the lifeblood of a performer. The same act could be used for years without changing it, because by the time it got around to the same theater five or six years later, the audience was likely to have changed or the act had become so famous that it was still in demand, much like a good movie draws repeat viewers.

Stealing acts was not uncommon, but it was not ignored. Because of the slower speed at which information traveled a century ago it was not easy to catch up with a thief. A performer may be telling his jokes in New York while a thief would be telling the same jokes in Philadelphia. Of course, the further away or smaller the town, the harder it was to catch up with an imposter. The more famous the original act, the tougher it was to successfully steal it.

One of the most famous examples of capitulation to a Pat Casey letter was a performer named Ben K. Benny, a successful comedian on the circuit during the 1910s and later a radio star. When Ben Bernie, a famous band leader, complained to Casey that the two names were similar enough to cause confusion and that he had been around longer, Ben Benny changed his first name to Jack and became Jack Benny for his remaining sixty years in vaudeville, radio, television, and the movies. It would be hard to argue that the change had any negative impact on his career.

CENSORSHIP

In the bigger theaters, where a show might be booked for an entire week, Monday afternoon was often set aside for a rehearsal so that the manager could preview all acts to assure they were within house decency standards. The house manager watched the entire show, noting any objectionable material that had to be cut. Sometimes an act was dismissed immediately for various reasons ranging from poor quality to indecency. The manager would send a report to the booking office of any objectionable material and the overall quality of each act. Any offending or poorly performed act could be cancelled at any time. After the theater union was established, the actor was still due his salary, but a cancelled act would be reported to the UBO for all future employers to see when they reviewed files.

The trade publication *Variety* regularly featured a column called "You Mustn't Say That," which featured material that was deleted from various acts. While certain things were prohibited everywhere— use of the words "damn" and "hell" and material that directly insulted physical afflictions, such as cross-eyes, lameness, and insanity—the code of decency, as it does today, changed with the geography. What was perfectly acceptable in Wichita might not play in Boston, and what passed muster in New York may not be acceptable in Dubuque. Interestingly, it was not always small town America which had the toughest standards. It was often the case that a performer who had gotten laughs all along the way would have to delete a line for the first time upon arriving at the Palace in New York.

The standard backstage warning to performers listed certain phrases which were forbidden on the stage. These offensive phrases included such things as slob, son-of-a-gun, and hully gee. On the Keith-Albee circuit, actors were warned not to offend any member of the audience lest he be cancelled. When in doubt, it was always best to check with the local manager before uttering a questionable phrase on stage.

There were limits to the degree of concern about offensive acts, however. Blackface was a negative, stereotypical reference to African Americans, portraying them as simpletons and clowns. It was usually performed by a white actor in black makeup. It was not censored anywhere, and, in fact, the best were handsomely rewarded for performing it. It was a carryover of the nineteenth-century characterization of blacks in the antebellum minstrel shows, which faded out as vaudeville rose at the end of the century. This negative stereotype of blacks carried on much longer, still existing in the 1930s on radio (*Amos and Andy*, featuring two white men portraying two simple black men, was one of the most popular radio shows of its day) and in motion pictures.

THE LINEUP

Each show was run more than once per day, and each run was referred to as a turn. On the vaudeville circuit, actors performed a specified number of turns. A show, also referred to as a set, was a collection of individual acts listed on the daily program. It was this "collection" that a customer paid to see. In the big time, there were typically seven to nine acts per show, and the house (theater) did two turns per day—an afternoon/evening show and a night show. In the small time, there were four or five turns in a day, and in the small-small-time, there were often more. A continuous house was a house that continually repeated the same show, possibly ten or twelve times in a day, each show lasting forty-five minutes to an hour. The audience could come or go at anytime during the day and stay as long as they wanted. This type of venue was also referred to as a dime museum. The name originally referred to the low admission price and the inclusion of some static attractions, such as might be found in a museum, though of the freak-show variety; later on it simply referred to the low quality.

The standard vaudeville show consisted of two halves separated by an intermission. In order to construct a solid show that would keep the interest of the audience throughout, each half had a headliner, although one half generally featured a bigger star. The most coveted spot on the bill was "next to closing," usually reserved for a headline comedy act. The second-best spot was the similar point of the first half of the program.

The top act on any bill was known as the headliner. This was the act the manager saw as the major attraction, and the one he would headline on the bill. The headliner usually earned the highest salary, had the best dressing room and the biggest ego. This act appeared second to last on the program but at the top of the bill and in the largest letters. If the theater had a marquee, the star's name was on it. This was the act around which the bill was built and advertised.

Leading stage actors were often featured headliners in short stints in the better houses while between shows. Often they would appear in abridged versions of shows they had played to great acclaim on the legitimate stage. While the original fear for some of the actors was that they would taint their careers by appearing on the bill with a bunch of vaudevillians, the lure of the dollar usually won out. The best of the legitimate actors took turns on the circuit for a few weeks here and there, at handsome salaries, usually far exceeding their stage pay. At the turn of the century, top stars could earn two to three times their regular salaries for two twenty-minute shows per day on vaudeville. While on the road, their first-class accommodations and travel were also covered. This usually resulted in an increased salary when they returned to the stage, with their demand in an alternate market now firmly established and their potential audience increased due to the additional exposure. The biggest names of the era, Lillian Burkhart, John Mason, and Ethel Barrymore were all attracted to vaudeville at one time or another.

Full-stage acts, which required a great deal of setup, were usually reserved for the closing spots of either half of the show. This allowed the stagehands time to disassemble the stage after the act. Prior to these acts, a single performer, a singer or comedian, usually performed using only the front half of the stage, so a curtain could be dropped and the stage set for the full stage acts.

The hardest part of a bill to fill was the comedian. A top-notch comedian was often the headliner and highest paid act on a bill, second only to a touring Broadway star. Good comedy acts were in such high demand that sometimes they even played two houses simultaneously, especially in the largest cities. It was not unheard of for a good comedian to play the Palace on the opening bill and then play in a neighborhood theater for the later bill. While they would not receive double salary for this (since they were only playing half the card in each house), they could earn a sizable bonus. There was good reason for the high status of comedians: the objective of a show was to entertain, and the most fundamental method of doing so was to make people laugh. Ultimately that is what vaudeville became known for.

Managers were responsible for the timing of the show, which was a function of the timing of each individual act. If an act ran long, or if a stage change did not go smoothly, or, even if the show started late for some reason, the manager would have to get it back on schedule; the house depended on a certain number of turns per day beginning at certain times, and in order to accomplish this, the acts had to stay on schedule. Also, if the show ran overtime, higher pay kicked in for the musicians and other staff. In addition, since the typical house ran concession stands between shows, a longer show cut into the time available to sell profitable concessions. Thus, it was not at all uncommon for a manager to approach an act and tell them to cut their show short. An act had to be flexible enough to shave a few minutes off a typical twenty-minute show when asked. This was dangerous for a number of reasons, chief among them the quality of the act. If the quality suffered, the audience would not be as pleased, and one of the measures of a good act was audience reaction. Audience reaction was most easily measured by the length and intensity of applause, which was observed by the manager and noted by him in his reports to the booking office. Of course, if an act ignored the manager's request to shorten up, that would also be passed on to the booking agent.

A typical eight-act set would begin with a dumb act (an act without singing or dialogue), such as an acrobat or animal act. Because the house was typically still filling with latecomers when the show opened, a dumb act would mean that there was no dialogue to miss. After the opener would come a singer or minor comedian, followed by a tab show (tabloid version of a stage show) or flash act, so called because of its "flashy" appearance. It was often a mixed gender act of singers and dancers with their own scenery and often their own conductor. The fourth slot, usually one before the close of the first half, was usually reserved for a good comedy team or notable singer. This was the headliner position of the first half. The first half closed with a song team or tab show, depending on what was slotted in the third spot. After intermission, in the sixth spot, another dumb act would follow for the same reason as the first act—people returning to their seats. This was a good place for a dance act or an acrobat, since the props could be set up during intermission and taken down during the seventh act, which was usually a solo comedian or singer. This seventh act in an eight-act bill was the headliner. The second to last act was reserved for the star on every bill. The show closed with another dumb act since many people left after the headliner. Animal acts or acrobats often took this spot, especially if they had involved sets that were difficult to erect and tear down. The headliner could be out front performing with the curtain down, while the final act was being set up behind the curtain at the same time.

The continuous vaudeville show was designed to run for twelve hours, with only short intermissions. During this time, each act would appear two or three times in the larger markets, four or five times in the smaller ones, and a dozen or more times in the lowest level theaters. The headliner act, if there was one, would only appear two or three times, usually in the evening, when the audience was likely to be largest. This depended in part on the relative bargaining power of the actor and the manager. In the heyday of vaudeville, top acts seldom played more than twice a day. However, during the dying days of vaudeville, with work hard to come by, even the headliners were willing to take what work they could get, although performers who were in demand by Hollywood or radio, such as Jack Benny or the Marx Brothers, had sufficient bargaining power to avoid such bookings. If they returned to the stage at all, it was under their terms.

The nature of a continuous performance was to allow customers to arrive at a variety of times and still see the whole show. The vast majority of the customers remained only for one full show. With a continuous show, the management would hope to sell out the house two to three times in a day, twice as often on holidays. On a typical day, a continuous house would open its doors before noon and close about 10:30 p.m.

Vaudeville eventually adopted the silent movie. As the popularity of films increased in the late teens and early 1920s, vaudeville theaters began incorporating short films into their programs. Films were the eventual successor of the medium, driving it into obsolescence in the early 1930s when sound came to the movies. As the popularity of films increased, the ratio of film to live acts increased. Economics drove this change. The demand for movies was greater, and they were cheaper to run than live acts. Before they replaced them altogether, even the larger houses were down to a couple of acts a day as fillers between movies instead of the other way around.

THE ACTS

Each house provided music ranging from an orchestra in the biggest venues to a piano player in the smallest. In between, you could expect a pianist, a drummer, and perhaps a violinist. In the smallest houses the musician was a part-timer, perhaps the local mortician— in which case the show might be delayed if an unfortunate accident had occurred earlier in the day. Besides playing before and after the show, the music served as an accompaniment for most of the acts. The musicians had to be able to adjust their playing to the timing of the act, be ready to ad lib if something went wrong on stage, and needed to be able to learn music quickly, since their entire score changed on a weekly basis. Bad musicians could hurt an act, and a poor act would be likely to blame the musician as a first defense. The musicians, of course, would counter that you cannot make a silk purse out of a sow's ear.

The same headliner who wowed audiences on the Palace stage showed up in smaller towns as well—albeit less frequently and for a shorter stay, perhaps only one or two nights on the way from one larger engagement to another. The real difference from an audience perspective was not the quality of the entertainment, but the frequency of the quality. The exception was the smallest, neighborhood venues, which tended to be training grounds for acts on their way up but seldom saw them once they reached the top. Many famous acts cut their teeth on small stages. Once famous, these acts would return on occasion to the small town stage as part of a circuit.

Celebrities were attractions in their own right and were often booked onto vaudeville tours, though perhaps for only limited engagements, that is, a season or two, depending on the staying power of their celebrity. Athletes were common examples, such as the latest star of the World Series or Olympic games. Helen Keller and Anne Sullivan played vaudeville for awhile, as did Mark Twain, baseball manager John McGraw, and John L. Sullivan, heavyweight boxing champion.

Vaudeville acts came in all sizes and shapes. If there was a chance that it would entertain someone, then an act was put together around the idea. Burke's Juggling Dogs, the Imperial Japs, and Singer's Midgets fit this description. Singer's Midgets were exactly what they sounded like; Leo Singer scoured Germany for midget children of poor families and signed them to a contract. He used an extra large Packard to drive his troupe of 25–30 midgets around the circuit. Comedy and dance teams were always popular and featured catchy names like Bimm, Bomm, B-r-r-r, Top and Bottom, Back to Hicksville, Kiss and Tell, Yes and No, and Ham and Eggs. Animal acts were also a predictable favorite. Just about any animal that could be trained eventually crossed the stage at some point. Exotic animals were especially popular, but farm animals, such as Drako's Sheep and Goats and Musliner's Pigs, earned their few minutes of fame as well.

Hadji Ali was one of the more unique acts on the circuit. He showcased his ability to regurgitate at will. The big finish featured a small house on stage. Ali would drink a gallon of water followed by a pint of kerosene. Accompanied by appropriately dramatic music from the orchestra, he would suddenly spit out the kerosene onto the house, which burst into flames, which he then doused by regurgitating the water. These novelty acts demonstrated that nothing was outside the realm of possibility for vaudeville. If it was entertaining and not offensive, it found a place on the circuit.

The Unique Theater, located in Chicago, lived up to its name by featuring what may have been the most unusual act ever put on the stage. Owner Dave Grauman placed a huge table on stage, laden with a feast provided by local butchers, markets, bakeries, and cafes. The curtain came up, and every member of the day's cast came on stage, took a place at the table, and spent the next hour eating and chatting with one another. The providers of the food got repeated plugs from an emcee throughout the feast, the actors got a free meal, Grauman got the appreciation of the actors, and the audience got to watch an act that they would not see anywhere else.

Vaudeville acts needed to be novel in order to attract attention and get the big break that would launch their career. An act needed to feature a new joke, new acrobatic routine, new song, or a better or more outrageous performance. However, once an act was accepted as worthy of the circuit, both actor and manager changed their mindset completely. An established act was never changed. Managers and actors recognized the audience demand for familiar, established, quality material. Established acts delivered the same show night after night, in city after city, for years on end. The more famous the act, the more rigid the expectations of the audience who wanted to hear and see their familiar favorites. To change a successful act was not only considered bad luck, it was also bad business. Audiences neither demanded nor tolerated deviation from the most famous acts. For example, the comic team Smith and Dale, who were together for more than fifty years, performed their "Dr. Kronkheit" routine the entire time. It became so familiar that backstage help would recite the lines along with them.

Performers could use the same act for years in vaudeville because the performance was live and only played to a relatively small audience at one time. Without the availability of film and satellite, the show could not be broadcast to another venue. At best, only a few thousand people could see any particular act in one day. Contrast that to the average television broadcast today that reaches tens of millions of people in one evening, and can be recorded to be played over again.

Entertainers trying to make an impression, especially if they were aware that managers or booking agents were in the audience, were known to bring in "claques," or hired fans. Agents could be retained to assure a group of "claques" would show up to loudly cheer and applaud specific acts. This practice was not just limited to vaudeville, but was also present on Broadway and in the theater and even opera houses of New York. Not all claques were hired. Sometimes a close friend or family member would organize one. Such was the competition in the industry that just about anything was used to get that first big break.

THE LEGITIMATE STAGE AND VAUDEVILLE

Vaudeville was certainly not the only staged live entertainment available at the beginning of the twentieth century. The "legitimate" stage was also strong. This included musical revues and plays of Broadway. Symphony orchestras and opera companies also existed. These were considered "classical" entertainment, whereas vaudeville was "mass" entertainment. The difference for the biggest stars was not so much salary, as status. Along with that status came a reduced work and travel schedule and better perks, such as private dressing rooms and first class travel and accommodations paid for by the theater company. In contrast, typical vaudeville stars seldom played in any town for more than a week, perhaps two for a major booking. On a typical forty-week touring circuit, a vaudevillian could expect to play in more than thirty venues.

The relationship between the "legits" and the vaudevillians was mixed. Stage actors tended to look down on vaudevillians as classless entertainment, while the vaudevillians saw their counterparts as snobs. However, each benefited from the existence of the other. The legitimate theater was the goal for many vaudevillians, and the appearance of a Broadway star on the program would often pack the house, improving the situation for all. For the Broadway actor, vaudeville served as an easy way to make some serious money in between shows, where they were typically headliners playing to adoring audiences, most of whom would have no chance to see them otherwise. Broadway was too distant or expensive. But on the vaudeville stage, they could see the great Barrymores or Sarah Bernhardt in an abridged ten- to twenty-minute version of their Broadway act. It also served the same training ground purpose as the small-time circuit did for actors. Some Broadway shows were broken into one-act shows and tested on the vaudeville circuit before opening. In later years, it was movies that might be test run on vaudeville. The Marx Brothers tried out several scenes from their film *Animal Crackers* before vaudeville audiences.

Acting styles in the theater differed from those on vaudeville. For a Broadway play, excellent acting skills were a must. The vaudevillian needed to be a good entertainer. Though related, the two skills are not the same. An entertainer must be able to grab and hold the attention of an audience for about twenty minutes, usually without the help of a cast. He or she must be able to gauge the audience and adjust as necessary to keep them entertained. This often required a slightly different performance from town to town and even from day to day within the same town. It was also possible that the performer would have to adjust the length of the act on a moment's notice from the manager. It required acting skill and spontaneity. In addition, there were different stage hands and musicians to adjust to each week, as well as the need to adjust content to meet local standards. This was a difficult and demanding task.

In the theater, a play is a story that builds to a climax, developing a plot and featuring a cast of characters. The star does not have to hold the audience's attention alone for the entire performance. In vaudeville, however, a typical turn lasted twenty minutes, and the star of the act had to be able to hold the audience the entire time. For most acts, which featured only one person, this meant there was no help, no change in scene or sudden plot twist, no other actors to help out.

The travel schedule for a theater actor was minimal or nonexistent, as the show played continuously in one venue. If it did go on the road, it tended to play longer in each city and travel to far fewer cities than a vaudeville act. While the travel grind was absent from the legit actor's routine, the daily grind was not. The evenings were longer than for the individual vaudeville act. The theater actor had to be on stage or backstage the entire time. Like the vaudeville actor, the theater actor played six or seven days a week. But, while the vaudevillian traveled to the next town after a week or even a day, the theater actor could go home every night. Generally, the quality of the acting was considered superior in the theater than on vaudeville, but the best vaudeville acts were certainly acknowledged as talented.

SALARIES

Theater managers were willing to pay top dollar to attract a stage star because their drawing power would pull many first-time viewers into the theater. The manager was careful to add a couple of well-established vaudeville acts to the same bill, as well as the standard variety of acts, knowing that this was going to serve as the first impression of vaudeville for many. If they were pleased by what they saw, they were likely to become repeat customers.

When hiring a stage star such as Ethel Barrymore at $5,000 per week, houses outside of New York City were almost certainly going to lose money for that week. This is an example of a loss leader. The theater planned to lose money when offering a show at a cost greater than the revenue they could generate. The hope was that the star would attract some first-time patrons who would then want to return in the future.

During the second decade of the twentieth century, the very top vaudeville stars were commanding salaries in the $2,500 to $4,000 per week range. Standard journeyman acts, those which could get regular work but were not headliners, were earning $350–$500 per week. Although these salaries seem generous for the time, the business did not make most vaudevillians rich. Consider the case of Charles Bickford, an average vaudeville performer earning $275 per week in 1910. This worked out to an $11,000 annual salary for a forty-week circuit, which was enormous compared to the $650 annual salary earned by the average American. However, significant expenses were paid out of that salary. Fifty dollars each week went to the writer-producer of his material, $13.75 went to his agent, another $13.75 went to the UBO for booking fees, and an average of $60 weekly was needed for rail fares. Another expense was tips, which were a necessity if he wanted to assure that his act would not be ruined by an "accident" such as a lost trunk, missed lighting cue, or damaged props. Many vaudeville stars claimed that stagehands and porters conspired against actors, demanding tips as payoffs for doing their jobs correctly. Bickford tipped about $10 a week. From his $275 gross, $127.50 was left. This came out to a much more modest $5,100 annual salary, still impressive for the time; but, out of this amount, he still had to pay his weekly room and board and any repair and maintenance costs associated with his props.

For top stars, the money on the circuit was good, but the theater meant more stable employment and less travel. Whereas a star on Broadway could count on the same show for months, playing in the same theater, the vaudeville star would spend those same months traveling from city to city on a weekly basis. The pay was better for many top vaudeville stars, but the cost of earning it was also higher.

Until the advent of national radio and sound movies in the late 1920s and early 1930s, vaudeville stars were earning the highest salaries in show business. Women and blacks could do much better in vaudeville than they could elsewhere. In the 1930s, during the declining years of vaudeville, Ethel Waters, a veteran of some of the toughest grinds on the black vaudeville circuit, was earning $3,500 per week. During the same time period, the four Marx Brothers earned the distinction of being the highest paid vaudeville actors, commanding $10,000 a week.

Salaries were constant across the circuit, so that if an act was booked on the Keith circuit, the salary was the same for each performance, regardless of city. Of course, the smaller the circuit, the smaller the salary. The small circuits also ran a greater risk of not getting paid, in large part because they consisted of more independent houses, which were more likely to be run on a thin margin.

LABOR STRUGGLES

The first actor's union on vaudeville, called the "White Rats of America," was established by George Fuller Golden and eight other actors in June of 1900. The name was taken from a similar English organization, where "rats" was "star" spelled backward. Originally, they accepted only men. A similar organization for women, the Associated Actresses of America, was later formed. In 1919, both organizations merged with Actors' Equity, the stage performer's union founded in 1913. The purpose of their organization was to protect their rights in response to the creation of the Vaudeville Managers' Protective Association (VMPA) earlier that year by Keith and Albee.

The Rats formed their own booking agency, which attempted to book circuits in independent theaters for its members. They were charged a 5 percent commission for the service, but the money went back to the membership. This system was in response to the VMPA monopolization of the booking system. The problem with the Rats booking agency was that it had access only to independent theaters, none of which were first-class houses.

On February 22, 1901, the Rats staged a successful protest over the new booking system established by the VMPA, walking out of theaters on the East Coast and in the Midwest. The western branch of the association quickly caved in, and two weeks later, so did the Keith-Albee branch, with Keith declaring that he no longer favored the commission system of booking.

The Rats victory was short-lived, however. Within a year, they had faded from existence, to be replaced by a fraternal organization known as the Star Legion, and theater managers quietly reintroduced the booking monopoly that would dominate the industry to its end. After their apparent victory in the booking wars, the actors tended to be reluctant to pay dues for benefits that they did not see. This would turn out to be the pattern of vaudeville labor organizations. They peaked at times of crisis, but waned when the crisis at hand was resolved.

By late 1916 union membership began to increase again primarily in response to new clauses being used by the UBO in performer contracts. The most egregious was the "cancellation clause" introduced by Gus Sun, owner of the Gus Sun chain of small-time theaters, the largest of the Midwestern circuits. This clause allowed a theater manager to cancel an act after the first show without any obligation to pay even that single performance salary, much less reimburse travel costs to the suddenly unemployed act.

A second clause used by theaters was quite the opposite: the "play-or-pay" clause obligated the theater to pay an actor once contracted even if the theater cancelled the act. On the other hand, it required the act to pay the theater the contracted salary if the act failed to show up. Albee used these clauses as bait, rewarding or punishing actors by inserting or removing them, depending on what he was trying to accomplish. It was in this environment that discontent among actors began to grow and with it the membership of the union.

As the list of grievances against management began to grow, the union called for a general strike in 1916. Albee responded by black-listing all known members of the Rats from any of the nearly 15,000 theaters under his control. Actors who were only suspected of being members were allowed to work but were given unfavorable routes, salary cuts, and had the cancellation clause, rather than the "play-or-pay" clause, inserted in their contracts.

That year the VMPA developed another weapon in an effort to entice actors to abandon their union by establishing a house union, the National Vaudeville Artists (NVA). Clauses were inserted into contracts requiring acts to join the NVA and not the Rats under penalty of cancellation of the contract. In a symbolic coup, the NVA acquired the clubhouse originally constructed by the Rats in the previous decade and turned it into their own. The clubhouse had living accommodations for several hundred, a cafeteria, billiard room, and barber shop. Dues were originally $10 a year, eventually rising to $25. The benefits included a life insurance policy of $1,000 and care in case of sickness or accident. In its first eight years, the NVA paid out over $500,000 in financial aid and life insurance claims. Perhaps the greatest benefit was the "play-or-pay" clause, which became standard in the contract of NVA members. Those who refused to join were subject to blacklisting and, if they were employed, could expect the cancellation clause to appear in their contracts.

The Rats struck in late 1916, honoring an Oklahoma City stagehand strike. The walkout soon extended to Boston and New York. After the stagehands settled, the actors stayed out from December until mid-January 1917 in an effort to establish a union shop. The VMPA fought back with a blacklist of striking actors. Albee rewarded actors who joined his organization with preferential UBO treatment, including replacing the cancellation clauses in their contracts with "play-or-pay" clauses.

The strike was costly to both sides. Actors were without income, and theaters were without established acts to draw audiences. The strike had cost theaters plenty, with the daily revenue of Keith theaters plunging from an average of $1,800 to $100. The union, however, was crushed, and managers won the victory. After settling their labor differences, actors and promoters jointly formed an organization to govern disputes. The right of collective bargaining was guaranteed for the first time in show business. They formed an organization that would settle disputes between actors and promoters, managers and other actors. All parties agreed that the decisions of the "board" were final and binding. The disputes included issues of copyright similar to those covered by the Casey Letters, in addition to broader issues regarding disagreements between actors and managers, such as cancellations and working conditions, and disagreements between actors and agents. During its first eight years, the board heard over 15,000 disputes, with only four moving to the regular courts of law. Rats membership succumbed to the blacklist and the company plan and though it hung on for another decade, by the Depression it had relinquished its charter.

ALTERNATE EMPLOYMENT OPPORTUNITIES

The biggest theaters stayed open year around every day, with the possible exception of Sunday in those communities with strict blue laws prohibiting the operation of many businesses on Sundays. Smaller theaters might run performances only on Saturday and two or three evening performances during the week. During the pre-air conditioning era in which vaudeville reigned, it was not uncommon for a theater to close for the hottest part of the summer—July and August. Amusement parks filled the employment gap for actors and most parks had a theater featuring two shows daily.

Another potential summer employment opportunity for acts, especially in the waning years of vaudeville during the 1930s, was the so-called Borscht belt, so-named because of the large population of Eastern European Jews who frequented the area. This popular vacation destination comprised resorts and hotels located in popular spots in the Catskill Mountains. A typical lineup featured a dance team, singer, and comedian. Salaries were low, only about $350 per week, but better than no employment at all. Sometimes, in lieu of a salary, an actor would take a week's free vacation for his or her family.

Those theaters that stayed open during the summer, such as the Palace, changed their regular offerings. Summer acts at the Palace were often signed for multiple-week runs on the assumption that the regular clientele was less often in attendance and transient theater-goers were more frequent; thus running the same acts still filled the house. Though these acts were booked for long runs (often four to six weeks), each week the theater announced that they were held over another week by popular demand in order to generate more interest for future shows. Because they were summer replacements and not the usual top-quality acts booked by the Palace, they were paid lower wages. Despite the lower salaries, actors liked the contract for the stability of income and the prestige of playing at the Palace.

It wasn't just summer break that provided employment alternatives for actors. Besides stage work, there were many opportunities for idle vaudevillians to earn some extra cash. These ranged from additional shows off the stage, such as cruise lines, resorts, and private parties, to endorsements. One of the most profitable, as well as controversial endorsements was a practice known as song plugging. Song plugging originated in the 1890s and proliferated throughout the vaudeville era despite attempts by the trade papers and managers to put a halt to it. Music publishers were aggressive in their endorsements to famous and not-so-famous acts to use their songs, either to be sung, or in the case of silent acts, as background music. The bidding was most aggressive for big-time stars like Fanny Brice and Sophie Tucker, who could earn hundreds of dollars a week for using a particular song. At its height, in about 1910, music publishers were paying out more than $1 million per year to vaudevillians to get them to use their songs on stage. Some of the acts made more money plugging songs than they did performing—not unlike some of today's top athletes, who can earn more from endorsements than their playing contracts.

The most prestigious alternate employment opportunity for a vaudevillian was the Ziegfeld Follies, created by Florenz Ziegfeld Jr. in 1907. It was an all-star lineup of some of the best vaudeville acts in an elaborately staged, well-rehearsed extravaganza. The Follies traditionally opened in New York in the early summer before touring the rest of the country through the winter. The annual extravaganza lasted until 1923. It was a successful concept that became a premier engagement for acts. Many of them appeared year after year with the Follies, which as its centerpiece, featured dancing women. Over the years, the company numbered between 150 and 175 actors and stage-hands and featured about 20 acts per show, usually including a silent film. The Follies were the most expensive, elaborate vaudeville show in existence. They were a financial success despite a weekly payroll twice that of the Palace. Tickets for the show, performed only once per day, were scalped for as much as $25, more than five times their face value.

BLACKS ON VAUDEVILLE

At the turn of the century, African American vaudevillians were for the most part prohibited from touring the circuit. A decade later, from the 1910s through the 1920s, the Theater Owners' Booking Association (known as TOBY), a black vaudeville circuit, evolved to match the talents of these performers with the demands for their work, largely to black audiences in the segregated American theater. For black female performers, the additional hurdle of sexism needed to be overcome.

Being a star on the colored circuit was far from a life of luxury. In fact, many black acts preferred the fringe of the white circuit to starring spots on the black circuit. The black circuit was underfinanced, seldom featured anything but split-week bookings, and racism in the South, where the circuit was concentrated, was much worse than the racism in the North.

Black actors were not totally absent from the major vaudeville circuits. The best black acts were courted by white vaudeville, and since the white circuit paid more, they often performed there instead of the black circuit. However, managers had an unwritten rule that only one black act would be allowed in any show, thus severely limiting the market on big-time vaudeville for them.

Theater managers sometimes seemed to be above the issue of race, but audiences were not. It is more likely that managers were not so much color blind as they were blinded by the color of money. If a black act was believed to be profitable, a manager could usually find a way to book it without offending his primarily white audience. Black face was one easy solution to this problem. Black actors often put on burnt cork and wore gloves so that the audience would not know they were really black.

There were some notable exceptions to the general intolerance of black acts by white audiences. The very best black acts toured on the white circuit but faced discrimination in hotels, restaurants, and aboard trains, even if the backstage atmosphere with other actors was more tolerant and open-minded. Actors tended to discriminate on talent more than skin color, an attitude that was decades ahead of mainstream America.

One of the leading black acts in the early twentieth century was the Whitman Sisters, a headline act on black vaudeville that regularly crossed over to the white-touring circuit. They were managed by Mabel Whitman, one of the sisters, who was the only black woman managing her own company at the turn of the century. It was rare enough for a woman to be in a managerial position, but a black woman was even more unusual. She fought racism, sexism, and corruption, provided a role model for countless others, and offered a rare opportunity for black performers to work for a black manager booking shows in the best theaters in TOBY. One of the most remarkable examples of her power was exhibited in Birmingham, Alabama, on July 11, 1904. Mabel Whitman insisted that black patrons be allowed to sit anywhere in the Jefferson Theater or she would not put the Whitman Sisters on stage. The Jefferson was typical in that it featured an upper balcony, the worst seats in the house, reserved exclusively for blacks. Her demands were met, thus resulting in the first time that Birmingham segregation codes were successfully challenged and overturned.

Along with the Whitman sisters, Sherman Dudley was one of the most influential blacks in the vaudeville business. A former vaudeville star, he was instrumental in founding TOBY. After his retirement from the stage in 1912, he moved to Washington, D.C., and began accumulating theaters and leases. He worked with both white and black theater owners to put together a string of theaters across the South, Southwest, and Midwest. By the mid-1920s TOBY theaters were strongly represented in towns like Jacksonville, Kansas City, Nashville, St. Louis, Memphis, and New Orleans, as well as some cities as far north as Cleveland. Through his theater ownership and influential column in the *Chicago Defender*, he fought racism and managerial corruption. He promoted refinements like fixed salaries for performers in lieu of the common practice of giving them a percentage of the house. This practice not only might leave the performer with little or nothing to show for their work under the best of circumstances, but was often the source of outright swindling by dishonest theater managers.

The efforts of Whitman and Dudley paid off so that by the late 1920s conditions had improved dramatically for black actors in TOBY. They had better living conditions and travel and performance schedules allowing them to stay in a city for an extended period instead of a grueling series of one-night stands. The Lyric Theater reflected this influence. The Lyric was the only New Orleans theater that permitted black audience members. As the only outlet for live entertainment for blacks, the 500-seat theater was regularly sold out. Interestingly, if the act was talented enough, whites would also attend, but they always sat in the upper balcony, segregating themselves from the blacks on the main floor.

THE DEMISE OF VAUDEVILLE

Vaudeville reached its peak in terms of organization, and perhaps quality, in the early 1920s, about a decade before the entire industry collapsed under the weight of competition from talking pictures. At the time, there were over 15,000 theaters in towns of every size. It was without a doubt the most popular form of mass entertainment in America. It was easily accessible, affordable, and appropriate for the whole family. The bill changed on a weekly basis and the most famous names eventually landed in even the smallest of theaters, adding a sense of commonality to it all.

In the golden years of vaudeville, Edward F. Albee noted that the medium was the most nationally representative form of theatrical entertainment, drawing from the artistic resources of every branch of the theater—grand opera, drama, pantomime, choreography, symphony, and farce. There was truly something for everyone, no matter the composition of the audience.

Hollywood moguls predicted that the motion picture would replace vaudeville. However, vaudeville adapted, including silent films as part of its program throughout the 1920s. Films did force some changes. The two-a-day standard became a four-a-day in smaller towns first, and eventually on the big time as well. The Palace was the last theater to hold out with two-a-days, with fewer and shorter acts arranged around a film or two. It wasn't until the advent of sound in the motion pictures that vaudeville was dealt a fatal blow.

The larger theaters in the biggest cities, like the Palace in Manhattan, continued to feature live entertainment with motion pictures, but by 1935 the industry had disappeared from the American entertainment scene, never again to reappear. It was not that vaudeville failed to adjust or misread the future, it was simply a victim of forces beyond its control. Evolution in technology and consumer tastes, and better alternatives for the best entertainers, victimized vaudeville.

Vaudeville was a victim of the motion picture industry on both the demand and the supply side of the equation. The demand for vaudeville shows fell off as demand for the movies increased. In addition, talent was drained from the stage to the big screen. Performers preferred the higher paychecks and reduced travel schedule offered by national radio networks and the movie industry. Finally, venues disappeared as theaters were converted from vaudeville shows to the more profitable motion pictures.

Charlie Chaplin was a prime example of why a vaudeville star would want to shift from the stage to the screen. His pay was better, the travel was virtually eliminated, the work schedule was more humane, and the exposure was more intense and brighter. A year of touring could not expose the vaudevillian to as many people as a single week in a movie theater. The early years of the movie industry, especially the talkies, relied heavily on vaudeville stars to fill roles. The stage featured seasoned and talented actors who proved ready, willing, and able to step into the movies. Consider the case of Al Jolson. Jolson was an accomplished veteran of the vaudeville stage. He is best known, however, for a relatively small part in a movie. His was the first voice heard in the first talking picture, *The Jazz Singer* in 1927. After the successful debut of *The Jazz Singer*, many top vaudeville stars (including such standouts as Jack Benny, Fred Allen, Edgar Bergen, George Burns, Gracie Allen, the Marx Brothers, W. C. Fields, and Bert Lahr) tried their hand at the movies, proved to be quite successful, and gave up the trouping life of vaudeville for a more sedentary movie lifestyle.

Aside from Charlie Chaplin, probably the greatest stage to screen success story was that of the Marx Brothers. They were highly paid headliners on vaudeville when they made their first movie, *The Cocoanuts* in 1929. Thereafter, they made more than a dozen movies, never returning to the regular vaudeville circuit.

Despite being gone from the entertainment landscape for more than a decade, the imprint of vaudeville was evident in the early days of television. Television variety shows in the 1940s and 1950s were patterned after vaudeville, and some even starred vaudeville performers, such as Milton Berle's *Texaco Star Theater*. Berle had been in vaudeville since childhood. The show was actually called *The Texaco Star Theater Vaudeville Show* when it debuted on June 8, 1948.

The demise of the Keith-Albee empire is symbolic of the decline of vaudeville. In 1927, Keith-Albee merged with Orpheum to form the Keith-Albee-Orpheum circuit. In 1928, Joseph P. Kennedy, patriarch of the Kennedy political clan, bought controlling shares in Keith-Orpheum and merged it with his own Film Booking Office (FBO). Kennedy had no interest in vaudeville; he just wanted the theaters, which he planned to convert to movie houses for the film booking interests he ran in cooperation with RCA. Kennedy forced out Albee, who died a rich and bitter old man in Florida, on the fringes of the now defunct vaudeville empire he ruled for more than a decade. Meanwhile, Kennedy merged Keith-Albee-Orpheum with RCA to form the film company Radio Keith Orpheum (RKO).

Radio was another threat to vaudeville but not a significant one until nationwide networks debuted in the late 1920s. Two factors affected vaudeville in this regard: the ability to stay at home and listen to radio instead of going out and the exodus of stars from the stage to the microphone, especially comedians.

It is no coincidence that the final deathblow for vaudeville came during the Depression. Though the industry was well on its way to oblivion by the early 1930s, the prevailing economic conditions ensured that it would not survive. The demand for shows fell sharply amidst the dire economic conditions, and theater owners resorted to cheaper fare. Straight films, absent any live acts, were much cheaper for theaters to supply. The result was the dramatic growth of the double feature and the extinction of the vaudeville show.

The end came quickly. By 1930, there were fewer than a handful of big-time vaudeville houses, down from about one hundred at the beginning of the decade. And they no longer resembled the big-time venues of only a few years earlier. No longer was the big-time theater the domain of the two-a-day. Rather, the only remaining big-time houses were playing at least three shows a day. The admission prices and actor salaries were lower, as was the overall quality. It became a tougher market in which to survive, and the best acts chose not to do so, turning to the better pay and less demanding travel schedule of radio and Hollywood.

In the spring of 1932, the Palace became the final vaudeville theater to abandon the two-a-day. It was the last two-a-day straight vaudeville house in the country. Tellingly, the house was nearly empty for the final reserved-seat, non-film performance in May of that year. Ominously, the date was Friday the thirteenth. Beginning on Saturday the fourteenth, the Palace went to four-a-day continuous performances, cut prices ($1 maximum seat price), and eliminated reserved seating. It was a desperate and unsuccessful attempt to save vaudeville. In November, the Palace succumbed and converted to a straight movie house.

While the Palace was the last of the big-time theaters to disappear, the small time was able to hold out much longer. It wasn't until December 23, 1947, that the last of the true vaudeville shows played. After continuous runs since 1919, the State Theater closed its doors. The State, founded by Marcus Loew as a small-time house, ran four shows a day. Many top talents played the State, especially toward the end of their careers, when they were looking to reduce the strain and cost of travel and build up their bank accounts. They traded in the higher top-notch salaries for the steady bookings at the State.

Acts which in 1920 had no problem booking a forty-week touring season, by 1928 had difficulty booking ten weeks. Vaudevillians were forced to compete for a limited number of radio and movie jobs. Others survived by playing one-night acts in small towns, gigs in resorts, or the occasional sideshow at festivals. Only the most successful acts are remembered from vaudeville, and then only because of their success in the movies and television.

As vaudeville faded away, so did its thousands of performers who disappeared into the forgotten realms of history. A few, however, succeeded wildly by successfully transferring their act to new entertainment media. In fact, some of the best-known radio acts were little more than sound versions of vaudeville comedy and singing acts.

Burns and Allen, Jack Benny, and Fred Allen all transformed their comedy skits to the airwaves. Milton Berle and Ed Sullivan hosted variety shows that resembled vaudeville in style, if not form: a variety of performers, changing weekly, gathering together to entertain an audience. The difference, of course, was that the audience now numbered millions, and the act, once played on television, was pretty much played out. There wasn't much of a market left for it once it had been played to a national audience in one broadcast. A successful performer now had to have fresh material every week. This was too much for most, and the new venue killed off more. Not all performers could translate their act from the big stage to the small screen. Some were unable to adapt to the new methods required by the new medium—the different type of audience, the different type of sound and camera needs, and the fact that for television they were not a life-size act, but an 8-inch picture. On the radio, of course, actors who relied on facial and physical expressions to express themselves were unable to survive.

CONCLUSION

While vaudeville was certainly a business, run by shrewd businessmen for immense profits, it was also viewed as an important contributor to the social and intellectual development of America in the first decades of the twentieth century. Millions of Americans each year, from children to their grandparents, rich and poor alike, attended vaudeville shows, the chief source of American entertainment before the radio and movie industries blossomed. It allowed people to escape from the everyday humdrum of their working life to a fantasy world where anything might be possible. From the fantastic acrobat acts to the astounding magicians to the lyrical singers and outrageous comics, vaudeville offered it all.

Vaudeville was also responsible for a cultural transformation in America. It was populated by people of very diverse backgrounds, primarily working-class immigrants, who used the stage to transform the stereotypical ethnic identities held by turn of the century America. Since they needed to appeal to a large audience in order to secure greater bookings and better circuits, they moved away from cultural offerings to broader, more multiethnic material. Other barriers were also challenged. While it was family-oriented, vaudeville often pushed the envelope of the Victorian code of sentiment, yet it was seldom so overt as to turn off those seeking a more genteel form of entertainment.

Vaudeville provided opportunity for many otherwise disadvantaged groups. Blacks, though they faced subtle discrimination on stage and overt discrimination offstage, still had better opportunities in vaudeville than in the rest of the American economy. The same can be said of women, who had access to more opportunities on stage than off during the vaudeville era. Both groups could earn more money and rise to higher status in vaudeville than elsewhere.

Although it may have disappeared from the American entertainment landscape, the impact of vaudeville is firmly embedded. Its overall impact on the American cultural canvas is equally important. While vaudeville is no longer with us, its presence will be felt forever.

——3——

Technology Transforms Entertainment: The Dawn of Recorded Sound

INTRODUCTION

At a convention of phonograph manufacturers in 1893 Thomas Edison proclaimed that he would live to see the day that phonographs became as commonplace in homes as pianos and organs. He was both confident and prophetic. Recorded sound has come a long way since that convention. What began as a few minutes of barely audible spoken text recorded onto a tinfoil-coated cylinder, designed to be used as a time-saving device in the office, has evolved into the iPod— the ultimate current form of personal entertainment in the form of a credit-card-sized computer which stores hours of selected recordings in electronic format.

Like the motion picture industry that would soon follow, the novelty of new technology simply sold itself. Records were sold by volume, not topic. Early on, the novelty of hearing prerecorded sound was enough to sell just about any recording. This was reflected in the selection of recordings available for sale: comical songs, monologues by famous or learned individuals, whistling, marching songs, and hymns. Talent was only a minor consideration when making a recording. The recording itself was the main event.

The promotion of recordings to the public has evolved into a complex and multifaceted process. The basic scientific principle of converting sound into an electrical current has evolved into a massive entertainment industry which has advanced on two major fronts in the twentieth century: art and technology. On the artistic front, the styles of popular music have changed and diversified from classical to jazz to rock and its many variations. As dramatically as the musical tastes of Americans have varied over time, they pale when compared to the technological innovations that have impacted the recorded sound industry.

Prior to mass production of the phonograph, the piano had been the main source of music in the American home. Because of its size and cost, the piano was limited primarily to middle and upper income households. When the phonograph first debuted, it too was marketed at upper-income households. Over time, however, its price dropped rapidly, and it soon found a place in American homes of all income ranges, largely displacing the piano along the way. But, before it could penetrate into a majority of homes, the radio came along and short-circuited its growth.

INVENTION AND EARLY INNOVATION

The Edison Speaking Phonograph Company was organized under Connecticut law on April 24, 1878. Although the company bore his name, Thomas Edison did not own it. He had sold his talking machine for $10,000 and 20 percent of the company's profits. This was not a bad deal for Edison, who was preoccupied at the time with his electric light company and could not devote the attention necessary to exploit the phonograph's profit potential. The company enjoyed tremendous growth, reaching its peak employment at the end of the first decade of the twentieth century at more than 10,000 employees.

The first Edison phonographs were heavy, handsome, well-built machines, weighing in at 50 pounds or more (contrast that to the credit-card-sized iPod). They featured hardwood cases and polished brass fittings. They were designed as furniture showpieces that would function seamlessly and last a lifetime. They were priced that way as well, retailing for $150 to $200 ($3,000–4,000 today).

The talking machine debuted to great fanfare. Demonstrations were arranged by the company in and around New York City and were attended by thousands of curious souls who paid an admission fee to witness the latest invention from the Wizard of Menlo Park. The success of the demonstrations led to national tours of the machine, which was leased out to local entrepreneurs who charged for similar demonstrations in their towns. These lease arrangements were commercially successful early on, but ultimately the novelty of simply hearing a recording wore off. This meant that a different kind of marketing strategy was needed. The result would be the recording industry we know today, centered primarily around music.

Edison did not acknowledge the relationship between the machine and recordings soon enough. His focus was on perfecting the machine itself, not on marketing the recordings. In a business sense, this would prove to be costly. Though he captured historical credit for the most important technological advances in the phonograph, he was never able to exploit them as profitably as others.

Part of the problem was due to his preoccupation with another one of his inventions—the electric light. This distraction allowed others to gain a foothold in the industry, resulting in furious competition between manufacturers, which defined the early industry. Edison made major contributions despite not devoting his undivided attention to it. He was behind the movement toward mass production of the "talking machine" by unskilled workers, decreasing the cost of construction, and ultimately making it affordable to Americans of every income class. Instead of relying on the craft system of construction, in which each unit of output was carefully put together by a team of skilled craftsmen, he relied on techniques of mass production, standardization of parts, and low-skilled, low-cost labor to assemble the machine. This assembly line production technique, which he employed in the best manner of Henry Ford, was in full swing by 1917.

Edison's original intent was to market the machines for business use. But this market never really developed. History, of course, shows us that it was the home entertainment market, unintentional as it may have been, that proved to be most profitable. Because the first machines were designed to be used by businesses, the technical problem tackled by their inventors was the reproduction of the human voice, particularly the male voice. Consideration was not given to the recording of musical instruments, and no concern was given to the ability to record sound beyond the range of the average male voice. However, once the machine demonstrated its potential popularity as an entertainment device, the technical problems that needed to be addressed changed to the reproduction of music.

Inventor Eldridge Johnson founded the Victor Talking Machine Company in 1901. He had perfected his trade working for the Berliner company, an early rival of Edison's in the phonograph business. His annual sales of talking machines climbed from 7,500 in 1901 to nearly 125,000 a decade later. While it was Edison who invented the phonograph, it was Johnson's Victrola which became synonymous with the evolution of the industry.

The recording industry at the turn of the century was dominated by three firms: Edison, Victor, and Columbia. Victor was the company founded by Johnson, and Columbia was another early large manufacturer of phonographs. Columbia got out of the manufacturing game in 1909, however, and focused exclusively on producing recordings for use on the machines. In time, they would become one of the largest and most influential companies in the entertainment industry when they eventually evolved into CBS. The three faced competition from a host of small competitors, but they were able to maintain their profit margins against this competition featuring lower cost and lower quality machines as well as recordings by unknown performers. The Big Three could do this because they were vertically integrated operations, dedicated to high-volume, low-cost production of talking machines sold through their network of national dealers to play recordings made by their recording studios.

This was not a trivial concern, given the variations in talking machines being produced. In the early days the differences were manifold: some using discs, others cylinders, and no uniform standard of either. There was no guarantee that cylinders, for example, could be played on competitors' machines. Another difference was the speed at which cylinders and discs revolved (measured in revolutions per minute, or rpm) during playing. Early recording speeds were determined almost randomly and could range from 50 to 120 rpm. It was critical to replay them at the same speed at which they were recorded, for even slight variations would result in noticeable changes in pitch. The rpm battle was fought over many years, and ultimately a single speed was never settled upon. As history shows us, the 78 rpm eventually gave way to the 33.3 rpm long playing record (LP) and the 45 rpm "single." Of course, both were largely replaced by magnetic tape, the compact disc, and ultimately digitized music devices in the form of today's iPod using various formats of sound files.

The beneficiary of the competition was the consumer. As prices dropped, demand increased, creating a mass market for the phonograph. Each year from 1900 to 1920, except for the depression year of 1907, sales of talking machines increased. This was the first example of technology-driven home markets in entertainment that would be repeated with radios, televisions, and currently computers.

The phonograph went through many changes, most in response to the demands of the marketplace. For example, as interest in recorded music grew, the demand for higher quality recordings grew. This led to a bifurcation of the market into technology and art. On the one hand those producing the machines focused on increasing the quality of the sound and volume. The latter was driven in large part by the increased popularity of using the phonograph to play music for dances. It was one thing for volume to be sufficient to allow a room full of seated people to hear it clearly; it was an entirely different matter to increase volume sufficiently for dancers to follow the tune.

The length of recordings was another subject of intense research. Early recordings lasted about two minutes. This was not sufficient for dances and became tedious in other situations. When the phonograph was novel, people did not mind changing the recording every couple of minutes. But after awhile this became a chore, and the demand for longer playing discs grew.

Standardization was the next important frontier. After getting machines into general usage, it was necessary to standardize the recordings so they could be played on any machine. Initially, manufacturers believed that controlling the supply of recordings was the key to long-term profitability. To that end, they found it worthwhile to create a system in which recordings were machine dependent, that is, they could not be played on rival machines. This required that the manufacturer also be a recording studio. As Edison would ultimately discover, this was a different business altogether, one that he ultimately would opt out of, focusing instead on his comparative advantage: inventing.

Initially the recordings were identified with labels of the manufacturers, not the performers. The early Edison rolls featured a picture of Thomas Edison on the cover. The identity of the singer might only be revealed through a recorded introduction at the beginning of the cylinder, if at all. By 1907, all that had changed, and the inventor was replaced on the label by the star, prominently becoming the focal selling point. No longer were consumers content to pay 25 cents for a sound recording of an anonymous singer, but they were willing to shell out as much as $5 for the recording of a specific star.

Manufacturers scrambled to sign up talented musicians to exclusive contracts in order to help sell their machines, which would then be the only source for the masses to listen to the music of world famous talents such as opera star Enrico Caruso. Caruso is credited with turning the recording machine from the business application originally foreseen by Edison into a source of home entertainment. His first recordings for Victor, on their exclusive Red Seal label in 1902, proved to be so popular that they raised the status of the talking machine to the level of a musical instrument. It began to be sold in high-end music stores along with pianos and violins and was purchased by discriminating consumers who could afford it.

As the phonograph gained in popularity, a variety of quality levels evolved to meet the demands of a wider market. The average consumer was targeted with lightweight, lower quality models in the $25–40 price range. These models were usually made by smaller companies, but Edison, Columbia, and Victor all made forays into the mass market as well. Ultimately it was the competition for this market which led to an all-out price war as the century drew to a close. Prices of basic home models dropped from $25 to $10 for tiny models such as the Edison Gem (weighing in at 7 pounds). This competed favorably with similar machines produced by Columbia and Victor. Even at $10, it was not a cheap piece of equipment. Ten dollars was nearly a week's salary for the average American family in 1910.

STANDARDIZATION

The evolution of the record disc, today epitomized by the compact disc, was by no means a certainty. There was no clear early advantage of the disc over the cylinder. Indeed, the two existed side by side for a long time. It was the demand for longer recordings that ultimately led to the demise of the cylinder in favor of the disc. The length of a recording was a function of the spacing of the grooves, which were easier to compact on a disc than a cylinder. Between 1900 and 1920, discs increased in size from 10 to 14 inches in diameter and recording length quadrupled from two to eight minutes. In order to accommodate longer pieces of music, record companies would package several discs together, and the listener would have to constantly change them. This package, or *album*, as it came to be known, was the original long-playing recording.

Although cylinder players were forced out of market production, many still existed in American parlors. Edison continued to manufacture cylinders for them throughout the 1920s, though in ever decreasing numbers. In 1914, 23 million discs were manufactured as compared to only 3 million cylinders. A decade later cylinders were an anachronism. The small number of remaining players did not make for a large enough market for retailers to carry cylinders. The final blow came in 1929 when the cylinder machine Edison invented ceased to be produced by his firm.

An even longer running battle was that of speed. The issue seemed to be settled with the near universal adoption of 78 rpm discs by all the major producers. This standard was not without its problems, however. It did not allow for long recording length, necessitating frequent disc changes for long pieces. In addition, the quality of the recording left something to be desired. This was a problem which merely festered until a confluence of events brought it to the forefront.

The war of the speeds erupted in the 1940s in response to changing technology, musical tastes, marketing, and an economy emerging from the Great Depression. Victory would rest on a handful of variables: how many machines could be introduced to the marketplace, how many hit recordings could be produced at a given speed, and who would produce recordings at what speed.

In the spring of 1948, Columbia introduced its new long playing records. The new format had a speed of $33\frac{1}{3}$ rpm, a 12-inch diameter, and twenty minutes of playing time per side as opposed to the industry standard of ten minutes. It obliterated the old 78 rpm discs from the market. Gone were the multiple disc albums which required a listener to frequently change discs to hear an entire piece of music. This was a big issue for lovers of classical music, which often featured pieces requiring several discs. Not only was it less effort to listen to these new long-playing vinyl discs, but the quality of the sound was vastly superior.

In addition, Columbia successfully marketed an attachment that allowed existing 78 rpm machines to also play the new LPs. They gave away the patent in order to broaden the market for their discs. Instead of joining, Victor went in the opposite direction, focusing on an entirely different market by introducing a disc with yet another speed: 45 rpm. The speed of 45 rpm had been chosen based on a mathematical formulation which, when considering the physics of the phonograph, produced the highest quality, distortion-free sound for a period of just over five minutes, long enough for most of the popular singles purchased by the increasingly important teenage market.

The next several years saw a "war of speeds," with Columbia pushing the 33 1/3 LP standard and Victor clinging to the 45 rpm single. The problem was that machines could not handle both speeds. Until technology existed to allow a single machine to handle both discs, the stakes for the industry speed standard were huge. With neither company ever to claim complete victory, they began to invade each other's territory. Victor released its first LPs in February of 1950, and one year later Columbia began to issue 45s. Ultimately the solution to the speed war was found in the successful development of a phonograph capable of playing variable speeds ranging from the obscure $16^{2}/_{3}$ rpm talking books to the early standard 78 and the newly popular $33^{1}/_{3}$ and 45 in between.

Victor introduced the 45 rpm rapid changer in 1949, upping the ante. It automatically dropped another record from a stack of singles onto the turntable, allowing the listener to select individual songs and the order in which they wanted to hear them. The listener could stack them all together and listen to them play one by one. This, of course, seems crude in comparison to the ability to customize songlists today on an iPod, but it was revolutionary at the time.

THE MANUFACTURING OF PHONOGRAPHS

The phonograph was a common piece of household furniture in the upper-income American household by 1910. It helped to transform the twentieth-century parlor into the twentieth-century living room— instead of a room to receive guests and sit in stately conversation, it became a room where guests might be entertained. One of the features of the early phonograph which kept it out of the American living room was that it did not look like it belonged in the formal setting of the parlor. The often grand, even exquisite, cabinets housing the mechanism were fine, it was the large, protruding amplification horn that was objectionable. The large horn was a definite improvement over earphones, especially for the purpose of entertaining, but it was unsightly and limited the phonograph's acceptance nonetheless.

The Victor Talking Machine Company was the industry leader in addressing this problem with the debut in 1906 of its Victrola model. Its outstanding physical feature was the absence of the unsightly horn that protruded from the top of other talking machines. Instead, the horn turned down, underneath the mechanism and was enclosed in a cabinet. The Victrola was totally enclosed, resembling a fine piece of furniture as much as a technological innovation and state-of-the-art home entertainment unit. The new Victrolas were a marketing success. Style and price (average $50) trumped performance quality. This was not much of a problem, however, since most purchases were made by first-time customers who had nothing to compare it to. Even though the new Victrolas represented a step backward in performance quality, they were a huge step forward in public acceptance.

Despite the sub-par quality of its sound caused by the internal horn, Victor had its greatest financial success in the years after its introduction. This had more to do with factors other than its appearance. It had locked up the greatest singers with exclusive contracts, possessed superior advertising and marketing departments, and held the patent on the important Johnson tapered tone-arm, a technical breakthrough that was valuable and highly desired by every manufacturer.

The recording industry began to decline in the 1920s, and from production to sales, the industry flagged. The problem, in a nutshell, was too many companies competing in a market that was already saturated. In 1914, 18 companies, with sales of $27 million, manufactured phonographs. Less than five years later, the industry had expanded to 166 companies with $158 million in sales. The expanding market and profit potential was only one factor enticing entrepreneurs. Another was the availability of patents, most of which had expired by 1917, thus removing a serious barrier to new entrants.

The high watermark for recordings came a few years later, in 1921. It would be another quarter century, following a Depression and a World War, before the $106 million sales mark set that year would be surpassed. In July of 1920, *Variety* recognized the importance of the recorded music industry by adding the best-sellers chart, which would ultimately become the "Top 40." But by the end of WWII, the number of recording companies would be drastically reduced, and by the end of the century, the industry concentration of global publishers would be so tight it would undergo several close looks by antitrust investigators and the production of phonographs would give way to other technologies.

The giddy heights of 1921 gave way to the depths of 1925. Record sales were less than half their 1921 peak, and for the first time since 1901, Victor failed to pay a dividend. Radio, the Great Depression, sound movies, and market saturation were all to blame for the slump in the latter half of the 1920s. Manufacturers were turning their resources to producing radios rather than phonographs. Little technological advancement was made on the phonograph during the 1920s because most of the effort went into radio production. Some even thought the day of the phonograph was over. The predictions of recorded music's demise, however, were premature. The industry would eventually roar back. It just required the right set of circumstances.

THE JUKEBOX

The "jukebox," though it was not yet called that, was first developed in 1889 by Louis Glass of the Pacific Phonograph Company. He equipped one of his Edison machines with a nickel-slot operating device and four listening tubes. He then had this machine installed in a San Francisco saloon. Each tube required a nickel deposit to activate a predetermined song. The ability to choose from a selection of songs lay in the future. It proved so popular, he quickly produced more and secured a patent on the device. Soon thereafter, Edison developed a machine that would allow up to six different songs to be played, but they rotated in a predetermined order and the listener had no choice of songs.

Competition bred innovation. After the market became glutted with Glass's slot machines, the development of gimmicks separated the machines in the competitive marketplace. Some developed pictures that would illustrate the song. In a crude forerunner to the nickelodeon, these song machines would drop cards designed to illustrate the lyrics of a song into view. In 1905, the *Multiphone* was introduced. For the first time listeners could select from a variety of songs. Also that year, the slot machine first came equipped with a listening horn, replacing earphones, thus permitting more than one person to hear a song with just one nickel.

While the original machines were located in areas where people already gathered, such as saloons, eventually places evolved that were solely dedicated to entertainment by means of placing nickels in pianos, phonographs, or motion picture machines. These so-called arcades became places of entertainment, and still exist today, though usually devoted to computer games.

The popularity and profitability of slot machines waned by about 1910. Home use of recording machines contributed to its demise, but another factor was the increasing popularity of the nickelodeon—a nickel slot machine that showed moving pictures. Nickelodeon parlors quickly displaced arcades in public demand. It would take another generation, a Depression, and prohibition to bring back the popularity of the machines.

The Depression increased the popularity of the coin-slot record machine, or "juke box." While the typical household could not afford a $400 phonograph, it might be able to afford the occasional beverage and song at a local watering hole. The quality of these machines had improved dramatically since their debut in the 1890s. By 1930, there were 50,000 in use. When prohibition was repealed in 1933, waves of patrons descended upon taverns and bars for socializing, and they demanded music. Coin machines were the perfect solution, and over the next few years, annual sales rose to 500,000 units. They were everywhere. Not just in taverns, but pool halls, hotels, restaurants, cafes, and beauty parlors. Anywhere people might congregate they could now listen to music.

This quantity of machines needed music, and it had to be replaced on a regular basis. By 1936, more than half of all records produced were destined for juke boxes. The Depression helped move music from public places into the home, where recordings were a cheaper alternative to live music performance for listening and dancing entertainment.

The softening market resulted in a decrease in sales by Edison from 140,000 players in 1920 to 32,000 in 1921. Victor was purchased by RCA. The merger was a major one, resulting in a new company called RCA Victor, which manufactured radios, phonographs, and combination sets. RCA became one of the great companies of the world. They also owned research laboratories and recording studios and in the next decade would add motion picture companies and theaters to their stable. Their research labs would be among the leaders in the development of television.

With the saturation of the record playing machine market, the emphasis switched from the sale of machines to the sale of recordings. All companies now had to stake their survival on their recording catalogue, which had to keep pace with the ever-changing tastes of the American public for musical style. This was a much different problem to master than merely mass producing machines at the lowest possible price, and not all companies were equally well suited to the task. Scores of smaller companies went bankrupt in the market shakeout.

Columbia saw the future as well, and in 1927, it purchased a small radio network, United Independent Broadcasters, in order to ensure an outlet to broadcast and promote their recordings. The new company was renamed the Columbia Phonograph Broadcasting System, ultimately changed to Columbia Broadcasting System, and is today known simply as CBS. The future was clear: the entertainment industry had become big business, and big business would grow to dominate it.

RADIO

Recorded music and radio suffered through a love–hate relationship. On the one hand, they competed against one another for the entertainment time and dollar of the American public. Listening to the radio meant that one was not listening to recorded music. Early radio broadcasts were most likely to be live performances. This, however, was an expensive pursuit and as the availability and quality of recorded music improved, recorded music became more prevalent. This occasionally led to legal wrangles. Record companies objected to radio stations playing their discs on the air, which they clearly labeled "not licensed for radio broadcast." On the other hand, it was free publicity for their new songs, so the protests were often faint, as negotiations between the record companies and radio stations regarding the payment of rights fees would ultimately show. The industry would learn to see radio as a strong complement, eventually going so far as to pay radio stations to play their music.

Radio and recording went from being substitutes for each other to complements in the entertainment industry, a metamorphoses that would later be repeated by the television and movie industries. Each found that they profited from the other. Recordings were cheaper and more efficient than live performance as a source of entertainment for radio broadcasters, and radio broadcasts became the primary method of advertising a recording to its potential audience. A song gained popularity through repeated play over a wide network of radio stations and became a "must have" for the American buying public, which then sought out a copy of the recording for their own personal library.

Radio stations began to move away from live and into recorded music as early as the mid-1920s. Some smaller stations in large cities relied on recordings for all of their music, playing up to eighteen hours of records a day, covering the time during record changes with commercials and chatter, rarely acknowledging the source of the music, as required by Federal Radio Commission rulings. As technology improved the quality of transmitting recorded music, it eventually led to the elimination of stations employing musicians to provide live music. The lack of royalties grated on performers and publishers for decades, even after they saw the benefits radio had on their record sales.

The radio became the in-home entertainment choice during the Depression. The number of households with radios more than doubled from 12 million homes in 1930 to 25 million in 1935, whereas only about 500,000 phonographs were purchased during the decade ending in 1935. While cost considerations of the Depression first gave rise to the use of prerecorded entertainment by radio stations, it was the drafting of large numbers of performers for World War II that really pushed its use into the mainstream. With the paucity of performers available for live broadcasts, radio stations were forced to rely on prerecorded music only. What they discovered was that as long as the quality was good, listeners couldn't tell the difference, so they didn't care.

The arrival of talking pictures in 1927 had a greater impact on the recording industry than just technology, it also changed the market structure of the industry. The movies produced popular music that recording companies wanted to sell. The rights to the music now in demand by the public belonged to the movie companies, which soon recognized a good market opportunity, and instead of partnering with the record producers, they took them over. Warner Brothers purchased a recording studio in 1930, consolidating the process. They now owned the music performed in their films, and they produced the recordings the film-going public grew to love. In turn, they promoted their music on their radio stations, just in case somebody had not already heard it in the movie theater. Warner Brothers grew from a nearly bankrupt $10 million company in 1927 to a $230 million corporate behemoth three short years later.

With the dawning of the Depression, more radio stations were willing to use recorded music in place of the more expensive live version, though the two national networks at the time, CBS and NBC, held out longer in their policy against "canned music." The first crack in their defense was the recording of shows which originally aired live on their stations. They tended to record these on discs, as they were convenient, durable, and easily transportable to other stations. It also provided for a cheap way to rebroadcast popular shows at a later time and even turn them into a source of income by leasing them to nonnetwork stations in the future. During the 1930s, the radio networks became the major users of recorded sound technology. The use of recorded versions of their own radio shows allowed a network to broadcast a show at the same local time in different time zones.

Amos and Andy, the first show syndicated in this way, could thus be aired at 8:00 p.m. in all time zones by means of having been recorded in New York and then sent via disc to member stations across the country for later broadcast. If it was more convenient for a station to air the show at a different time, its availability on disc allowed for that possibility. As networks grew in importance and proliferation in the market, their reliance on prerecorded entertainment grew. Today, little broadcasting on radio is live, especially music.

The Depression hit the industry hard, as consumers revealed to phonograph and record makers that despite their advertising attempts, they considered recorded music a luxury, not a necessity. By 1932, sales had declined to $11 million, barely 10 percent of a decade earlier, leading to the bankruptcy of many small manufacturers. Radio sales were not much better, although that medium was considered a necessity, since it was the source of much of the news obtained by Americans. Sales of radios dropped from $500 million in 1929 to $302 million in 1930.

Recording studios closed, performers were released from contracts, and artists joined the long lines of migrants westward to California. They had their sights set on Hollywood. Not Herbert Yates, however. Where others saw misery, he saw opportunity. Where others were selling, he was buying. Taking advantage of Depression era fire sale prices, he began buying up bankrupt record companies. Yates owned Consolidated Film Laboratories, which also bought up small bankrupt film companies. He purchased these companies and consolidated them as the American Record Company (ARC). In just three short years of bargain basement purchasing, ARC became the largest record company in the United States, with annual sales of 6 million records by 1932. By comparison, RCA-Victor sold only 3 million records that year.

While Yates was buying up small recording studios, the English investor Ted Lewis swooped in and purchased pressing plants, the actual manufacturers of the records, and recording studios to obtain a foothold for his British label, Decca records. He set about changing the industry, ending the two-tiered approach whereby premium recordings sold for 75 cents to a dollar and lower tier recordings sold for 35 cents. He sold everything for 35 cents. Yates quickly matched this strategy, and the two men dominated the recording industry during the Depression. The industry had moved from the era of the inventor, like Edison and Johnson, to the businessman, where it remains today.

Performers also fell on hard times. Even top stars like blues sensation Bessie Smith found their demand wanting. Though she was paid a standard fee of $3,000 for a recording session in 1928, she was willing to do the same work for a mere $50 just three years later (if she could find someone willing to pay her even that much).

As the country emerged from the Depression, the recorded sound industry flourished. Flush off of a Depression, and coinciding with an improvement in technology that allowed for the growth of recorded discs for the broadcast of music, the recorded music industry took off. Record companies now advertised the availability of their recorded music that was already heard on the radio. The tag line, "music you want, when you want it," became a familiar theme as record companies appealed to Americans who had more disposable income available for entertainment to buy their own personal copies of the music they grew to love from the radio.

During the 1940s, the prominence of recorded entertainment grew to the point where 75 percent of all broadcasts over radio were recordings. This era gave birth to the "disc jockey," the live broadcaster who chatted to, or sometimes with (via call-ins), the audience in between introducing recorded songs to play. This format still exists today in most markets, although it has been replaced at some stations with totally prerecorded entertainment.

After WWII, television became the preferred medium for introducing a hot new release. Performers appeared on variety shows, such as the *Toast of the Town*, hosted by Ed Sullivan, or the *Colgate Comedy Hour*. Ultimately, shows devoted to music, such as Dick Clark's American Bandstand, which debuted in 1951, and then cable channels like the music dedicated channel, MTV, would arise.

The introduction of MTV in 1981 created a new era in sound. Now music became a video show as well. The cooperation of Time-Warner and American Express created it as one of the first dedicated cable television channels catering to a small but homogenous audience. Television took over where movies and radio had preceded it in the promotion of musical tastes, and it proved to be much more powerful. Because of its reach and its audience of baby boomers prone to buy music, MTV turned good songs into hits virtually overnight.

Like the radio stations that received free records in turn for publicizing music, MTV did not pay to produce or broadcast its videos. The videos were provided by the artists and publishers. The cost of a music video was much greater than a record, but the results could be fantastic. A 1982 survey of retail record dealers by *Billboard* found that new acts debuting on MTV could expect an immediate 10–15 percent increase in album sales.

The success of MTV led to imitators, such as VH1 and The Nashville Network. Some were 24-hour dedicated music channels; others featured music video programming. The market became more competitive and a familiar pattern emerged. Established artists could now sell their videos to television stations and then benefit additionally from the sale of their music promoted by the video. New artists would pay to finance their own video and then through a major distributor hope to strike a deal that would get it aired on television just to get the exposure that would give them the break they needed.

RESIDUALS AND COPYRIGHTS

Because the phonograph was originally viewed as a passing fancy, no serious thought was given to copyright issues. The only person paid for a recording was the musician, who received a one-time fee for the actual recording. Composers and lyricists were not paid for the privilege of recording their work, and royalties were a future topic of discussion.

In 1909, the Copyright Act was revised, creating new protection for music publishers, authors, composers, and songwriters. A new royalty was mandated at a rate of 2 cents for each mechanical copy of a song made, be it cylinder, recording, or paper music roll. This was known as a mechanical royalty. Perhaps most importantly, it provided enforcement of the unauthorized performance clause by providing a minimum damage claim of $250 for anyone found to be in violation.

Victor pioneered the royalty basis of payment in order to sign the greatest artists to exclusive contracts. The royalty method was adopted by other companies and extended to a broader range of talent, not just superstars, as the competition to sign talent heated up. For the most part, the matter of payment to performing artists has been determined in a competitive market. To an unknown artist, the fact that he or she has been signed to make a recording by a major company is much more important than the actual pay, so royalties may be low or even nonexistent. For an established star, however, royalties are an important bargaining point.

The playing of records on the radio led to legal challenges on the issue of copyright infringement. These legal battles persisted throughout the century, but the early ruling, that copyright ended with the sale of a record, was never changed. It meant that if a record was purchased by the station, it could play it as often as it liked without any obligation to pay royalties. Thus, a popular piece could be played thousands of times over thousands of stations without any further payment to the performer or publisher. Of course, as songs became more popular, the public began to show more interest in buying them, which did lead to royalties for the rights holders. During the down markets of the Depression years, these benefits were not as readily obvious to the performers and publishers, who spent considerable time, energy, and money in court fighting for changes to copyright laws. Ironically, a couple of decades later they would again be in court, but this time fighting charges of antitrust violations for paying radio stations to perform their music. This "payola" scandal is discussed at greater length later in the chapter.

The Music Publishers Protection Association (MPPA) and the American Society of Composers and Publishers (ASCAP) were formed to protect their membership from unlawful use of their music, among other things. The collection of royalties on the performance of music, whether it was owned by the writer or publisher, has been a persistent problem. One of the controversies has hinged on where the collections should be made: at the point of performance, or at an earlier, wholesale level. In the early twentieth century, before the available technology that makes it easier and cheaper to monitor such events, just recognizing that the music was being performed without a royalty payment was a major challenge. License fees were collected from places ranging from movie theaters to hotel lounges. What made the job even more difficult was that some of these venues had trade organizations of their own, which actively fought for the right to perform the music, or at least defer the obligation of collecting the royalty to a different party.

Many attempts were made to curtail the use of recordings by radio, or at least require the payment of royalties. Legal challenges were one avenue, so was market pressure. The formation of the National Association of Performing Artists (NAPA) in 1930 was done for the original purpose of eliminating the free use of recordings by radio stations. Groups such as NAPA and SARA (Society of American Recording Artists) and ASCAP attempted to bring radio stations in line either through legal challenges or ill-fated attempts to withhold music.

James Caesar Petrillo was president of the American Federation of Musicians (AFM) during the period when talking pictures, the Depression, radio, the decline of vaudeville, and the jukebox were throwing masses of musicians into unemployment. At the time, performers were bit players. The copyright laws explicitly covered the authors, composers, and publishers but not performers. With rampant unemployment in the industry, however, Petrillo realized that musicians had no bargaining leverage. This changed with the advent of WWII.

The AFM, which represented most of the performers of recorded music, went on strike in August of 1942, virtually shutting down the production of newly recorded music. It was the first general strike by the AFM against the recording industry, but it would not be the last. The crux of the strike was union wages and working conditions, but also included an insurance fund for out-of-work musicians. The AFM won concessions from publishers on all three points, though it took more than a year to get them. During the first part of the strike, despite the almost total stoppage of new recordings, publishers did fine by selling backlogs of production created in anticipation of the strike.

AFM members went on strike again on January 1, 1948. This time the strike centered on the distribution of royalties, in addition to the issues of working conditions and union scale. Studio musicians returned to work a year later. During that time, their fate was sealed by the arrival of improved taping technology. Their existence was doomed by the announcement in February of 1948 that ABC Radio Network was going to an "all talk" format for its nighttime programming. The industry was further stunned when Bing Crosby, the most marketable star in the field, decided to change the format of his weekly show from live performance to tape. The dam was broken, and the rush to tape was on. It would be years before technological advances made equipment affordable enough for home use in large enough quantities to justify mass production of tapes, but once it did, tapes quickly outpaced records. But, the final deathblow to records would be put off until the dawning of the compact disc (CD) and the arrival of the iPod.

The legal challenge facing the producers in the 1980s became one of home taping, using the by-then cheap and readily available cassette tapes. The industry blamed its sagging sales on the illegal copying of its albums by home tapers. Despite research which indicated that the heaviest album buyers were the people doing most of the taping, the producers pursued legal remedies in court. Clearly, there was no way to monitor home taping. Instead, the recording industry wanted a tax put on tapes which would pay a royalty to the recording industry on each blank tape sold. The future of tapes was all but determined by the introduction of the Walkman in 1980. The cassette tape was displaced by the personal CD player, and further replaced by iPods. The issue remains the same however: how to maintain control of copyrighted music. While taping is an irrelevant issue today, computer file sharing legal battles against companies like Napster are not new. Before, they were fought with radio stations and cassette tape manufacturers. One heavy piece of ammunition that delayed the imposition of a tax was evidence that home tapers only used about half of their tapes to record music. The other half recorded other things, from work to baby's first words.

After a decade of legal battles, the producers finally won a victory with the passage of the Home Audio Recording Act in 1994. The act put a 2 percent surcharge on the sale of digital audio tape recorders and a 3 percent surcharge on blank audio tapes to be placed in a fund to be distributed to record companies, artists, music publishers, and songwriters via a complicated formula worked out in advance. The long-term impact of this is likely to be inconsequential in view of the obsolescence of the system. A similar bill has not yet been crafted to address the problems of electronic music file sharing. Even though copyright laws have been found to extend to the computer, policing continues to be a big problem.

MUSICAL STYLES

When the demand for a star exceeds the demand for the product in general, the bargaining position of the star increases. From the beginning, it was to the advantage of recording companies to enter into exclusive contracts with stars for their marketing potential, which naturally led to riches for the stars in the greatest demand. World renowned tenor Enrico Caruso was the first to get a royalty for every record sold and was paid a $2,000 annual "retainer" by Victor to ensure that he would record only for them. In addition, he negotiated a separate deal for each recording session. His recording in 1907 of "On with the Motley" from the opera "I Pagliacci" became the first million-selling album. Over the lifetime of their agreement, Caruso and Victor would earn millions for each other. Though he gained fame on the stage, Caruso earned most of his income as a result of his recordings.

Another trend that began to pick up by the end of the nineteenth century and would totally overtake the industry by the end of the twentieth century was the source of most popular music in America. At the beginning of the nineteenth century, when sheet music was the only source of music for the home, only about 10 percent of purchased music in America was of domestic origin. By the end of the century, that figure had risen to 70 percent, and by the end of the twentieth century, American music, as part of the broad category of entertainment, was the second leading export in the American economy. In the nineteenth century, European music was considered more "cultured" and appealing to sophisticated listeners. It didn't hurt that most of the music was also not copyright protected, making it cheap to reproduce. The latter fact was in no small part due to the refusal of the original American Copyright Act of 1790 to recognize copyrights on foreign printed materials.

New York City was the center of the recording industry, and the recording industry was the center of musical styles. By rapidly responding to new music and committing it to cylinder and disc, the recording industry accelerated the pace of change in musical taste in America by the 1920s. The growing popularity of blues and jazz at that time is an example.

American music flourished during the first World War, when the supply of European classical stars dried up. The shortage of European stars impacted the American market in two ways: exposing the recording companies' reliance on foreign stars and exposing more American musical talent, especially in different types of regional music such as bluegrass, jazz, and blues. It was the beginning of a fantastic period of growth for American regional music.

Jazz emanated from the Deep South, most famously from New Orleans. By the time it reached the recording studios of New York and the living rooms of Americans, it was refined and toned down for mass audience appeal and almost always recorded by white musicians. It differed from its origins in that it was scripted and did not rely on the improvisation that characterized the jazz of the Deep South. This was necessary given the strict time constraints imposed on a recording. The heavy early role of percussion instruments in jazz also had to be toned down or it would have drowned out other instruments in the primitive technology of early recording studios.

The taming of jazz was but one step in the recording industry's effort to transform black American music into something the general public would be willing to buy. This sales job has progressed from the early days of negro spirituals through jazz, rock, and rap. The record industry was the key to making the music of black Americans the popular music of the world.

Black performers seldom worked for royalties when their music was being popularized in the 1920s. Part of this was due to discrimination and part to good business. While some blues and jazz music became highly popular, much of it did not, and recognizing which tunes would fall into the hit category was not easy. As a result, publishers legitimized the practice by arguing that many of the songs lost money, so those that were huge hits had to pay for the rest, and the only way to do that was for the publisher to retain all the rights to reproduction. Top performers, such as Bessie Smith, could earn as much as $200 a song, whereas run-of-the-mill or unproven talent was paid the standard fee of $25 per song. Performers seldom complained, since the typical royalty share they would have gotten on their share of mechanical royalties would have left them worse off than the flat fee given the expected average sale of the recordings. Of course, if the musician had a big hit, they would have been better off receiving royalties, but the risk would have been theirs. True stars eventually graduated to a fee-plus-royalty contract which arose out of competition among publishers for top flight talent.

Throughout the century it has been the independent companies that have taken the lead in recording fringe, or cutting-edge musical styles. They often cater to a small but devoted audience of specialized music lovers, such as rhythm and blues, gospel, or classical, and are better able to respond quickly to changing musical tastes. Recognizing the growing interest in rock music, they quickly moved to record what have become some of the industry classics, and in retrospect its most important hits. Elvis Presley, for example, recorded his early songs on the independent Sun label. Bill Haley released "Shake, Rattle and Roll," regarded as perhaps the first true rock and roll hit, with Essex, an independent, in 1953. This song went on to sell over a million copies in 1954. As rock and roll began to catch on, independent labels slowly built the momentum of its popularity into more airtime on the radio, more shelf space in retail stores, and wider recognition. They slowly developed the distribution network that is the lifeline of the recording industry today.

The success of the early independents encouraged copycats, and the number of independent studios proliferated during the 1950s, and began to have an impact. The last few years of the "pre" rock period, 1948–1955 were dominated by the four largest producers, who accounted for 75 percent of the hits on the *Billboard* top-sellers chart. Over the next three years, however, their share of the top hits fell to 36 percent. By 1960, there were more than 3,000 different record labels in the United States. Most were one-hit wonders, but there were about 500 established operations. The one-hit wonders did not have their own studios. Instead, they would rent time in a recording studio, record a song with the artist they "discovered," and, for less than $1,000, would have a master disc ready for duplication. At about 10 cents a copy, records could be made, a little hustle got some airtime or space on a jobber's rack, and the rest was up to the public. Most of these never sold another record, but the fact remains that thousands of different labels were represented.

In the fall of 1953 the music world felt the first ripples of a tidal wave that would rock the industry. A young trucker from rural Tennessee went to the Memphis Recording Service, a small-time record studio catering to local bands, and recorded two songs as a birthday present for his mother. Elvis Presley had just made his first recording without any fanfare.

A year after recording his mother's birthday present, Elvis made his first commercial recording. By the end of 1955, he had begun a revolution coined "rock and roll" by disc jockey legend Alan Freed and had turned the industry on its ear. Presley tunes were selling more copies in one day than most songs sold in a lifetime. He recorded five different million-copy sellers and sold in excess of 10 million records in just over a year, accounting for over two-thirds of Victor's entire sale of singles. Despite his popularity, Elvis wasn't immediately appreciated by the critics. One New York newspaper complained that he couldn't sing a lick and made up for his vocal shortcomings with weird and suggestive dancing.

Another factor which helped rock and roll establish acceptance in popular culture was the industry's ability to successfully whitewash it. The industry term was "covering." In an America still divided starkly along racial lines, the early rock movement saw clean-cut white teens singing songs originally made popular by African-Americans. Elvis Presley and Bill Haley were perfect examples of pioneers in rock and roll who were wildly successful, originally singing "black" hits. The fact remains that the original singers were not going to be able to be promoted nationally, especially on television.

What really differentiated rock from other musical styles was its impact on the record industry itself. It was the product of independent record companies, which had almost died out due to a combination of events since the Depression. The technical revolution of electric recording favored large companies that could better take advantage of the large setup costs of establishing new studios. The Depression itself weeded out the smaller and weaker firms, and the shortage of shellac for making records and the reduction of recordings made during WWII forced most of the rest to shut down. The few that survived catered to specialized audiences for jazz or classical music and often rented facilities from major publishers for pressing their records.

At the time that rock began to rise, another technological change made it possible for small recording studios to revive. Magnetic tape recording was a much cheaper system to install and maintain, and it was superior in sound quality. It meant that virtually anyone with some skills and a tape recorder could make a recording. Gone were the days of expensive disc cutting machines. They were replaced by talented producers with an ear for popular music who made recordings with inexpensive professional grade tape recording equipment, and who were ready to share the latest musical sensation with the world.

Rock music was also helped by the declining importance of radio in the American home. The 1950s saw television replace radio as the focal point of home entertainment. That meant radio stations would have to seek a different audience to survive. The mass market audience was gone, replaced by television. Instead, radio stations sought out niche audiences—smaller but more homogenous audiences, such as teenage fans of rock and roll music. In addition, rock and roll adopted television as a new medium for promotion. The long-running hit show "American Bandstand" launched the career of numerous rock stars. Many of them had only one hit, but the show was the source of their success.

By the time they landed on American soil for the first time in 1964, the Beatles were already the greatest thing to hit American music since Elvis. Their record sales surpassed a million dollars a month. Elvis, the Beatles, and then Michael Jackson were three music superstars who single-handedly changed the fortunes of the industry. The Beatles went on to revolutionize the way albums were recorded. For Jackson, it was his video and recording of *Thriller*, the best-selling solo album in history, with sales topping 25 million units, resulting in $120 million in sales for CBS in 1983 alone.

MARKETING AND DISTRIBUTION

The 1930s saw the rise of creative practices used to increase sales. In the early part of the decade, RCA Victor began a publicity scheme of sending gratis copies of new recordings of black artists to newspapers and magazines for them to review. This served as the primary means of publicity for the company for the remainder of the decade. Eventually, this changed to free copies for radio stations, which was only a short step from paying radio stations for favorable airtime for songs.

In 1938, the record club debuted. RCA Victor launched the Victor Record Society in a successful effort to rejuvenate its classical lines. For $6 a year members got access to discounts from the RCA catalog, and for joining they got a free record-playing attachment, valued at $15, which could be plugged into any radio. The music club was modeled after the successful book clubs then in existence.

Columbia used its marketing might to raise the stakes in the free music to station games by spending nearly a million dollars in 1947 to produce, distribute, and purchase airtime on 537 radio stations for a new show featuring Martin Block, America's best-known disc jockey, that introduced newly released recordings. Block eventually outgrew the show, going on to a million-dollar-a-year network disc jockey job. He and Columbia paved a new path, however, setting the stage for publishers paying stations to feature certain music.

The role of local disc jockeys increased in importance through the 1950s. They were the source of most of the new music heard by the consumer. This market shift led easily from providing free music to radio stations to directly paying disc jockeys to favor certain recordings on the air. This "payola" scheme involved cash and material goods, spread to thousands of disc jockeys, cost the publishers millions of dollars, and ultimately led to restraint of trade charges against the major publishers.

Paying for the privilege of getting a song performed did not originate with radio. "Plugging," as it was known, was a scandal in the vaudeville industry. Performers were paid to include certain songs in their acts. The popularity among publishers of plugging eventually became a Frankenstein monster. The price of popularizing a song could exceed its total sales revenue if a bidding war for popular talent erupted and the song did not catch on as hoped. If plugging wasn't purchased, the song would be less likely to achieve "hit" status. Plugging, however, did not guarantee a hit. It just meant that more of the publisher profits were being paid to performers.

In 1955, the federal government launched a probe into the practices of the major publishers, hinting at violations of antitrust law. At issue were the shipment of free records to radio stations, price discrimination, and price cutting and fixing. While nothing came of the probe, it served notice that an eye was being kept on the industry. Four years later, the Federal Trade Commission (FTC) filed the first of an eventual one hundred complaints against record manufacturers and their distributors. Chief among the charges were several involving the practice of paying disc jockeys for airtime to favor certain selections, resulting in these songs being played as often as ten times a day. No public hearings were ever held. Instead, the major publishers all agreed to consent orders, which essentially meant they agreed not to do again what they did not formally admit to doing in the first place. All sides came away feeling like winners. The FTC felt they had ridded the marketplace of an evil, and the publishers admitted nothing and suffered no bad publicity in the form of potentially damaging hearings.

By the end of the 1950s, the music market experienced a music glut. There were approximately 700 distributors attempting to get airtime for 100 new singles each week. Airtime was the only way to generate sales, but with that many new issues, each song could only be played once a week, if they were all to get played. That left no time for oldies or repeats. This glut was a problem for retailers as well, who received about 5,000 new releases each year, less than 10 percent of which would sell as many as 100,000 copies, with the occasional hit coming in at 500,000 to a million. Sixty percent of all new releases sold less than 3,000 copies, not enough to break even on their production.

LPs gained favor by producers in the 1950s as profit margins grew. It cost about the same to produce an LP as it did for the equivalent amount of singles, but few singles ever sold enough to recoup their costs, whereas LPs did. Listeners bought LPs they heard promoted on the air by disc jockeys for the one or two favorite hits they recognized. A few LPs had numerous top singles on them, as in Michael Jackson's *Thriller*, but that was rare.

During the 1960s an average day saw twenty new singles and ten albums released, all competing for the same radio time and rack slots in stores. Despite the popularity of television, the real key to exposure was radio airtime. It was here that the public at large would get exposed to the greatest number of songs, and it was on radio that a song would live or die. Just as important as cheaper and better quality technology, it was the change in radio stations that was important to the success of rock and roll. The shorter length of time of rock songs meant more of them could get played on the air, and it meant more opportunities for disc jockeys and radio station managers to reap benefits from producers seeking to get their songs on the air.

After public exposure on the radio, the next step for the marketers was to get the public to purchase the music from stores. While it was easy to pick up various radio stations from one's home simply by changing the dial, it was more difficult to find the music in local stores. The most obvious example was the rhythm and blues of the South, considered by some northerners as "negro music" and thus not stocked. However, when white teenagers who heard the music on the radio began demanding these records, it was profitable for stores to stock them.

Local radio stations, by necessity and circumstance, were much more responsive to their local audience's tastes than national distribution chains. The change in focus from mass-market appeal to niche audiences changed the focus of distribution from one-size-fits-all to a local market. This made it more expensive for national distributors and returned the advantage to small producers who could focus their distribution on the specific markets that favored their product. It put the relationship between the distributor and the local station manager or disc jockey at center stage.

As changing technology reduced the cost of starting a studio, independent studios thrived. The big advantage they had over larger studios was their flexibility. Instead of a rigid corporate hierarchy of owner, producer, promotion manager, and technician, independent studios had only one or two people filling all of these positions. It made it easier for them to adjust to changing tastes in the market. Stars gravitated to them because they were not required to sign exclusive long-term contracts, but sign on for specific recordings. This left them free to move on or even simultaneously record elsewhere.

Capitol Records, founded in 1941, was one such independent producer. Despite the ill timing of its birth, it made it through WWII and became one of the leading music publishers in the United States. Capitol got its foot in the door by pioneering the practice of providing free copies of its records to radio stations in the hope that the airtime would lead to the publicity necessary to generate sales. It expanded on the strength of an eight-million-dollar capital infusion through a stock sale and was poised to meet the increased demand for its records. Capitol's rise led to the formation and eventual success of several other independent record labels, each following the example of Capitol by specializing in a type of music for which there was a niche demand. This included labels devoted to jazz, hillbilly, or country music. They followed the other example of Capitol by distributing their new releases freely to radio stations. Many of the small producers also survived by hiring staff writers to compose and perform their own music, which they then sold to BMI (Broadcast Music Incorporated), the new licensing organization, for a flat fee, transferring all air rights to BMI. This money was then used to build and establish their own catalogs of music.

A major problem faced by independents was the "covering" of their hits by large producers. Especially if the independent specialized in African American music, a hit was often co-opted by a bigger label. The larger producer then had a white artist record it and used its vastly superior distribution network to flood the market with their version of the song. Even when the independent provided a free copy to radio stations and received the publicity, the copy that customers often ended up buying was recorded by a different artist for a major label.

The challenge the independent producer faced was the same that independent film producers faced: distribution. It was, and still is, easier to make a recording or movie than to get it into the hands of the public. This is where major producers held the real advantage. It was not in technical know-how, or equipment, or the uncanny ability to spot talent. Rather, it was in promoting and distributing talent. They had distribution networks to get recordings into the retail market, on radio airwaves, and in Broadway stage shows, movies, and television.

They also initiated changes in the distribution system. Under the old regime, record retail stores were aligned with one or more of the major recording studios, taking contracted deliveries of records from them. The independent producers used a different system of "jobbers," similar to independent distributors, who leased rack space from retail stores and grocery stores, where they would set up record racks and stock them with the most popular hits from the independent producers. These "jobbers" would purchase the records from the producers and sell them in various outlets for a profit. They represented several labels, and because their income was a function of total sales, they had an incentive to be up-to-date on the latest musical trends, ensuring that the most popular hits were always on the racks. The "jobber" was the ultimate commission salesman, whose earnings were a function of the number of records sold.

Another problem was that leading independent studios were subject to become prey for large corporations. Warner Records bought

Reprise in 1963, added Atlantic in 1967, and Electra in 1968. Within a decade, this strategy of "if you can't beat 'em, buy 'em" vaulted Warner to a position as the second largest record company in the United States, just behind Columbia. As the 1960s marched into the 1970s, what had begun as a period of innovation and proliferation of independent studios, ended with essentially the same number of independent labels. This was misleading, however, because the labels were concentrated in the hands of a small number of large corporations.

This wave of conglomeration was essentially the same as what had occurred in the 1920s. The industry pattern repeated itself many times over the decades. Independent producers arose in answer to the stifling of creativity artists felt at the hands of large corporations. They promoted new artists, being the first to recognize the popularity of new groups and styles of music. As they became profitable and successful, they attracted the interest of the large players, who inevitably bought them out, "sanitized" their trademark musical style into mass marketed appeal, and moved on, ready for the next round of mergers when new independents came on the scene. Originally new technology made it difficult for independents to compete, but over time decreases in cost and improved quality of technology made it easier for them to thrive. Inevitably, however, a new innovation would come along, starting the cycle over again. In the 1980s it was video. By the end of the twentieth century it was the computer.

Independent producers were responsible for the majority of music produced by 1970 and were the nearly exclusive source of innovative music. The big media conglomerates of CBS records (previously Columbia), RCA, and Capitol, however, accounted for 50 percent of the market. Wildly successful groups like the Beatles had pioneered the move from corporate to independent studios, where they could better control the method of their recording. Now the only thing most large record companies were used for, at least by big stars, was distribution of the albums recorded at independent studios and financed by independent producers.

Retail stores, jobbers, and specialized record stores were the primary outlets for new music. By the mid-1960s there were some 15,000 racks in supermarkets alone. Big producers also sold a large amount of material by mail via catalogs or record clubs. With over 200 record producers in business, distribution was a key problem for all but the largest. Independent regional distributorships arose to meet the needs of some independent producers. By the mid-1980s, many independent producers had conceded the distribution market to the majors. While they still produced albums, few distributed their own product.

One survivor was Sam Goody, the king of discounters. He added records to his New York City novelty shop business, buying used records from jukebox operators. He eventually graduated to offering a huge selection of new releases. He obtained his stock at an average price of under $2 an album and sold them at just under $3 each, which was more than $1 less than the regular market price. His profit margin after overhead was impressive, but it was the volume of sales made possible by an inventory numbering in the hundreds of thousands which proved his strongest point. The majors sued to stop his practice of discounting when it began to hurt their own bottom line, but they were unsuccessful in court. When they attempted to cut him and similar discounters out of the loop by refusing to sell to them, Goody pioneered the practice of transshipping.

Transshipping occurs when a retailer ships a discounter unsold portions of its stock of new releases. Retailers were allowed a return privilege, but they had to wait six months to recoup their money. If they didn't want to wait that long, they could ship their excess to discounters for cash on the spot. Another reason not to return materials to the producers was due to the method producers had developed for allocating new releases. Retailers got quantities of new releases based on past shipments less returns. If a hot new release was anticipated, a retailer did not want to jeopardize its share of the inventory, so instead of returning unsold material, the retailer sold the inventory at a discount. This kept the discounters in business, gave ready cash to the retailers, and kept them in line for their future shipments, thus frustrating the publishers. Discounters often paid as little as 50 percent for their transshipments from retailers, for whom selling at a loss to discounters simply became a cost of doing business.

The distribution of music is currently undergoing a revolution as a result of the proliferation of personal computers and Internet access. At the dawn of the twenty-first century the biggest challenge facing music studios is the Internet. The ability of consumers to share music files with one another over the Internet and to copy and load music onto personal music devices (e.g., iPod) means that studios are losing control over the distribution and sale of their music. This issue is not yet resolved, but will certainly define the production, distribution, and consumption of music well into the twenty-first century.

THE RECORDING STUDIO

An album is recorded at a studio by the artist, sometimes with technical assistance provided by a producer. After the recording session, they physically create the record, tape, or CD, and then distribute the recording to the retailer, who in turn sells it to the customer. Retailers are sometimes eliminated in favor of direct sale via the Web, mail catalog, or club.

The early twentieth century saw the perfection of the duplicating process, which allowed for the low-cost recording of mass quantities of the same songs. The birth of the recorded music industry marked the beginning of the popular appeal of the phonograph. Eldridge Johnson, founder of Victor, recognized that the ultimate demand for talking machines would be a function of the availability and quality of recordings to play on them, and he set out to perfect a process of mass producing quality recordings. The commercial benefits of this invention were quickly obvious. The perfection of a low-cost, high-quality recording was a key to the proliferation of talking machines in American parlors. Prices of recordings dropped from $2 to 50 cents in the first decade of the twentieth century as millions of the recordings made their way into American homes.

Original recording was dedicated more to reproducing original sounds rather than mixing various tracks to create the perfect, though "artificial," sound. In this case the original setup of microphones and arrangement of band members was important. Early recordings focused on concerts performed before a live audience. Two requirements had to be balanced—the placement of microphones and band members for recording purposes against the placement of the same for maximum audience enjoyment. The emphasis on early record sales was the best possible reproduction of an actual live performance. Only later did mixing and multiple tracks take over with the goal of producing the perfect blend and balance of sounds—something that could never be done in a live performance.

Early recording was more art than science and would remain that way until standardization and improved technology removed some of the guesswork. Variables such as the temperature of the wax onto which the grooves of the disc or cylinder were being cut, the pitch of the voice being recorded, and the distance of the singer and instruments from the diaphragm (the precursor to the microphone) all impacted the quality of the final product. The studio recorder had to worry about where and how to position each person in the band to achieve the best balance on the recording. And, furthermore, the result could not be monitored from a mixing studio, it could only be determined by listening to the final product. If it wasn't good enough, the process had to start all over again. No dubbing, remixing, or balance adjusting could be done. The electronic marvels of modern studio recording were well in the future.

Before the dawning of magnetic tape, the prohibitive cost of running a recording studio kept their numbers at a minimum, thus giving significant bargaining power to the producers. The studio became part of the process of mass producing music. Artists were still valued for their talent, but they no longer controlled what was recorded. The recording manager would determine what songs would be recorded and who would record them. Marketing managers would determine the release strategy of the recordings, and corporate executives would determine the long-run strategy of the combination of types of music to record, who would record it, and the pattern of marketing and distribution.

A typical session run by the corporate studio split the day into three recording sessions. During a session, an artist would come in and play for three hours. The engineers in the booth used the available technology to maximize the quality of the recording. The artists did not worry about volume, mix, or other technical issues. They did not have to record a completely flawless take, because after the session, the technicians could splice together the best parts of each take to produce the perfect piece. They could also add elements later to enhance the recording. Often the artist would take direction from the engineers and marketing executives on how to record a piece, what to record, and how to promote it. As the popularity of stars rose, their ability to influence these decisions rose as well. The rise of independent producers facilitated the ability of artists to control their own destiny.

Advances in radio broadcasting changed the way in which music was recorded. By the mid-1920s, the old recording diaphragms were gone, replaced by the electronic components that we would recognize today in a recording studio, such as microphones and control panels.

The microphone was an improvement over the diaphragm, but it did not solve all the problems. It was still critical how band members were arranged and where microphones were placed. However, now the microphone could be used to broadcast the sound to loudspeakers in the control booth, so the recorder could more easily determine if the balance of sound and volume were as desired. Since the recordings were still made by cutting grooves into a wax disc, there was still concern over the sudden change in pitch or volume, which could affect the way the grooves were cut. In addition, the temperature of the room containing the disc was critical, so the wax would neither be too hard or too soft.

The 1950s saw the dawning of multiple-track recording. Les Paul, of guitar fame, experimented with new technology to record multiple tracks of his guitar playing onto a master tape of his wife singing. It took more than a decade before the technology improved enough to turn dubbing into a science. Until that time, the cost of the technique made it rare.

It was the change in both technology and the social structure of studios which revolutionized the recording industries in the 1950s and 1960s. Two-track recording became four-track in the early 1960s and continued up to thirty-two tracks by the 1970s, with virtually limitless dubbing possibilities. It was now possible for the same artist to sing multiple parts and play several instruments on a recording. More tracks increased the ability to make changes, enhancements, or deletions after the recording session, resulting in higher quality recordings.

The physical production of records also benefited from advancing technology. Computers allowed the cutting of grooves into the discs to be constant for an infinite number of cuttings. Gone were the days when human touch was required to provide the right amount of pressure and human ingenuity was needed to determine how to adjust that pressure for changes in volume and pitch on the original. Now the computer could make the necessary adjustments and perfect copies could be replicated infinitely.

The next major evolution in recording was the advent of magnetic tape. While tape did not improve the quality of the recording itself, it dramatically improved the ease of editing. All that was necessary to edit a recording on tape was a sharp blade to cut the tape and some adhesive to splice it back together.

Tape recording began to replace disc recording in the industry in the late 1940s, but it took a decade to completely replace the inferior system. The holdups were stations and studios that had recently purchased or upgraded their disc recording systems and their reluctance to invest in another new system so soon. In addition, some simply waited for the wave of anticipated improvements and cost reductions in the medium before buying in.

While tape recording had long been used in recording studios and radio stations and businesses, it did not become a popular method of listening to music until the late 1960s. It was first popularized as the eight-track tape cassette. The eight-track was originally designed by the Lear Company (producer of luxury jets) in 1964 as an ideal method of customizing the music you listened to in the car. It was easy for a driver to put the track into the car player and simultaneously watch the road. The problem with the technology was its difficulty in allowing the listener to pick out a specific song on the track. This was somewhat easier on a cassette tape but nothing like the ability to do so on a compact disc. The CD, because of its virtual indestructibility, has rendered tapes obsolete. Repeated playing of a tape weakens it, decreasing the quality of the recording as well as the structural integrity of the tape, making it more prone to breaking or stretching. The CD has no physical contact with the player, as it is "read" by laser, thus making it unlikely to ever wear out. It remains to be seen how the CD will fare against the newest revolution of storing music digitally in personal computer files.

Ironically, all of these sophisticated advances in technology led to a new revolution in music in the 1980s which depended on using turntables and intentionally distorting the sound, causing scratches and hisses that were an integral part of rap music. The music depended on deejays to spin record turntables backward, slow down the speed with their hands, and scratch the surface of the records. Technology was now being used to make the music, not record it, and it was intentionally being misused in order to create the final product.

As early as the Great Depression, well before the advent of sophisticated sound studios, two theories of recorded music evolved and have been debated among artists, marketers, and technicians ever since. The two sides in this argument are the purists and the perfectionists. Purists prefer the actual performance, warts and all, recorded as authentically as possible. Perfectionists prefer the most perfect possible sound, which today involves remixing, synthesizing, editing, and enhancing, sometimes beyond recognition of what was originally performed. Extremists in the purist camp regard such electronic enhancement as fraudulent.

The 1960s saw a shift in the balance of power in the studio from the producers to the artists. Many of the new hit tunes were written by singers who recorded their own compositions, including making the decisions about the technical details concerning remixing and editing. The selection of material to be recorded and how it would be marketed was no longer the sole responsibility of the producer. Even the ownership of music had changed. ASCAP's monopoly on music publishing was broken in the 1940s when radio broadcasters, tired of paying high royalties to ASCAP, created Broadcast Music Incorporated (BMI) to serve as their own music publisher, ultimately holding the rights to most of the music created during the 1950s.

Another area of conflict exists between the artist and the corporation. On one side are the recording stars, often portrayed as the artists, pure and devoted only to the quality of the final product of their artistic expression. On the other side is the corporation making the recording, providing all of the technology, the studio, and the expertise to make the highest quality (from a technical standpoint) product as well as marketing and distributing it. These two sides often conflict over the number of takes, the balance of sound, the selection of songs, and the choice of marketing strategies. The bigger the star, the more influence he or she has on the process.

During the 1960s there was a convenient merging of desires by production companies and recording artists. Production companies, strained by the pressure of producing thousands of new songs and trying to cull a few hits from among them, were looking to simplify their business and concentrate on what they did best: distribute and promote. Performers wanted artistic freedom to produce unique sounds and personal expressions. This led to an evolution in the business whereby the most successful artists formed their own production teams, leasing equipment and studios from the producers to produce their own master tapes.

The Beatles were trendsetters in the way that artists began to use the studio. Rather than view it as a place to go and record previously practiced and rehearsed songs and then let the technicians polish them by dubbing and editing the various takes and tracks, the Beatles began to use the studio as the place where they created their music and rehearsed. They moved into the control booth, practicing with technological innovations on their sound.

Their first album, *Please Please Me*, released in 1963, was recorded in one day. *Sgt. Pepper*, on the other hand, was a watershed album, taking months and hundreds of thousands of dollars to record just four years later. It became the norm in the recording industry. Part of the attraction of the high-tech wizardry performed on new "artistic" albums was lost on old monophonic, low-fidelity players. In order to fully appreciate these innovations, they required the advances made to high-fidelity, advanced electronics and stereophonic sound.

The music business has evolved into a two-tiered world involving superstars and everyone else. Recording studios get into bidding wars over superstars, resulting in long-term, lucrative contracts with large advances, artistic control for the artists, big potential losses on mediocre work, but huge paydays for the biggest hits, making the whole system somewhat risky, but ultimately profitable. For everyone else, the system is much tougher. Many young stars are willing to pay for their own recording costs just to get exposure. If they can land a contract with a major producer, it is usually for one year with an option at the discretion of the producer for up to four more years.

NEW TECHNOLOGY

The military was the source of many new techniques in recording technology. Their efforts to improve communications, preserve messages, and capture sounds from the enemy were valuable defense tools during WWII and were transferred to profitable improvements in home and theater entertainment after the War. Among the many innovations that owe at least their genesis to the military was magnetic tape recording, which in time became the music industry's cassette tape.

Cassettes were produced commercially first in the 1940s, shortly after the end of WWII.

Tape not only proved to be a substitute for records, but it became a superior method of making records as well. It allowed for multitrack recording, cheaper and easier editing, and led to experimentation in recording. For example, one performer could record him or herself singing lead and backup and playing all the instruments, among many possibilities. The Beatles were famous for some of their recording studio innovations. Digital recording would take this one step further.

The Phillips Company introduced the compact cassette in 1964 and did not protect it as a proprietary technology. Instead they allowed and even encouraged others to license its use. The requirement was that the same standards would be adhered to by all users of the license to make them compatible in all machines. By the end of the decade, the Phillips cassette was the industry standard, played on machines manufactured by more than 80 companies and having produced nearly 2.5 million units worth $150 million in sales.

The shortcoming of cassette tapes was the hissing produced during recording. Ray Dolby developed a method for reducing the noise which could be incorporated into existing machine technology, thus avoiding costly redesigns. The cassette recorder became the technology of choice in the mid-1970s, replacing the bulky, costly reel-to-reel system in home stereos. It remained a mainstay and central feature of stereo systems until the CD began to replace both it and records. Currently, CDs are in danger of being replaced by electronic music, which can be directly downloaded onto computers.

The precursor to today's iPod was the Walkman, the first of the now ubiquitous personal music devices introduced by Sony in 1979. The Walkman was a small tape player with attached headsets which allowed consumers to carry their personal choice of music wherever they went. It was not exactly pocket-sized, but it could be easily carried in a purse or a bag or hung on a belt, making it portable, lightweight, and personal because it used headsets instead of a speaker. It rose in popularity, and the sight of headset-clad teens became commonplace. This ultimately evolved into the sleeker, smaller earplugs of today. Today's iPods hold much more music, do not require cassettes or CDs, and can be updated easily and frequently. The quality of sound is also superior, and as mentioned earlier, it does not wear out.

The CD debuted in 1982 as an expensive, upper end alternative to records. It featured higher quality sound, and the standard 4.5-inch disc could hold much more music, up to seventy-five minutes, than a record with grooves on both sides. The absence of physical contact during playback meant the discs would never wear out. Along with this innovation came the laser-operated remote control, ushering in the era of the couch potato. The average American could now be entertained by video and audio technology of the highest quality without having to get up from the couch—except for snacks, a problem which was solved by the invention of a recliner with built-in minifridge.

By the end of the twentieth century less than 10 percent of recorded music sales were LPs. Most of it was CDs. Though the CD made record albums obsolete, it was in danger of being eclipsed itself by music stored directly onto playing devices such as the computer and the iPod. There is nothing to record on in the iPod, just a collection of electrons stored for personal use. And the vast quantities of music that can be stored on the pocket-sized iPod is staggering, with even budget versions holding thousands of songs.

The industry now centers on the computer. Digital sound has come to the forefront, and the greatest challenge facing it is how to retain control over the recorded product once it is produced. Computer file sharing systems like Napster and handheld devices like the iPod have revolutionized the industry. Listeners can share music files over the Internet and download libraries of music onto their computers and handheld devices, bypassing the marketplace altogether. While this type of music sharing violates U.S. copyright laws, it is difficult to enforce and expensive to monitor. One way the music industry has attempted to police their copyrights has been to focus on the activity in file sharing on college campuses and threaten legal action against the college if they do not undertake to stop the sharing.

Despite changes in the types of music preferred by the listening public and the different means of delivering music, the industry looks remarkably like it did a century ago. The main issues are still the same. Manufacturers seek to push the envelope and deliver the highest quality sound possible. Performers still strive to express themselves through their art. Producers compete for the opportunity to promote and distribute the best-selling stars, and consumers clamor for the best equipment to listen to the best music. Despite all the advances in technology, or perhaps because of them, the same problem besets all the players in the industry: how to control the rights to the final product. The dawning of the computer age in the recorded sound industry is not likely to solve this problem, only to complicate it.

—4—

Motion Pictures and the Rise of Big Business in Entertainment

INTRODUCTION

In 2000, nearly one and a half billion people went to the movies, over 70 million videos were rented, and an estimated 30 million households saw movies on pay cable channels. Not including movies shown on television and airplanes, a conservative estimate would show nearly two billion pairs of eyes watched a movie. With a population of 280 million in 2000, that works out to just about four movies per person. If we consider only the population between the ages of 10 and 80, that would be five movies apiece.

This kind of market penetration would have been hard to imagine a century ago. In 1901 the movie industry bore little resemblance to the splendor of Hollywood as we know it today, comprising a smattering of storefront operations primarily limited to large cities on the East Coast. These were the first movie theaters. They resembled videogame arcades more than theaters, with each machine serving only one person at a time. The popular price for viewing one of the films was 5 cents, hence the parlors became known as nickelodeons. It was a fledgling industry in a number of ways. Movie stars were unknown, temperamental directors nonexistent, and buckets of overpriced buttered popcorn awaited the birth of an entrepreneur like Orville Redenbacker.

At the dawn of the twentieth century, the movie industry was dominated not by movie stars, directors, and producers, but by inventors and business moguls. Since then, while the power in the industry has ebbed and flowed from the stars to the studio executives to the agencies, the spotlight has never faded from the movie stars who have captured the imagination and adulation of the public eye. The early days of the industry were dominated by inventors such as Thomas Edison and William Dickson. Today, the industry revolves around the likes of Brad Pitt and Jennifer Lopez, and executive Michael Ovitz. But at its heart, it is the same industry, delivering the same product: diversion from life's everyday problems through a story preserved on celluloid.

The movie business is unique. Its product is constantly changing, and the demand for it is unknown when it is produced. Movies can be produced within a certain genre, say a Western, a comedy, or a horror film, as an attempt to signal to the audience what type of film to expect, but they must by nature be a unique product, or there will be little demand. The market for the second showing of the same movie is thin indeed. The closest that a studio can come is the sequel, which is a risky market as well. The demand for the original is well known, thus a demand for the sequel can be predicted to a certain extent. However, the studio runs the risk of going to the well once too often in this scenario, or failing to live up to the expectations of the audience if the original was a big hit.

THE INVENTIVE ERA

On April 14, 1894, the first kinetoscope parlor opened in New York. It was a machine that allowed one person to peer through what looked like a pair of binoculars to view a short moving picture with no sound. A syndicate, headed by A. O. Tate, Thomas Lombard, and Erastus Benson, opened the parlor. They were the first to commercialize what has now become a multibillion dollar industry, after striking a deal with Thomas Edison. Within a year kinetoscopes were popping up in storefronts of their own and as attractions in stores, hotels, and saloons in major cities across the country and abroad.

Within two years the motion picture projector was simultaneously introduced by the Lumiere brothers in France and by Thomas Edison. Edison put his, called a Vitascope, to a public test for the first time on April 23, 1896. The projector began displacing the kinetoscope and quickly transformed the industry into what we would recognize today as a "movie," at least in form if not content.

The invention of sound pictures came shortly after the invention of moving pictures. The kinetophone, also patented by Edison, combined his phonograph with his kinetoscope. However, this early combination of sound and moving pictures was too clumsy to be marketed. It would be more than a generation before the commercial viability of sound with moving pictures would be achieved.

By the turn of the century commercialization was in full force. Commercialization was rapid and evolved as quickly and sporadically as the technology. Businessmen, particularly the inventors themselves, were quick to recognize the commercial promise of the kinetoscope. They moved to monopolize the potential profits by tying up the technology necessary for making and displaying the pictures. The early years of the movie industry were dominated by patent battles and lawsuits surrounding the attempt by various individuals to monopolize the industry by controlling the hardware. The industry paid little attention to the actual movies that were made, focusing instead on controlling the means of making and displaying them. In fact, such little regard was given to the quality and substance of the movies themselves that they were sold by the foot. Films were valued only by how long they ran and how new they were, not by the actual content.

The decade of the 1890s was marked by rapid innovation in the industry, with competing and increasingly better cameras and projectors quickly coming on the scene. In addition to the development work of the Lumiere brothers and the constant tinkering of the Edison labs, other significant advances were made, including those of a company called the Mutoscope and Biograph Company, which invented the biograph projector. This projector was notable for the size and clarity of the picture it was able to project—which allowed it to be used in vaudeville theaters as part of the entertainment bill. This projector quickly replaced the kinetoscope. Early films were made on one reel of film, 50 feet long, resulting in a show of less than two minutes. Several films were shown when moving pictures came to vaudeville, since a "turn" on the circuit was typically fifteen minutes long. Films were produced primarily by the projector manufacturers and sold as stock film priced by the foot. By the turn of the century, the price was about 10 cents per foot, dropping as the film aged and more people had seen it.

Traveling businessmen introduced motion pictures to small-town America. They would haul their projectors and films from place to place, setting up at fairs, vacant storefronts, or tents, wherever a crowd could be gathered. They would show their films, collect their money, and move on to the next town. The most popular films showed scenes that the typical viewer was not likely to see. This meant exotic locales, since the average American did not travel far from home in the late nineteenth century. Early films had such gripping titles as *Niagara Falls*, *Horseshoeing*, *Highland Dancing*, and *Locomotive*. The titles were accurate descriptions of the contents.

Though the name nickelodeon was coined from the price of the original theater, the price quickly increased to a dime in most places. Nickelodeons were seldom permanent in the early days, just rented storefronts. They were hot, stuffy, uncomfortable, ugly, and packed all day long. Once the supply of available films was exhausted, the exhibitors moved on. The arrival of permanent theaters had to await the rise of distribution companies which could assure theater owners a steady supply of fresh film subjects necessary to attract repeat customers to a permanent theater.

The early format for these showings was, not surprisingly, based on the vaudeville circuit. While the main attraction was the motion pictures, there was usually an accompaniment of live acts—singers, comedians, and lecturers. This format was pioneered by early nickelodeon promoters such as William Fox and Marcus Loew, who would go on to become titans in the Hollywood film industry.

The first film that truly told a story was *The Great Train Robbery*, produced by Edwin S. Porter and released in 1903. It was unique both because it was a story with a plot and because it was an astounding 1,100 feet in length—more than 20 times as long as the standard movie. It featured several things that we take for granted in modern movies, including editing, character development, and plot. It was the first film that viewers today would likely recognize as a movie.

The first distribution companies appeared in 1902 in San Francisco. Harry and Herbert Miles saw a need for a service, and they formed what would become the first of ultimately only a handful of distribution companies which would dominate the industry to this day. They set up a business that dealt in films—not producing them, but simply distributing existing films among theaters in order to maximize the profitability both of the film, by assuring it got the widest circulation possible, and the exhibitors, by assuring that they got a steady supply of fresh material. Within five years about 150 such distributors were in business across the country. Within two decades, a mere eight would control the entire film industry.

Once a steady stream of films could be assured, permanent theaters appeared. Harry and John Davis opened the first one in Pittsburgh in 1905. They turned a storefront into a theater by setting up about a hundred chairs facing a wall, on which they showed films to paying customers. The growth of theaters was astounding. They were so popular they often played to sold-out crowds nearly around the clock. Within a year, more than one thousand opened across the country, and by 1910 there were more than ten thousand. By this time the standard length of the movies had increased from under two minutes to about fifteen minutes. That year approximately 26 million Americans attended the theater each week. On average, every American saw a motion picture once every six weeks, more often in larger cities like New York, where more than 25 percent of the population attended each week.

With thousands streaming into theaters each day, a steady supply of new films was needed to accommodate the public demand. This was met by scores of filmmakers, who churned out short films in rapid order, made copies in labs, and sold them to distributors, who then circulated them around the globe. Since films were silent, there was no language barrier, and the market rapidly became truly global. The production of films showing subjects from far-flung corners of the globe were especially popular with a viewing public that was unlikely to wander far from home, much less traverse an ocean.

Films were demanded by consumers because they were new and had not yet been seen, not because they were exciting storylines or featured favorite actors or special effects. As new films were released, older films decreased in interest, since they had already been seen. These films were then sent to smaller theaters, in smaller towns, where they had yet to be viewed. To this day, that is how the release schedule of films works. New films open in the largest theaters in the biggest markets, where they can play to the greatest number of people, at the highest possible prices, in the shortest period of time. After they have exhausted the demand in these markets, they move on to successively smaller and more remote markets. The difference now, of course, is that films are marketed for their plot, stars, and special effects, not simply because they are new.

THE PERIOD OF MERGERS

The increasing sophistication and size of the market quickly led to specialization and division of labor—key ingredients in efficient and cheap production. The industry soon could be divided into three major sectors which still exist in much the same fashion today. Those three sectors are the production of films, the distribution of films, and the exhibition of films. Today we call them the producers, the studios, and the theaters.

Industry Structure

The production aspect of the industry is the making of the actual films. It involves the cameras, the film, the movie stars, and directors. The distribution level of the industry is akin to wholesaling. There are many familiar companies involved with distribution, companies such as MGM, Warner Brothers, and Fox. Finally, the exhibition end of the spectrum is the finished product as we see it in the movie theater. This is the point at which the product is consumed by the viewing public.

Although the production and exhibition ends are familiar to most, the distribution sector is not, yet it is arguably the most important. This is the aspect of the business which is now, and has historically been, the toughest to break into. The distribution level is an oligopoly. It has been dominated by a small number of firms since the formation of the General Film Company in 1910.

The distribution aspect of the industry is the act of getting the finished product from the producers to the exhibitors. The movie theater is the exhibitor of the final product—the film itself. It is the distributor who solves the problems such as transportation and inventory management for the theaters. The wholesaler is responsible for satisfying the demands of both the producers, who want to get their films shown in theaters, and the retailers (theaters) who want their seats to be full of customers.

If we think of producing, distributing, and exhibiting as three stages of a process, we can picture them as a column. At each stage, there are a variety of firms competing with one another. At the turn of the century, for example, there were dozens of companies holding different patents, producing different movies. These movies were sold to thousands of exhibitors through dozens of distributors. The distributors made sure that fresh, original production was cycled through the various exhibitors, so that exhibitors got new pictures to sell, yet the previously produced pictures remained in circulation as long as possible.

In many ways the industry in the early twentieth century was similar to the twenty-first-century film industry. There are still the same three stages, and the most competitive and least profitable of those levels is the exhibition level. The distribution level is still the toughest to break into. While the monopoly position of the General Film Company was destroyed, rebuilt, and destroyed again over the past century, the distribution business is still an oligopoly. At the turn of the century, two thirds of the new releases in North America were handled by only five distributors (Disney, Fox, Paramount, Universal, and Warner Brothers).

The Mergers of the Film Companies

The legal battles involving patents came to a head in 1908 with the organization of the Motion Picture Patents Corporation (MPPC). It was formed through a horizontal merger of ten major companies that held most of the important industry patents. This merger included Edison, Vitagraph, and Biograph, the largest of the corporations, as well as several smaller companies. The patents were for cameras, films, and projectors.

A horizontal merger is a merger of the companies at any one of the stages of production. A vertical merger would be the merging of a production company with a distributor and possibly also an exhibitor. In other words, a horizontal merger involves companies that were previously competing in the same business, whereas a vertical merger combines companies that were previously doing business with one another at different stages of production.

A merger works to the advantage of some and the disadvantage of others. In the motion picture industry, a horizontal merger of the producers benefits those producers in the merger to the extent that they are no longer competing with one another. The merger is more likely to hurt those who do business with the newly merged firm. Instead of having the benefit of dealing with one of a number of competitive firms that compete on price, service, and quality of product, distributors are now faced with dealing with only one company in a take-it-or-leave-it environment.

In 1910 a vertical merger combined the production and distribution levels of the industry. The MPPC purchased 68 distribution companies and merged them into one company, called the General Film Company (GFC). This created a virtual monopoly in the production and distribution sectors of the industry. The exhibition level of the industry was still extremely competitive, with more than 10,000 theaters in operation. The exhibitors competed against each other, and this situation was exploited by the GFC. The theaters were forced into exclusive dealings with the GFC out of fear of being blackballed if they were caught showing films from one of the few remaining independent distributors. The exhibitors were kept in line by paying license fees to the GFC for the right to exhibit their films. This was a valuable right, since the GFC controlled so much of the traffic in new films, which were the lifeblood of a theater in the major markets. Without access to the newest films, an exhibitor would be unable to compete. The only exhibitors who could afford not to deal exclusively with the GFC were those small, economically insignificant storefronts in second and third-run markets who did not show current releases anyway, but purchased films that had already been in wide distribution.

With control of the industry in hand, the GFC proceeded to change the practice of renting films to theaters. Instead of theaters and distributors bargaining over film costs each time, the GFC set fixed prices, based on the revenue potential of the theater. In essence, they divided the market into first-run and subsequent-run theaters. First-run theaters got new films first and paid a premium price for them. Theaters in small and rural areas with less box-office power paid lower prices and waited longer for new films. They made do with older films that had already played in the big city.

93

Independent Producers

The film trust composed of the MPPC and GFC, however, did not last long. Ultimately, the independent producers and distributors were able to make a large enough crack in the armor of the trust to bring it down entirely. In part, this was due to a changing marketplace. True to form, innovation is not the strongpoint of a monopolist, and it certainly was not for the film trust. Their failure to anticipate market changes ultimately led to their demise.

Independent producers were historically kept in line by the difficulty they had in finding distributors for their films, and ultimately exhibitors, given the threat of blackballing by the trust. Their rise coincided with important changes in the industry. Primary among those changes was the evolution of the movie star system, the use of famous actors to market a film, and the metamorphosis of the industry from a novelty, showing generic motion pictures, to one telling stories.

D. W. Griffith, a director with Biograph is the father of the "feature film." This was a method of filming and writing that combined novel filming techniques with well-developed stories featuring plots and character development. In other words, what modern film-goers would recognize as the primary components of a movie. Prior to Griffith, the standard technique of filming was to stand a camera up on a tripod and run everything in front of it. The focus and angle didn't change. The only thing that changed was what passed in front of the camera. Griffith began to use the camera itself to help tell the story. He changed angles and positions, creating a variety of scenes, and employed creative writing to allow for a plot to develop and characters to take on greater depth. The result was a product which was noticeably different from the standard fare being offered by the trust. This product differentiation allowed for the growth of an identifiable producer, Griffith, with a specific company, Biograph, to develop a name brand for itself and thereby create a specific demand for its product, which was noticeably different from that of the trust. Griffith pioneered the movie industry as we know it today.

Griffith and Biograph were able to accomplish this as much by stealth as by talent. Because the trust monopolized the control of motion picture cameras, film, and projectors, independents had to rely on foreign companies for equipment and film. In an era when international copyrights and patents were often violated, this was not difficult to do.

Producing a film, however, was only one step in the process. Getting it into the hands of exhibitors was another. In order to accomplish this, independent producers needed to work through independent distributors. Again, it was profit-oriented small businessmen who recognized a market niche and exploited it. The independent distributors recognized the potential demand for feature films. They correctly predicted that the public demand for these feature films represented the growth of the industry and its future. The trust was unable to survive because of the inefficient system of distribution that a homogenous film supply required. Selling film by the foot and circulating the most recent footage among theaters was not the best way to exploit the profits of a feature film. The price and distribution mechanism for feature films was a function of market demand and required a different distribution strategy, one the independents recognized and mastered, unlike the trust. The trust was passed by and eventually collapsed.

In 1912, William Fox and his Greater New York Film Rental Company was the only film exchange not under GFC's control. He had been a licensee of the MPPC, but refused to sell his distribution company to them, and was blackballed. He countered by filing an antitrust lawsuit that eventually brought down the trust. In the meantime, he began to produce his own films. The MPPC appealed the decision but lost in 1918.

The MPPC was found to be in violation of the Sherman and Clayton antitrust acts in 1915. These statutes were the backbone of antitrust legislation used by the U.S. government to police markets and curb oligopolistic and monopolistic behavior. The statutes gave the federal government the power to force companies to divest some of their assets if the government could prove they had lessened competition in a market. The government could also seek fines and treble damages for behavior deemed to be monopolistic.

The MPPC and GFC trust, reeling at the hands of the independents, was formally put to rest in 1918 as a result of antitrust action. Both the distribution and production trusts were dissolved, returning the industry to the chaotic competition that existed at the beginning of the century. By this time, however, the industry had matured. The films being produced were more than mere motion pictures. They had grown into feature films with compelling plots and well-developed characters, featuring recognized movie stars, and created by well-known directors. The film talent was now in a position of power, able to extract economic concessions from the front-office businessmen.

In 1919 Adolph Zukor's company, Paramount, formed by the merger of Paramount, Famous Players, and Lasky in 1916, became the first fully integrated company producing, distributing, and exhibiting motion pictures. Zukor added the final piece with the purchase of theaters. Owning theaters was not part of his original plan. Their purchase was in response to the organization of many of the largest theaters into purchasing blocks allied against his highly profitable scheme of "block booking," a practice that would become common-place a decade later. Zukor sold his annual production of films, a few of which starred his most prized asset and America's most beloved movie star, Mary Pickford, in one block. In order to get the coveted Pickford films, theaters were forced to buy the scores of run-of-the-mill films that had little or no appeal on their own. To defend against this ploy, many of the largest theaters formed a cooperative to negoti-ate the purchase of his films. They were only interested in the better films, mostly those starring Pickford, and refused to buy his blocks of films, thus shutting out much of the lucrative first-run market to him.

The Star System

Another avenue which changed the nature of the industry was the growth of the movie star system. Until the end of the first decade of the twentieth century, actors in films were primarily anonymous characters, either completely unknown or known by a sobriquet, such as "The Girl with the Curls" (Mary Pickford), "The Imp Girl" (Florence Lawrence), or "The It Girl" (Clara Bow). This degree of anonymity served to keep actor salaries down, because it dampened the audience demand for any particular actor. If the audience did not know who an actor was, then it was much easier to substitute someone else for that actor if he or she increased their salary demands or demanded special treatment. On the downside, however, the anonymity of the actors made it difficult to capitalize on them for marketing purposes. It was not possible to advertise a film starring Mary Pickford if nobody knew who she was.

The growth in popularity of individual actors can be demonstrated by the growth in actor salaries. In 1908 the standard salary for an actor was about $2 for a day's work. More talented actors in slightly higher demand by the filmmakers, such as Mary Pickford, could earn as much as $5 a day. As actors became identifiable to the public and the demand for specific actors developed, the salaries of the top actors skyrocketed. For example, in 1911 Mary Pickford's salary was $175 per week, and within five years it exploded to $10,000 per week. Ultimately, Pickford would become one of the most powerful figures in the movie industry.

The demand for individual actors was fueled by a strange publicity stunt staged by Carl Laemmle, founder of Universal Studio. In 1908, he sought to generate some publicity for his movies by starting and then denying a rumor that his most famous actor, Florence Lawrence, known to the public only as "The Imp Girl," had died in an automobile accident. In the process of creating the rumor, The Imp Girl's name became well known. The ploy worked, creating publicity and demand by consumers to see the films starring the recently "deceased" star. It also demonstrated the powerful draw individual actors had with the public and their immense marketing value.

Mary Pickford had similar ideas. She suggested that Biograph, the company she worked for in 1908, capitalize on her name for marketing purposes (and for Mary's profit as well). When they refused, she accepted an offer of $175 per week from Carl Laemmle to join his company. He earned back the money by capitalizing on her name and publicizing her in his movie releases. Mary became one of the first film superstars whose films could be marketed on the basis of her presence in them.

The star system that emerged resulted in handsome paydays for actors. Mary Pickford was perhaps the most spectacular example, but other top draws were earning fabulous salaries. Charlie Chaplin was given a million dollar salary and a signing bonus for switching companies in 1916. Six-figure salaries plus profits from films were common offers to the top stars of the day. In addition, D. W. Griffith achieved the same kind of fame and fortune as a director.

United Artists

The creation of United Artists (UA) in 1919 can be seen as the turning point from the old trust system to the new star system. United Artists, an independent distribution company, was created to allow independent producers, who regarded themselves as artists in the new medium of the moving picture, free reign to express their creative endeavors. The company was formed by five of the biggest stars in the industry at the time: Mary Pickford, Douglas Fairbanks Sr., D. W. Griffith, William Hart, and Charlie Chaplain. The creation of UA is significant for what it represented to the film industry. The founders believed the movie industry was about creative endeavors and quality stories with good acting. They believed that a quality product would sell. Instead of focusing on creating a movie for the lowest cost, which the major distribution companies emphasized, UA catered to the independent producers who had an artistic vision, and as it turned out, a workable economic plan. Instead of minimizing cost, these artists focused on maximizing quality, correctly guessing that a high-quality product would have a much greater demand and the higher costs of production would ultimately be recouped in the marketplace.

UA proved to be a success, primarily because it did what it was formed to do: distribute high-quality movies. Critics agree that some of the finest work ever produced by the founders of UA was done during their years there. The first picture the company released was *His Majesty, the American,* starring Douglas Fairbanks. This was followed by some of the greatest films of the silent era, including *Little Lord Fauntleroy* starring Mary Pickford in 1921; the classic Douglas Fairbanks adventure tales *The Mark of Zorro* (1920), *The Three Musketeers* (1921), and *Robin Hood* (1923); and Charlie Chaplin's *The Gold Rush* in 1925.

Despite this success, UA was in trouble by the mid-1920s, as the move by distributors to acquire theaters gained momentum. The initial attraction of UA was to allow artists the freedom to produce their own pictures. While it was quite profitable, it was a risky business, since these stars essentially became independent contractors and did not have a salary to fall back on. It was difficult to convince others to follow their lead and, as a result, they began to suffer from a shortage of product and difficulty in finding theaters in which to exhibit it. The company was saved by a businessman named Joseph Schenk, who was made a partner and chairman of the board in 1924. Schenk was not an outsider to the industry. He was married to actress Norma Talmadge, and his brother-in-law was Buster Keaton. He had the industry contacts and the business acumen that UA needed to survive. He formed the Art Cinema Corporation, a company wholly owned by Schenk and his partners. This production company became a primary source of material for distribution by UA, solving their problem of too few movies. The production company produced famous pictures with major stars.

Schenk solved the outlet problem the same way he solved the input problem—by forming his own company and dealing exclusively with UA. In 1926, he formed the United Artists Theater Circuit, a publicly held company separate from UA, which began to purchase first run theaters across the country. This move forced other theater chains to recognize UA pictures, giving them negotiating power. Of course, the quality of the films being released by UA and their ultimate audience appeal was also of great help.

THE MOVE WEST

Today, Hollywood is synonymous with the movie industry. When one thinks of movies, images of California and the great studio lots in Hollywood are brought to mind. Even though many movies are now shot on location outside of Hollywood and its environs, the association is still relevant. The studios and soundstages are located there, and the agencies and movie stars still congregate near it. In addition, the television filming industry is also centered in Hollywood, giving added luster to its image as the movie capitol of the world.

California was not always the film center. The early movie industry was centered in the greater New York metropolitan area because that was where the production of equipment and the patent-holding corporations were located. West Orange, NJ, was home to Edison Labs, holder of numerous film-related patents and hence a logical place to film. Not until the early 1920s did filmmakers begin to migrate to the distant shores of California in large numbers. When the patent wars had ended and the focus of the industry had irrevocably shifted from mass producing moving pictures to creating feature films, the utilitarian reason for locating film companies in New York also faded. The lure of California was manifold: better weather, nonunion labor, cheap land, and a varied landscape.

At this time, nearly all filming was done outdoors, and in most instances, artificial lighting was not a suitable substitute for natural lighting. In California, the number of days of sunshine greatly outnumbered the number of sunny days in New York. In addition, the seasons were much more temperate, allowing for outdoor filming throughout the year.

Labor was cheaper in California, primarily due to the abundance of nonunion workers available. Ironically, many movies are now filmed outside of Hollywood for the same reason. The cost of unionized labor in the film industry has driven many film companies and producers to leave the area and film on location elsewhere. Canada has become a favorite location because of its relatively low cost of labor. Since labor was and is the major cost of most films, this is no small consideration.

The cost of land was also a consideration. Real estate in New York was at a premium in 1920 (as it has continued to be). The burgeoning film industry was expanding and found it both difficult and expensive to do so. Cheap, abundant California land provided a ready solution.

Another advantage was the geography of the West. Ocean, desert, and mountains coexist in a compact geographic area. This provided a dramatic and varied canvas for the filmmaker, who relied heavily on location shooting and sunshine for filming.

By the end of the decade no production companies were left in the East, though the financial offices remained there. In fact, that is still true. While the production facilities are centered on the West Coast, the financial arms of the companies are located in New York. The move of the production studios to California established Hollywood as the center of the film industry.

THE SILENT FILM ERA

Prior to the arrival of sound, acting was a very different profession. Because no voices or sound effects were available, actors had to use exaggerated physical movements and facial expressions to convey emotion. Dialogue was represented only by the occasional use of title cards inserted with written dialogue.

The process of making a film was also very different. Without sound, filming itself was much easier. An entire dimension of movie making could be disregarded. There was no need for quiet on the set. Background noise was irrelevant, and directors could shout out stage instructions to actors during a scene. There was no concern for the noise made by equipment or stagehands during filming, and sometimes an orchestra was hired to provide mood music or entertainment for the cast and crew. Actors often spoke the lines that were written on title cards, but of course their voices were never heard by the audience.

Film stages did not have to be soundproof and in fact were often opened to the elements to let in more light and ventilation on warm days. Large doors would be opened on either side of the stage for indoor filming. Filming on location was also easier because no concern need be paid to extraneous background noise—only visual aspects needed to be controlled.

Film studios date from the early 1890s. Natural light, however, was required for filming, so when possible, the use of expensive, confining indoor studios was eschewed in favor of cheaper outdoor stages. Since films were silent, the surrounding noise level was of no consideration.

The Theaters

The movie industry evolved and movie theaters evolved with it. By the second decade of the twentieth century, movie theaters resembled what we would easily recognize today. In the biggest urban areas, deluxe theaters with multiple balconies, gold trim, elaborate decorations, and large plush seats, resembling opera houses and symphony halls, were constructed. These appealed to the upper class more than the nickelodeon, which was clearly aimed at the blue-collar worker, though it did attract many curious upper-income Americans. This evolution was complete by the time of the First World War. The old nickelodeons and the one-reelers were replaced by theaters showing feature length films that were often the entire evening's entertainment, though some vaudeville exhibitions remained through the end of the silent film era.

During the era of silent films, there were dozens of producers, but few high-budget, high-quality films produced each year—at least relative to total production. While a producer might put out fifty to seventy films in a year, only one in ten was likely to be of the high-quality, first-run variety. And typically, only the largest of the producers would produce any of these films. The few "blockbusters" would open in the largest, first-run theaters. Oftentimes they doubled as stages for vaudeville or variety shows, and they were generally located in the heart of the major cities. These theaters accommodated thousands of patrons, and the shows played nearly around the clock, so that there was a nearly continual flow of people in and out the door.

The admission price for these theaters was the highest it would be for the showing of a film. As a film moved on to secondary theaters, the price dropped, as did the grandeur of the surroundings. Evening and weekend showings of the films would often be part of an evening of entertainment, coupled with a stage show and perhaps even an orchestral performance. Like a film today, the silent film would play in the first-run theaters as long as there was sufficient demand. A good draw might play for months before moving on to the second-run circuits.

The Movie Stars

The rise of the artist-filmmaker, the demand by the public for identifiable stars, and the breakup of the film trust swung the pendulum of power from movie executives and inventors toward the movie stars. The period from 1910 to 1927 was one in which the greatest stars earned fabulous salaries, lived outrageous lifestyles, and imposed their will quite readily on the industry. While the period from the 1930s to the 1950s is often referred to as the industry's golden era, that is from the perspective of the financiers and the film critics. From the perspective of the actors, the first golden era consisted of the two decades before the Great Depression and the coming of sound. This was an era when actors were able to demand salaries and perks that were limited only by what the market could bear. Instead of fixed daily wages, they were able to earn exorbitant salaries and bonuses. By 1916, Mary Pickford, one of the top stars of this era, was earning $10,000 a week. She made five films that year and earned an inflation-adjusted salary in excess of $80 million. This compares very favorably to the $20 million per picture that today's top stars command.

THE ARRIVAL OF SOUND

In today's surround-sound, stereo-enhanced, special-effects driven industry, it is hard for the modern viewer to imagine that the total sound for a movie used to be the accompaniment of a piano in the theater. Fancier theaters and more upscale settings sometimes used an orchestra, but a piano was more common. This was soon to change, however. Inventors worked hard to perfect the ability to combine sound and picture in an economical fashion. While pictures were silent, dreams of sound were alive and well.

The first commercially successful combination of sound and film, known as synchronized sound because it was produced along with the picture and not accompanied by a pianist or orchestra in the theater, was in *Don Juan*, produced in 1926. The soundtrack consisted of orchestral music only, no talking. It was, however, a harbinger of things to come. Once the technology was perfected that allowed for the synchronization of sound and picture, adding the live voices of actors was next. The red-letter day for sound in the movie industry was October 6, 1927. On this day the first movie with spoken dialogue debuted. *The Jazz Singer*, produced by Warner Brothers, featured only limited dialogue but had a cataclysmic impact on the industry. Al Jolson proved to be prophetic when he uttered the first spoken words heard in a movie: "Wait a minute, you ain't heard nothin' yet."

Warner Brothers Studio released the first talking picture more out of desperation than innovation. The studio was having major financial problems, having lost some of its market to the new-fangled radio receivers appearing in American living rooms in increasing numbers, with resulting poor performance of its recent films. The inclusion of dialog in a movie was a gamble because of the tremendous expense involved. Not only were production costs higher—a whopping $500,000 to produce *The Jazz Singer*, with its limited sound—but the movie could only be shown in theaters that were equipped to play sound pictures. Compare this to the cost of silent films, which started at about $4,000 for low-budget pictures and averaged $60,000. Even the priciest silent films cost less than the $200,000 needed to make low-budget talkies. Not only did Warner Brothers have to pay to create the movie, they had to renovate the theaters that would show it. A movie with its own soundtrack required special equipment that could project the sound in the theater. Not only was the release of the talkie expensive, but its distribution was limited to the few theaters that Warner Brothers could initially afford to renovate.

Incredible as it may seem now, the arrival of sound movies was not greeted with enthusiasm by many in the industry. The expense of renovating theaters and production stages to accommodate sound was staggering. At roughly $25,000 apiece, studios faced a $40 million renovation bill. Producers and theater owners were reluctant to make these sizable investments for what many considered a passing fancy. Actors were not thrilled with the innovation either, since it dramatically changed the acting profession and would prove to have a differential impact on actors' careers as they struggled to adjust to the new techniques required for acting with dialogue.

By the end of the 1920s, vertical integration of the movie industry was beginning to reappear. This time it focused on the exhibition end of the industry as well as the production end. Distribution companies were purchasing movie theaters in order to have a guaranteed market for their product. By 1928, the top eight studios owned over 1,600 movie theaters. While this represented only a fraction of the total theaters in the industry, it was a majority of the first-run theaters in the largest cities. Independent theater owners, who were primarily located in smaller, second-run markets, could not afford to gamble that sound was more than a fad. They had to wait until the turning point came, when it was obvious sound was here to stay. In the meantime, they were only able to show silent films.

Beside the theater conversion costs, the studios were facing the daunting task of having to convert their studios for sound production as well if this fad were to become a reality. With sound, the act of shooting a movie changed. The stage and equipment had to be redesigned to eliminate noise. The manner of directing and shooting had to change, and location was more difficult. Shooting outdoors now involved attempting to eliminate unwanted sound from the natural world. It was one thing to shut the extraneous noise out of the studio, but quite another to eliminate it during location shooting.

Producers were also less than thrilled with the prospect of sound because of the new challenges it imposed on filming. Microphones were very sensitive, picking up extraneous noise such as the sound of feet shuffling across a stage and the camera moving to a different position for filming. Innovations in equipment and filming technique were necessary to accommodate this new technology. Filming late at night helped to reduce noise outside the studio from automobile and foot traffic, while allowing for doors to be left open to facilitate air circulation. The alternative, shooting indoors with doors closed, proved to be exhausting due to the high temperatures of the California climate and the lights in a stuffy, enclosed, sound-insulated studio. Fans to help circulation were out of the question due to the noise. This is the era which spawned the famous director's command, "Quiet on the set!"

Because of the sensitive microphones, actors were forced to change their style of acting, favoring static styles that reduced the amount of noise from stage movements. The movement of the camera itself was also a problem, and until suitable technology could be developed, it meant that early talkies required a stationery camera. This meant that actors not only couldn't move much, but there could only be a few of them in any one scene. The placement of microphones and camera dictated the type of scripts that could be used.

The early technical problems were successfully dealt with by film-maker Rouben Mamoulian. He introduced multitrack recording—"multi" meaning only two early on, but still quite an innovation. Multitrack recording is the process of recording multiple tracks for different sounds and then combining them in the final film. For example, instead of trying to film the dialogue of two actors in an action scene while the shooting and car crashes are going on, the dialogue is recorded separately. The music that is heard in the background of movies is also recorded on a separate track. In the final version of the movie, the sound level of each track can be set so that the decibel level of the gun shots, the car crashes, the dialogue, and the music are exactly the way the director wants them.

Despite this improvement, another stumbling block faced by studios was the large stock of silent films in their inventories awaiting circulation in smaller, second-run markets and lucrative foreign markets, with some even awaiting initial release. If sound became the rage, what would happen to these silent films? Of particular concern was the impact of sound on the international market. With silent films, the cost of converting a film to the language of any other country was cheap. On average, it cost about $10,000 to convert a film for global release. It involved changing only a few dialogue cards from English into another language. With sound, however, films would either have to be dubbed with foreign speaking actors, or forego the international market altogether. Either prospect would be expensive. The cost to convert a film to another language increased to $70,000 per language.

Finally, the impact of sound on actors proved to be inequitable. Some thrived in the new medium, others were unable to adjust. Up until this point audiences had become familiar with actors' faces and dramatic styles, but they had not heard them. Radio was still in its infancy, and few actors were crossing regularly between the two media at this point, so few actors had ever been heard by their adoring fans. Some did not have voices to match their dramatic abilities. Clara Bow, the "It Girl" of silent picture fame, was one of the great leading ladies of that era. The dawning of sound, however, marked the downfall of her career. Her heavy New York accent did not play well with the parts in which she was cast, and her voice led to a downturn in her career.

Another famous casualty was an actor named Emil Jennings. Jennings won the first Academy Award for best actor in 1927–1928 for his films *The Way of all Flesh* and *The Last Command*. His thick German accent proved to be his undoing, and just a few years after winning his awards, he was gone from the American film industry forever. He returned to Germany where he continued his career as a bit actor. His greatest claim to fame after this was his appearance in the acclaimed German film *The Blue Angel*, where he was upstaged by a young actress named Marlene Dietrich, whose throaty German accent would prove a hit in Hollywood.

Besides voice problems, acting styles were also made obsolete by sound. Whereas silent films required exaggerated and flamboyant gestures in order to visually display emotion and intent, sound required almost the opposite. The over-the-top gestures were noisy and distracting. Thus actors had to contend with new acting styles as well as vocal problems. Talking pictures required dialogue and more natural movement, something that not every actor could adjust to easily.

Perhaps the most famous collapse was an actor named John Gilbert. During the silent film era, he was MGM's leading man. Sound proved to be his undoing because of the combination of his voice, which was not as masculine sounding as his image, and his contract fight with Louis B. Mayer, head of MGM studios. The fight was a precursor to the type of power that was being concentrated in the hands of studio executives. The result was that Gilbert went from being the most desirable leading man in the industry to a blackballed outcast who had trouble finding work. Gilbert was married to a young actress named Ina Claire, whose star was rising just at the time Gilbert's was descending. As a result of his failing career, Gilbert became an alcoholic recluse and died at the age of 38. His story was made famous by the movie *A Star is Born*, originally released in 1937, remade in 1954, and remade again in 1976. Gilbert was replaced in the leading male role by a then unknown Clark Gable.

Some actors, such as Gable, saw their careers skyrocket with the dawning of sound. The most prominent example was a young actor named "Steamboat Willie." Willie's silent film debut in 1928 was upstaged by his later appearances in sound films. Ultimately, he would star in hundreds of short and feature length films and successfully transform his career into one of the greatest multimedia success stories of all time. He is better known by the stage name he eventually took: Mickey Mouse.

Despite all of these potential hurdles and reservations, sound quickly took over the industry. The first all-talking picture came less than a year after the debut of *Jazz Singer*. *The Lights of New York* was released in July of 1929 by Warner Brothers. That was the last year in which silent films outnumbered talkies. Within a year only one in four films were silent. By the end of 1929 more than half of all theaters had been converted to sound. By July of 1930, about 80 percent of theaters showed only talking pictures. By 1932, only 2 percent showed silents, and by 1934 they were a thing of the past. A new era had dawned for movies, and it forever changed the landscape of the industry.

Sound was only one of the cataclysmic changes at the end of the 1920s that dramatically changed the industry, swinging the balance of power once again in favor of the executives at the expense of the actors. Only the largest studios could afford the conversion to sound, which required huge capital outlays. As a result, mergers occurred or smaller distributors simply went out of business. The era of the Studio System had dawned.

THE STUDIO SYSTEM

Evolution of a New System

By 1930, complete vertical integration dominated the industry. Unlike the integration in the earlier part of the century, this vertical integration included not only production and distribution, but exhibition as well. The largest distributors controlled the production of pictures through their soundstages and long-term contracts with actors and directors. They also controlled the exhibition side of the industry with their ownership of the largest first-run theaters in the nation. The return to an integrated industry was made possible by a number of factors, among them the economies of scale resulting from technological changes in the industry, the shift in the balance of power from actors back to studio executives as a result of sound, the public's move from rural areas to cities, and the economic hardships of the Great Depression.

The change in the balance of power and the onset of the Great Depression changed the status of contracts with actors. Instead of being "free agents" and signing on to make individual pictures with various companies depending on their time and interest, actors were signed to long-term contracts with studios, who then used their stable of stars to produce pictures built around the talent at hand. These actors and directors were paid annual salaries and their contracts often specified a minimum and maximum number of films they would be required to make. The actors became fixed costs in a production process. This was a much better deal for the studio executives than for the actors, who lost their bargaining power. Exacerbating the situation was the nature of the contracts, which were long-term with options at the discretion of the studio. The oligopolistic nature of the industry allowed for collusion between the studios, which helped to keep wages down and prevented actors from moving between studios. If an actor was released or refused to sign a contract, he or she could be blacklisted from the industry. Actors sought comfort in long-term contracts which protected them from the uncertainty of the new talking picture format as well as the cruelty of the Great Depression. This was no small concession during a period when as much as 25 percent of the labor force was unemployed.

Increasing urbanization decreased the size of the second-run theater market. As Americans moved into big cities, small rural theaters lost their customer base, and the size and economic significance of the second-run circuit evaporated. As it faded away, the distribution strategy employed by the studios also changed. A smaller secondary market meant fewer outlets for second-run films and less cycling of big production films. It increased the emphasis on bigger productions which would pull in a bigger audience in a shorter time span. This helped to emphasize the drive to accumulate large first-run theaters. Possession of these theaters guaranteed an outlet for the exhibition of these major productions. The move was toward fewer pictures, but bigger productions. This pattern would evolve slightly as vertical integration matured and the double feature became a staple.

The Studios

The industry was controlled by the "Big Eight" studios, which were themselves divided into two types. The fully integrated majors included Paramount, Fox, MGM, RKO, and Warner Brothers. They owned theaters, distribution networks, and studios that employed the talent for making the movies. The "Little Three," Columbia, Universal, and United Artists produced films, but did not own first-run theaters. United Artists was unique among the Big Eight studios as a distribution arm for independent producers. It had no talent under contract and owned no theaters.

Paramount owned the greatest number of theaters (1,500), which caused them some financial problems during economic downturns as the cost of maintaining a large number of theaters was great. However, it also meant that they realized huge profits during economic upswings.

Warner Brothers struggled during the 1930s due to their extensive theater holdings and heavy investment in nonfilm assets, such as radio and music production. Their investment in sound films and technology was a risky financial gamble that paid off and ultimately saw them through the lean Depression years.

MGM was the most successful studio during the Depression. One important reason was their small number of theaters, which were the primary cause of financial problems for other studios. They owned a scant 125 theaters, all of them premier first-run film palaces in major metropolitan areas. Equally important was their ability to repeatedly gauge the public's taste for movies. They produced a disproportionate share of top-revenue grossing films during the 1930s. With their stable of stars, the MGM slogan "more stars than in the heavens" seemed to be true. From 1930–1933, when other studios were awash in red ink, MGM was in its glory. They released nine of the twenty-five top grossing films during this period, including *Anna Christie* (1930), *The Guardsman* (1931), and *Grand Hotel* (1932).

The fate of UA was both helped and hindered by its unique status among the majors. As a distribution company for the independent producers, it did not own any theaters, thus avoiding the pitfalls the Depression brought to the theater-holding studios. However, UA also had no stable of talent it could rely upon to produce movies. It had to depend on the ability of independent producers to generate a steady stream of output for release. As box-office revenues declined, so did the number of independent producers. As a result, UA went through some lean years when it did not have a regular supply of films to release. It lost money during the Depression, but managed to stay afloat, and eventually emerged unscathed.

Columbia survived the Depression years with a stronghold on its position as the biggest of the little three. It never lost its focus, and instead of succumbing to the mad rush to acquire theaters, it concentrated on producing movies. In particular, it concentrated on exploiting its comparative advantage: fillers, shorts, newsreels, and B-pictures (low-budget films used as the second half of a double feature). Without a big stable of high-priced movie stars, this was a natural market for Columbia and a lucrative one. They did come out with the occasional hit, such as 1934's Academy Award winner for Best Picture, *It Happened One Night*. But for the most part, they were content to profit from the lower end of the market.

The relationship between the big five and the little three was symbiotic. The major studios did not have the capacity to produce enough films for their theaters in a year, especially after double features became the norm. The gap was filled by the little three. Because the major five dominated the first-run theaters, the other studios could not afford to produce much in the way of first-run films. As a result, their primary focus was on producing the large quantity of B-grade films used as second bills and filler films in between new first-run releases.

The integrated majors each produced about forty to sixty movies per year, about half the industry total, but accounting for 75 percent of the first-run product. Even though they owned less than 15 percent of the theaters, their films accounted for 70 percent of the total box office. The theaters they did own were concentrated in major urban areas, constituting the bulk of the first-run market. The little three of Universal, Columbia, and UA produced films, but did not own first-run theaters.

Independent production during the studio era was difficult because the integrated majors shut them out of the first-run theaters. It was made even more difficult by the smaller independent theaters, which often refused to show any film that had not played in a first-run theater. If a smaller theater exhibited a film without a prior run (i.e., produced by one of the majors), it would risk losing access to any of the films produced by the majors. The decline of the studio system led to a proliferation of independent producers. Before the Second World War, there were few independent producers. In 1945, 40 were listed in the trade journals. In 1946, the number increased to 70, and within a decade that had more than doubled to 165.

Government Aid

The U.S. government was very helpful to the movie industry, as it tried to be to many industries during the Depression, with passage of the National Industrial Recovery Act (NIRA) that was signed into law in June of 1933. This Act legalized many anticompetitive activities in the interest of avoiding the cutthroat competition that the government saw as a contributing cause to the economic turmoil. The Act was eventually overturned by the Supreme Court, but not before it had a major influence on the way the movie industry was organized. Ultimately, Hollywood became heavily unionized, from the Screen Actors Guild down to the more than one hundred labor unions representing Hollywood employees today. However, the NIRA reinforced the monopolistic structure of the industry. This structure stayed in place until well after the war.

Among the practices protected by the NIRA were those involving block booking, blind bidding, and minimum price controls. Block booking was the practice of selling blocks of films together. In this way a studio could package a highly desirable film with a few lower quality films. Theaters were forced to buy the whole package of films to get the one they wanted. Blind bidding was the practice of selling films to theaters without benefit of preview. A star or director with enough box-office appeal could be used to sell a forthcoming film without benefit of previewing it first. The studios required second-run theaters to maintain minimum admission prices in order to protect the first-run market. Since the interest of the theater was to bring in as much money as quickly as possible, the pricing of the product could not be too significantly different between first and second-run theaters in big cities. If the price was too low in the second-run theater, then some people would not be willing to pay the higher price for the privilege of seeing the film a bit earlier.

With a vertically integrated industry, it was not difficult to force nonaffiliated theaters to comply with the block booking or blind bidding systems. If they did not, they would be shut out of the major picture market. They would have been forced to rely on a steady diet of B-pictures from independent producers, with the possible exception of an occasional big-budget picture by an independent producer released through United Artists. The large number of small, independent theaters, almost exclusively located in small markets, had no marketing clout against the Big Eight.

Double features were popularized during the Depression as a way to get more patrons in the theater. Prior to this, the typical format was a feature film, a newsreel, and a few shorts. In 1931, about 10 percent of theaters showed double features; by the end of the studio era in 1947, more than 60 percent did. It changed the way studios produced movies, but ultimately did not increase attendance. It did, however, change the customer's expectations. The standard trip to the movies came to include the main feature as the culmination of an evening's entertainment that included a serial, a newsreel, and a B-picture.

The newsreels served a dual purpose. They informed the public about the current news, including a regular dose of Hollywood gossip, which also served to generate publicity for the industry. During the heyday of the studio system in the 1930s, Hollywood was one of the largest sources of news in the country, second only to New York and Washington, D.C., in the amount of press coverage it received. In addition to hard newscasts, movie fans thrived on the supply of gossip provided about their favorite stars, behind-the-scenes business, tidbits about forthcoming feature films, and the latest hits. In the era before the Internet and hundreds of cable television channels, the movies were the central common entertainment theme of the nation. As a result, Hollywood was brought to the attention of nearly every American household. The news and gossip were relayed via newsreels, press releases, and magazines devoted to the industry.

The Effects of the Great Depression

While all the major studios survived the Depression, some fared better than others. They all saw profits decline. Profits were pinched for studios because sound had increased the cost of movies to a range of $300,000 to $800,000 (up from approximately $60,000 for the average silent film). However, the hits were only bringing in $300,000 to

$500,000 in the domestic market, and foreign box-office revenue had dwindled significantly. Some survived only by selling off assets, such as theaters or subsidiaries. Others, like Warner Brothers, survived because of the diversity of their business.

The arrival of sound had both changed the balance of power in the industry and increased the advantage of the well-capitalized company. The cost of converting studios and theaters to sound, arriving roughly at the same time as the Depression, meant the small operators had trouble surviving. The need for large capital outlays to purchase sound equipment, convert stages to soundproof them, and equip theaters with sound projection systems forced most of the small companies out of business.

Directors and Producers

Centralizing production into a small number of studios reduced costs. Producers were able to juggle a number of projects at once, film equipment was in more constant use, which included everything from the cameras to the soundstages and the editing room equipment. In addition, a greater specialization and division of labor emerged to increase efficiency. This is particularly evident in the changing role of directors and producers.

Under the independent system, a producer controlled the production of pictures and took responsibility for hiring actors, directors, stagehands, technicians, and writers. In addition, the producer either owned or rented a soundstage and oversaw the development of the film from beginning to end. The business side of the company was also overseen by the producer, who had to budget the production and negotiate the distribution of the film. The director, on the other hand, was responsible for the creation of the individual film. While the producer was organizing the flow of films for the company, the director was responsible for the details of a specific film, overseeing the budget, actors, and actual filming. Directors were thus very powerful, exerting great influence over a film, primarily from an artistic perspective.

The studio system saw a change in the relative balance of power between these two roles. Under the studio system, a director was one of a number of specialists employed by a studio. A studio might have several directors, each of whom worked on one picture at a time. They were responsible only for completing it on time and within budget. They had responsibility for artistic control of the final product, but little else. Often they had little or no say in choosing the actors or changing the script, though more influential directors did hold some sway over their producers.

The producer under the studio system became the organizer. He was responsible for bringing together the writers, actors, and directors employed by the studio and sorting them out into a series of filming projects. The goal was to produce a certain number of films, each with a set budget and anticipated audience and revenue goal. The producer organized the assets of the company in order to maximize profits. This was very much the role of a manager. Their job was to make the most of the talent assembled on their lot—sorting through the available storylines, deciding which to film and when, choosing the directors, finalizing the scripts, and picking the cast.

Under the independent production system, a producer needed to hire actors and directors specifically for each film. Thus, a contract would have to be worked out for each person each time a film was made. Since the availability of actors and their final negotiated salary changed with each picture, the cost of employing them was variable. If the producer wanted to film fewer pictures, he hired fewer actors, thus the total amount spent on actors decreased. If he wanted more films, he needed to hire more actors, thus the cost increased. In other words, the total cost of actors varied with the number of films produced.

Actor Contracts

Under the studio system, however, the on-screen talent was all under contract. The basic contract paid an annual salary to an actor for a set length of employment, usually one year. Actors were paid to act, but not hired for a specific film. In this way, the studio producer's job was much different. Instead of hiring the best actor he could get for a part, he already had the actors and needed to sort them out for the various projects he was producing at any given time.

The contracts were very one-sided. They were annual contracts, renewable by the studio through an option clause arrangement employed in such a way as to make them nearly infinite in length. This tied up the talent with specific studios. The domination of the industry by the Big Eight made it even easier for a studio to control its talent. All the firms were physically located near one another, and all the executives knew each other well. Thus the informal labor market was very strong. If a studio wanted to keep an actor whose contract had expired, the word would be floated to the other executives, who had a gentleman's agreement to respect one another's talent wishes. Thus a studio would make an offer to an actor, who would find it was the only one available. No other studio would make a competing offer. Once a contract was signed, it was renewable, at the studio's discretion (called an option) for up to seven years. If an actor got out of line during the time of employment, he or she would be suspended. The duration of the suspension was added to the length of the contract. Thus an actor could not sit out an unfavorable contract. Sometimes a studio would have an idle actor because they did not have the right part for them in current production. Rather than leave the actor idle, the studios employed another strategy that became commonplace—leasing an actor to another studio. The actors would earn none of the rental price, only their regular salary.

A particularly rebellious star might be fired and blackballed with a few simple phone calls to the other studios. Consequently, the star would find him/herself virtually unemployable in the industry. The small, independent producers were an option, but they typically produced only low-budget films, so it was not a lucrative deal. Blackballed stars were on the downside of their career unless they repented and begged their way back into the graces of the studio.

The seven-year contract contained six-month options. The studio decided each six months whether or not to renew them for another six months. The contract required the actor to act in whatever movies the studio deemed best and to go on publicity junkets to promote pictures, give interviews, and dress, act, cut their hair, even change their name, all at the behest of the studio. In short, it was the actors, not so much the movies, that were marketed. The studios defended these contracts in the name of the expense of developing actors. Not all actors panned out, and the expense of training had to be made up by the studio. Besides, actors were handsomely paid, well above the national average, especially considering that the nation was in the midst of the Great Depression. Shirley Temple, for example, earned $350,000 a year and Greta Garbo made $7,000 per week. Nonstars did not earn this kind of salary, but they still did relatively well compared to the average American. In 1933 the median salary for actors was $4,700 per year. The average wage in the United States that year was $1,045 for those lucky enough to have a job.

The Screen Actors Guild

The Screen Actors Guild (SAG) was formed in 1933 in response to the attempt of studios to cut actor salaries by 50 percent. SAG failed to receive recognition as a bargaining agent for the actors by the National Labor Relations Act, so Hollywood ignored it. Not until the actors threatened to strike in 1937 was it taken seriously by the studio moguls. In the negotiations for recognition, SAG won concessions from the studios, such as minimum levels of pay for actors, continuous employment guarantees, and minimum rest periods between calls. The studios averted the threat of a strike at virtually no economic cost. Future negotiations proceeded along similar paths, with SAG settling for gains the studios gladly gave up. The perks that SAG won cost the studios little, but gave the union a sense of accomplishment, improved morale, and made life on the set more tolerable. It also gave the union a footing in the industry, which it would be able to exploit to a greater degree upon the eventual breakup of the studio system.

The actors were composed of different types of performers. Extras were trivial players who were often hired on a daily or weekly basis. These are the actors, usually with no speaking parts, who make up the crowd and passersby in the background. They were paid little, received no screen credit, and were never certain their scene would make the final cut of a movie. This was the largest class of actors and the one most aspiring actors started in, hoping to be discovered. In reality, the majority of these actors earned their living in another profession, as a waiter, gas station attendant, or secretary, making ends meet while they waited for their big break. For the vast majority of extras, that break would never come.

The largest group of actors who could realistically hope to make a living in the profession was stock players. These were the actors who had been discovered young, upcoming, and promising. Not all would make it, but they were recognized as having potential. They were under contract, typically the renewable six-month option. This group also included actors at the opposite end of the spectrum: seasoned, experienced, older actors who would either never become stars or were faded minor stars. They were, however, useful, versatile, and cheap enough to keep under contract and use in a multitude of minor roles. They earned $50–350 per week during the Depression.

Featured players were at the level just beneath the stars. They also had contracts, but they received screen credit, were often featured in publicity tours and advertising, and played substantial, though not star, roles in films. Their contracts usually specified a range of films they would be in and might pay on a per picture basis.

Stars, of course, were the elite. They received the highest pay, as well as trivial perks that separated them from the other classes of actors: private dressing rooms, personal attendants, and their name in big letters, perhaps above the title of the movie in advertising and on screen. Many of these perks cost the studio very little, but they did keep the stars' egos in check.

Studios typically had fifty to one hundred actors under contract at any one time, only about five or six of whom received star billing. These individuals changed over time. A star could fade and still be kept as a useful contract player or eventually be released.

Stars lived a lifestyle that was the envy of most Americans. Movie magazines thrived on stories of their profligate spending. Unbeknownst to most people, these lifestyles were promoted, if not manipulated by the studios. They encouraged lavish parties, grand homes, and conspicuous consumption. Feeding the gossip mill of the picture magazines was free publicity for the studios. They often extended loans to their stars to help with their oversize standard of living and encouraged them to spend lavishly and publicly. Sometimes they even went so far as to script their very public personal lives for studio-marketing advantages. This was not an era of liberal sexual tolerance, so the privates lives of gay stars were elaborately covered up. Rock Hudson, for example, was required to date Mamie Van Doren, a screen sexpot of the day, for the sake of the studio.

B-Pictures

New methods of marketing and producing accompanied the new organizational structure of the industry. The integrated majors focused on a strategy of producing low cost, or B films, to cover fixed costs and producing high-cost, high-yield films to make the profits. The major independent producers were primarily concerned with the high quality end of the spectrum. They rented studio production facilities and negotiated distribution deals with the studios, oftentimes with United Artists, which remained an independent distributor to fill just such a niche.

There was a guaranteed market for B-films on two fronts. First, the studios owned theaters, thus they could show any of their films, and they did so, keeping the theaters filled in between major hits. Secondly, for those studios that did not own theaters, they sold these low-budget pictures in a package deal with their blockbusters. This made for a guaranteed audience. Independent theaters were subject to these negotiating tactics and had little choice, since they did not have a guaranteed source of films. In order to keep movies in their theaters, they had to book what the studios offered.

The classic B-picture is the Western, a whole genre of filmmaking unto itself. Despite the huge number of these films made, the stereotypical Western is a B-picture. They were the cheapest genre of films to make and became the staple of small production companies. They were cheap because so many of them relied on the same stock footage. They could be filmed outdoors in the California hills and deserts and required only minor script variations on the same common theme, which was that the bad guy terrorizes, the good guy arrives, and the good guy gets the girl.

B-pictures cost from $50,000 to $200,000 to produce. First-run pictures averaged $400,000 but could cost twice that for a major production. B-pictures typically rented for flat fees and served as second features or fillers between releases of major pictures. Their role for the studio was to fill their theaters between first-run films, provide a second feature to enhance demand, and basically cover the fixed costs of the theater. They didn't make much money, but because they sold for flat fees and not shares of the box office, as the first-run films did, their revenues were predictable.

CENSORSHIP AND THE MOVIE INDUSTRY

Because of its enormous impact on the film-going public, the movie industry has been one of the most controlled industries in America. Films were essentially monitored by three levels of varying enforcement. The first was an internal industry board, known as the Production Code Administration, established by Will Hays in 1924. The board monitored the content of each film along its production life, beginning with the script and ending with the release of the final product. Its goal was to remove potentially offensive material before it got too far along to cause any problem with the completion of a film. Sometimes this included suggesting methods of handling potential criticism if a controversial scene was left in the film. The studios enforced this as a way of forestalling stricter practices from the government.

The second formal level of monitoring came from state and municipal censorship boards. These boards had the authority to order the removal of any scene from a movie or prohibit its exhibition within the geographic area of their authority. This was a serious threat and could be problematic, since there was not a basic list of prohibited scenes. The board had the authority to deny anything it found objectionable. Today this would be unthinkable. The movie industry now enjoys the same First Amendment rights to free speech as the rest of the country.

The final source of censorship came from organized "watchdog" groups. These groups still exist today. They have no formal authority over the movie industry, but they do wield the power of publicity. Their ability to organize a boycott of a movie must be considered when including potentially controversial scenes or subject matter in films.

Frequent clashes occurred between groups representing small-town America, major cities, and studios. The first-run theaters in large cities catered primarily to adults and generated most of the revenue. Therefore the standards for these movies were considered differently than those for rural and middle America, where families were the audience, and big city "smut" and "sophistication" was not considered virtuous.

THE DECLINE OF THE STUDIO SYSTEM

It was the rise of television that spelled the end for the double feature and the B-movie, as well as a host of production companies that survived on the B-movie. The mid-1950s also saw the return of antitrust legislation, which forced diversification of the major studios and dissolved the near-perpetual contract arrangements they had with the stars. As the era of "free agency" in talent returned, the B-picture was priced out of the market. Finally, with so many entertainment options opening up in the postwar boom, consumers began to demand quality instead of mere quantity for their dollar. The cost of supplying B-pictures increased, their demand waned, and a chapter of American movie history drew to a close. The industry was going through another major organizational shift, the last one of the century.

World War II cut off the European market for Hollywood. Business shifted from Europe to Latin America, which had been largely unexploited. However, this did not make up for the lost European business. Fortunately for the film industry, the American market was recovering from the Depression. By the time America entered the war, the economy was in full recovery mode, but the massive government programs geared toward war production left the country with a relative shortage of goods to purchase. Consumers turned their dollars toward entertainment. Domestic film rentals increased by more than 70 percent from $193 million in 1939 to $332 million in 1946.

With the prohibition on block booking and blind bidding as part of the antitrust suit, it was no longer economically viable to produce B-pictures. Not only did studios not have fixed cost labor, there was little demand for the B-pictures. Theaters did not have to buy them to get the first-run material anymore, and consumers were not as interested in B-movies, since TV could provide equal or better quality at lower cost.

The improved business had other impacts on the market. The increased demand meant that movies played longer in theaters. The result was a decrease in the number of films made and an increase in average revenue. In 1939, 388 films were released. In 1946, this was down to 252. The smaller market opened up more possibilities for independent producers and made the production and release of their product less risky. As a result, their number and output increased during the war years. Favorable income tax laws also helped. Tax breaks were available for producers or stars who operated their own production company.

Postwar movie theater attendance began to drop, declining by about 50 percent during the decade following the end of the war. Numerous causes for this can be cited, beginning with the diversion of leisure budgets to other expenditures, particularly those unavailable or scarce during the war. The GI bill sent record numbers of veterans to college, and the rising birthrate kept more families at home in the evening with the radio or television as entertainment. The need to take their children or hire a babysitter increased the cost of movies to these families, and they responded by attending less frequently.

Unlike much of the rest of the American economy, the movie industry did not enjoy rapid growth after the war. As Americans moved to the suburbs, refocused on family, and spent their money on long-overdue consumer-durables purchases put off during the war, the movie industry became an afterthought. Also, as television began to hit its commercial stride and the cost of television sets came down to an affordable level for the average American family, their concept of entertainment began to change. As a result, the decade after the war was in some ways even worse for Hollywood than the decade before the war. The antitrust lawsuits, the rise of television, and the change in consumer behavior all contributed to the decline of the movie industry. Attendance dropped, 4,000 theaters went out of business, studios sold off assets, ranging from real estate to film libraries, and dramatically changed their production styles. Gone were the newsreels, B-pictures and shorts; all would be replaced by television. Instead, studios produced fewer and "higher class" pictures. Finally, payrolls were cut, as producers, directors, and actors were no longer signed to contracts by studios, but instead signed contracts for specific films.

Studio Diversification

The studio system was not only doomed by changes in the economy, but by the attitude of the public as well. After the war, a thriving American economy was much less tolerant of anticompetitive practices and organizations. As a result, challenges were made to these organizations, and they collapsed. The movie industry was no exception. The system was attacked on two major fronts: vertical integration and the perpetual form of contracts between studio and star.

In 1943, Olivia de Havilland challenged the contract that she had signed with Warner Brothers. An issue was whether the studio had the right to extend the contract beyond its original seven-year length. The studio claimed it had that right, since de Havilland had spent part of that contract under suspension, and thus had not fulfilled the seven-year term. De Havilland argued that a suspension, during which time she was not paid because she was not working, should not lengthen the contract. The studios had been enforcing this type of contract for the better part of the past two decades, so they believed they stood on solid ground. The courts disagreed. The result was a victory for de Havilland, the first step toward stars regaining power.

The other war being waged on the studios was a renewal of the antitrust lawsuits brought early in the century. Whereas in the first case, the government broke up the horizontal merger of the film trust, this time they challenged the vertically merged studios. They focused on the links between production and exhibition, forcing studios to release their stranglehold on the theaters by selling their holdings. The Supreme Court heard the Paramount case in 1948 and ruled against the movie industry. Paramount and RKO were the first studios to comply with the diversification ruling, in 1949. By 1959 all the studios had sold off their theaters. This divestiture essentially satisfied the court order against monopoly practices like block booking and blind bidding.

With the forced divestiture of the five integrated majors, studios now had soundstages sitting empty and no new films to distribute. Without a theater chain, a studio no longer had a guaranteed outlet for its pictures. Without control of the first-run theaters, they no longer had leverage over the second-run theaters. Gone was the ability to block book and blindly sell their lower quality films with their blockbusters. This led to a decrease in the quantity of films produced, creating a surplus of soundstage availability. They began to fiercely court independent producers to put these assets to use. Before the breakup, their control of the industry effectively shut independent producers out of the market, but now they were necessary for the very survival of the studios. Now that venues to exhibit independently produced films were opened, such films became more popular. It was a chance to make money, exert artistic freedom, and even avoid taxes. Generous loopholes in the income tax laws allowed wealthy Americans, including many actors and directors, to significantly reduce their tax obligations if they owned an independent production company. In 1949, independent producers produced 20 percent of 234 films released by the eight majors. About half of those were released by UA. In 1958, 65 percent of new releases were produced by independent producers, less than a third released by UA. Independent producers were capturing a larger portion of the market with more venues available for distributing those pictures.

However, the distribution arm of the industry was what remained in control of the studios, and ironically, it was what kept the industry an oligopoly. As the market shrank in the face of changing American entertainment patterns, the presence of the distribution arm became more important, and it was more difficult for a newcomer to enter the industry. The minimum efficient scale for a distributor required capital to finance twenty to thirty films per year and a worldwide distribution network. In the 1950s it required about $25 million per year in overhead costs to maintain a studio. The capital necessary to finance films was another $50 million, and this was in an era of shrinking production, hence only a few studios could exist in the market—about the same number as had existed before divestiture. So while divestiture was meant to return all aspects of the movie industry to competitiveness, the nature of the production side was such that no additional studios could afford to break into the industry. While the number of independent producers increased over time, the number of distributors did not. By the mid-1970s, the majors captured 90 percent of the total box office, approximately the same percentage as they controlled when the original antitrust action was filed against Paramount. Today the top six studios account for more than 80 percent of the box office. The difference is that studios now produce few movies, instead they finance their production by independent producers in return for the right to distribute them.

Marketing Innovations

From 1946 until 1962, box-office attendance dropped 73 percent, but in the face of increased ticket prices that were partly attributable to an upgrading of the quality of the movies, box-office gross only fell by 48 percent. Hollywood responded by filming more color movies in the 1950s as another way to differentiate itself from television. The novelty wore off after a few years, and Hollywood returned to the cheaper black and white films for awhile until the advent of color television forced Hollywood's hand in the 1960s. By then, television had also become an important secondary market for Hollywood movies, and the symbiotic relationship between the movie and television industries was born.

In order to compete with television, Hollywood introduced such innovations as 3D movies and wide-screen pictures. The former proved to be no more than a fad, while the latter ultimately helped to revive the industry. Special effects and cinematography which exploited the wide screen helped make the movies a viable competitor to television. The quality of the picture was certainly greater in the theater on the wide screen than it could be on the television. This held true until the advent of large, flat screen televisions and home theater technology. However, the high price of this technology has kept it a small part of the market and still has not made serious inroads into the movies.

Drive-in theaters were one area of growth in the industry. Immediately after the war there were fewer than 300 drive-ins. Ten years later there were over 4,500, ranging in size from 200 to 2,500-car capacities. Although insignificant in terms of revenue at the conclusion of the war, they accounted for 20 percent of all film rentals by 1958. Drive-ins wedded two American passions—cars and movies, adding another dimension to a night out on the town.

By the 1970s the industry had evolved into its present-day form, with the majors operating essentially as bankers and distributors. They provide the financing to independent producers in return for the rights to distribute their pictures. Some own production stages, which they lease or use primarily for television production. While they don't control the industry from top to bottom as they once did, the distributors are still the least competitive sector of the industry. Few of them exist, and until a method of distributing films is developed that can bypass the old studios, all producers and theaters must deal with them. They are still a powerful force to be reckoned with, they just aren't as visible to the movie-going public as they once were.

THE MODERN ERA OF MOVIE PRODUCTION

The Conglomerate Era

The last decades of the twentieth century saw a change in the ownership pattern of movie studios. Non-entertainment-oriented conglomerates purchased studios as a way of diversifying their portfolios. Some of these purchases were disastrous and nearly bankrupted their hosts, primarily because they didn't understand the nature of the movie business. Gulf and Western (oil industry) purchased Paramount, Trans American (insurance industry) bought United Artists, and Coca Cola purchased Columbia, which they later sold to Sony. The most famous of these purchases may have been Ted Turner's purchase of MGM from hotel magnate Kirk Kerkorian. Turner kept the most reliable source of profits, the film library, which he brilliantly exploited through his television empire, and sold off the rest.

The purchaser of a movie studio buys valuable nonphysical capital, such as the name brand, the distribution networking skills, and clout. The physical assets include a sound stage and a library of old films. The name brand and the distributing clout are used to distribute movies made by independent producers in the new era. The soundstages are rented out to movie and television producers and, as Ted Turner demonstrated, there is a large market for old films on television, VCR, and DVD.

These pairings did not always go well, in part because the corporations purchasing the studios had no film background and tried to run the studios like they ran their own businesses. The film industry is not like the production of any other good. The creative process involved in making a film cannot be standardized for efficient, low-cost mass production. Formulas for films are not always successful and cannot be reliably employed to churn out profitable products in the long term. For every series of successful films, like the long-running James Bond series, there are dozens of ideas which die with the first sequel or fade when the original bombs at the box office. Finally, the purchase of high-quality inputs does not necessarily mean a high-quality output will result. Hollywood history is littered with expensive failures starring high-profile stars. *Cleopatra* in 1963 (starring Elizabeth Taylor and Richard Burton, two of the biggest stars of the time), *Heaven's Gate* in 1980 (a would-be epic directed by Academy Award winner Michael Cimino), and *Ishtar* in 1987 (starring Dustin Hoffman and Warren Beatty) are but three examples. These films were all predicted to be box-office hits, but are remembered today only because of their spectacular failure.

Studios also pursued this strategy, diversifying their own portfolios by getting into other businesses. In many cases, they did this by embracing the enemy, television. It was a logical relationship, since television and the movies were so similar in their production techniques. The initial cooperation was in the use of soundstages. Studios leased their stages to television producers or produced television shows on their own. In other cases, studios branched out a little further in the entertainment industry, purchasing more distant entertainment-related packages that eventually gave way to the conglomerate era in the movie industry. Examples include Disney, which moved into theme parks and purchased professional sports teams, and Fox which started its own television network.

The problem with running a movie studio has always been one of balancing business acumen with artistic talent. Financiers have proven adept at cutting costs in the movie business, but have seldom shown the artistic flair necessary to produce the products the public demands. It takes a good working combination: an artist to produce quality pictures and a financier to balance the books. This combination has been in place since the early days of the industry. The problem has always been who has the final word. Does the businessman get to pull the plug on the cost of producing one last multimillion dollar scene, or does the creative genius get to include that last scene which he/she knows will elevate the picture to the rarified level of box office blockbuster?

The Modern Studio

Specialization exists in Hollywood to a greater degree than before. The breakup of the studio system led to the rise of agents as the central force in the industry. They replaced the old studio producer as the "dealmaker" who put the picture together. Now each phase is carried out by a separate firm instead of under the roof of one company. Agents serve the function of the dealmaker. They represent actors, directors, and screenwriters, and serve as the conduit to put all of these parts together for a producer, who will then finance the movie and distribute it.

In this modern era, studios do not make movies at all. They own soundstages, which they lease to television and movie producers. These producers are independent contractors, striking individual deals for each of their pictures, or sometimes signing multipicture deals with a studio. The studios also provide the financing and distribution services for producers. In return for financing a film, the studio gets to distribute it. The studio then earns its profit out of the box-office returns of the film, which it shares with the producer and the theater.

Agents represent writers, directors, and actors. Producers put movies together, and studios finance and distribute them to theaters, which in turn show them. Agents, producers, and studios work with each other to put a picture deal together. A producer secures a storyline, develops it into a script, and lines up the talent to act in and direct it, while also securing financing from a studio. Studios finance films that they think will be profitable in return for the rights to distribute them. The distribution rights are the way the studio will earn their money back. Theaters want films in high demand, though the biggest expected blockbusters will be the most expensive to get. That is, they will earn the smallest percentage of the box office and have the least generous terms of renewal of the film due to the competition. The best deal for a theater is an unanticipated box office hit, like *Blair Witch Project*. A sleeper like this is rented to a theater on more generous terms; the exhibitor gets to keep a larger percentage of the box office and has more control over how long they can renew the film. An unanticipated hit can be box-office gold for the theater and may have a much greater impact on the bottom line than the latest installment of *Harry Potter* because of the favorable lease obtained by the theater.

Studios are placed in the role of gamblers in the current environment. They must try to guess the popularity of a movie based only on a sketch of the storyline and its projected cast. The hotter the story idea or the recent record of the producer pitching it or the talent signed to appear in it, the tougher the competition among studios to secure it. The making of a film is a gamble because little is known about it before release, including the final cost of production.

United Artists, for example, was nearly bankrupted in 1980 by the deal they signed to finance *Heaven's Gate*. The director, Michael Cimino, was fresh off Oscars for best picture and best director (*Deer Hunter*, 1978). The studio ultimately found itself in a contract which allowed Cimino virtual *carte blanche* over the final cut, resulting in a multimillion-dollar-budget overrun and a film that was so long it lost much of its appeal at the box office. The result was one of the costliest failures in Hollywood history, taking in a paltry $2 million at the domestic box office, while costing $44 million to film.

Theaters

Theaters are independent as well, though a recent trend has seen some studios beginning to purchase small numbers of theaters again. Primarily, the theaters are individually owned or franchised in chains, which own large numbers of theaters across the country. The theaters bargain with the studios for the rights to show films. They may bargain for any film they want, from any studio. In practice, however, competing chains in larger cities tend to deal regularly with the same studios. A deal for a first-run film will usually include a geographic monopoly agreement. The theater, or theater chain, secures an agreement that the film will not be sold to any other theater within a certain geographic distance of the purchasing theater for a set period of time after the theater finishes showing the film. This reduces the likelihood that second-run theaters charging a lower admission price will siphon off some of the demand for the film.

In addition to distance, the theater will bargain over time. A movie may stay in a theater for only a week or it may play for months. Most films play for a few weeks. In 2000 the average film played for eight weeks during its first run. During this time, the box office revenue is shared between distributor and exhibitor on a sliding scale. The earlier in the run, the larger the percentage of the box office the distributor keeps. The division of box office is on the order of 90 percent for the distributor in the early weeks of an engagement. The longer it is shown, the less of the box office is taken by the distributor, although the size of the audience generally decreases as well. Distributors typically protect themselves against box-office losers by contracting for a percentage of the box office or a minimum payment from the theater.

Because theaters are independent and the box office is but a minor source of revenue, they focus their business on total entertainment for the customer. Theaters make most of their money on the sale of concessions. While the seven- to ten-dollar ticket is a steep admission price, the theater keeps little of that. On the other hand, that six-dollar box of popcorn can earn about $5.50 in profit. Since the distributor and the exhibitor both know that the theater owner earns his profits at the concession stand, they both understand the incentive for the theater owner to reduce ticket prices and entice people to spend their money on food and drink instead. In order to get around this problem, first-run movies are leased to exhibitors with minimum ticket price requirements. Exceptions are made for child tickets or matinees, but not for movies with large anticipated demand.

The movie industry is one of prognostication. A typical studio will release an average of thirty to forty movies in a year, and their fortunes usually rest on one or two blockbusters. Without one, it is unlikely they will make a profit. With a *Titanic*, bonuses will flow and careers will be made. Hot new actors and directors will emerge, with agents commanding and earning higher salaries for them in their future pictures. As a result, some studios will lose money on the next picture that is made on the assumption the hot actor will carry the film. When this fails to happen the large cost results in a loss for the studio. Nobody has yet been able to predict the film market on a regular basis. Eventually the hot actor or director will turn out a film the audience simply doesn't like, and the studio holding the bag will pay. This will then lead to a decrease in the demand for and price of the talent in question, including studio executives, who are in the same type of cyclical market. Their demand and pay is closely related to their most recent success at obtaining the distribution rights to blockbusters.

A movie is generally released in theaters before TV or video, because the theater is the way to generate the greatest amount of revenue in the shortest amount of time. In the movie business, time is money. With an average film production cost close to $50 million and about half that much more to advertise, and with an elapsed time from beginning until release of one to two years, it is critical that the studio recoup the money it invested as quickly as possible. As technology evolves and the availability of pay-per-view movies reaches a greater percentage of American households, it is likely that pay-per-view will become a more important source of income, perhaps displacing the theater as the quickest and best source of revenue for studios. It will probably never replace the theater, however, because going to the movies is a unique experience. And as the movie industry has demonstrated over the past century, it is nothing if not resilient.

After the domestic theater, the typical film moves overseas, then to cable television such as HBO or Cinemax, to video, network television, a second cable run (most likely on a nonpremium channel), and then syndication for local stations. Each of these has a window of time for its appearance after initial release.

The run-clearance-zone system of movie distribution existed during the distribution oligopoly heyday. The name of the system came from the method of distributing a new film. It ran exclusively in a first-run theater in a certain geographic zone. When it was finished in that theater, it cleared out and did not play in any other theater in that zone for a set period of time. This "clearance" allowed the first-run theater the chance to attract as many of the customers for the film as possible. The longer a market cleared before a film returned to a second-run theater, the fewer potential customers there were who would put off seeing the film until it showed in a lower-priced theater. A new picture debuted in the biggest, first-run theaters in the big cities. After a certain period of time, perhaps as short as a week depending on the picture, it was mothballed for a few weeks or months, before reappearing in secondary theaters in the big cities and theaters in smaller cities. After a run in these theaters, it was pulled, cleared again, and then released in smaller theaters. This pattern repeated until the movie finally played in the smallest, most remote theaters.

This system worked well with an audience that was differentiated only in its demand to see a picture when it first debuted or by how long they had to wait to see it. With television, the audience demand changed. Hollywood responded by changing its marketing technique. Now a movie had to be advertised as a "must see" event. In order to capitalize on such marketing, the movie needed to be released on a much wider basis. Instead of initial release in a select number of theaters in the largest cities, movies were released on a more massive scale, opening in 1,000–2,000 theaters. With the explosive growth of multiplexes (movie theaters with multiple screens), it has become possible for very highly promoted films to open on several thousand screens simultaneously, as cineplex owners can show the same copy of a film on multiple screens with staggered starting times to accommodate the large crowds turning out for anticipated blockbusters.

Television changed the distribution pattern, shortening the theatrical release schedule, and accelerating it. After the movie was removed from theaters, it was sold to network television, generally about eighteen months after closing in the theater. The networks purchased the rights to show a film a fixed number of times over a set period of time. Depending on the movie, this might be once within a year of purchase (for newer films) or three or four times over five years (more common for older films). Technology also changed the way the distribution system worked. A whole new level of home entertainment was created with the arrival of the VCR and the proliferation of cable and satellite television, which allowed for interactive viewing, pay television, and selective private, in-home viewing of movies.

The typical movie is still released first in the theaters, but it is now followed by nearly simultaneous release in foreign theaters and on pay-per-view. The latter two generally follow theatrical release by only about three months. After a period of about three months of exclusivity for these outlets, the picture is then released for the home video market. Television does not enter the picture until one or two years after theatrical release, with cable television getting the first shot, followed a year later by network television. Five to six years after the movie has been shown in theaters, it may begin the television cycle again, with a re-release on cable and then a move to syndication. The point of this cycle is to maximize profits by releasing the movie in such a way as to maximize the revenues at each stage. This is done by pricing the product such that those with the greatest demand to see it will pay the highest price rather than wait until it comes out in a cheaper format.

The home-video market got a boost when a federal court ruling in 1979 upheld the 1976 Copyright Act's First Sale Doctrine. This states that the first purchaser of any copyrighted work can use it any way they see fit as long as it was not duplicated and sold for commercial purposes in violation of copyright laws. Only about 15 percent of American households had VCRs in 1984, but within two years this percentage had increased to 50 percent, and by 1986, for the first time, the revenue from the sale of videos equaled the box-office gross. The secondary market still exists for films, but it is largely in the form of video and pay-TV release, though some second-run theaters are also on the tail end of the distribution network. Another change by Hollywood has been their pattern of release. Instead of releasing new films on a regular pattern throughout the year, they concentrate their offerings on the big movie-going times of year: Thanksgiving and Christmas holiday seasons, beginning of summer (Memorial Day) and mid-summer (fourth of July). These are times of the year when school is out and more children and young adults are able to spend time in theaters. New movies are still released throughout the year, but the anticipated blockbusters are concentrated during these holiday seasons when movie attendance is greatest.

Decreasing Output in the 1970s

Hollywood entered a period of financial crisis in 1969 that shook up the industry like nothing since the arrival of sound. By this time, Hollywood had entered the era of the blockbuster. The standard approach of each studio was to produce a couple of dozen films each year with the aim of covering the operating costs and overhead of the studio, while relying on a large investment in a blockbuster to determine the profits for the year. This worked fine as long as the blockbuster was a hit.

The relationship between the movie and television industries made this problem worse by dampening the demand for marginal quality theatrical releases. By 1969, the networks were airing feature-length movies or made-for-TV movies seven nights a week. The market became saturated, and viewers became much more selective, choosing quality over novelty, suddenly raising the stakes in the blockbuster game. The investment in an anticipated blockbuster occurs before the payoff and if the studio guesses wrong, instead of the blockbuster setting the profit level for the year, it will determine the size of the losses.

In the face of staggering losses, Hollywood responded by cutting its production roughly in half during the 1970s. All of the major studios survived, with the only casualties coming from amongst the ranks of the independent producers, but their method of operation came into question. One lesson learned from the box-office drought of the 1970s was that only about ten or twelve movies a year dominated the annual box office for the industry. These "megahits" were the movies that took a studio from the brink of disaster to financial salvation in one year. As it turned out, however, predicting which movies would achieve this status was not at all certain. Careers and fortunes were made and lost gambling in this manner. It led to a new method of producing films—the era of imitation. Studios began to copy their own and other studios' successes by producing sequels and copycat films. The highly successful *Godfather* was followed by *Godfather Part II* and *Godfather Part III*, marking one of the early sequel success stories. Beginning in the mid-1970s, the majors began to devote about 10 percent of their annual production to sequels. A hit movie today is virtually guaranteed to come back with a sequel in the near future.

By the end of the 1970s, two new outlets for movies opened up, providing a source of additional income for the studios. The home video and pay television industries provided new and much needed sources of income for Hollywood. Both concepts had been around for many years, but they didn't become profitable until technology evolved to more profitably exploit them.

Instead of acting as a substitute for the movie theater, the video and pay cable markets have evolved as a complement. While a certain segment of the population will wait for a movie to appear on video or television rather than pay the higher price to see it in the theater, this segment is no different than those who were willing to wait for the picture to come to the lower-priced neighborhood theater. Instead of buying movie tickets, they purchase the movie on TV or video. However, movie theaters have provided a boost of a different sort for the ancillary market. The demand for ancillary markets is related to the performance of a movie at the theaters. Success at the box office is the primary determinant of video success. The successful box-office performance of a movie serves as a strong signal for videos. In addition, the rise of ancillary markets has elevated the status of the theater from the only exhibition form to the first and foremost exhibition form. In other words, the status of the theater has risen in the eyes of consumers along with the proliferation of outlets. Showing movies at theaters is clearly still crucial to the industry.

Cable television also made serious inroads into the Hollywood market when HBO began a new concept called the "prepurchase" in 1977. They agreed to pay for the rights to certain films before they were released. In other words, they purchased the rights to air the films based on the script and cast. This became a common way to finance films, especially among small independent producers who traditionally had trouble attracting financing from one of the studios. With the prepurchase market fully developed, it was much easier to get a film produced. Instead of having to convince one of a few studios to commit a large chunk of its limited budget to one picture, an aspiring producer could approach a number of potential downstream buyers and presell the rights to the film for their venue, be it video, pay TV, or foreign theatrical distribution. These buyers needed films to fill their airtime, video outlets, or theaters, so they were willing to buy the product. The resulting effect on the market was to decrease the financial exposure of an independent studio and thus increase the supply of films, especially those by lesser known directors and/or featuring lesser known actors.

The ability to presell rights to movies benefited the independent producers and the smaller production companies. Small studios such as Orion Pictures and Cannon grew and succeeded because of it. In that way they did not need the massive amounts of capital necessary to fund pictures in their entirety. These "mini-major" studios prospered by preselling the video rights and pay cable rights to films before production, using these proceeds to finance the film. The downside to this for the producer was that if the film was an unexpected box-office hit, the prepurchaser of the rights would get the windfall. Of course, if the film performed below expectations, the prepurchaser took the loss.

The independent producers of today differ from their predecessors. The post–World War II independent producers worked outside of any studio, but were completely dependent on the studios for financing.

The present crop can exist without any interaction with the studios until it comes time to hire a distributor. As a group, independent producers provide about 300 pictures annually, representing nearly two-thirds of total output each year.

The other impact of preselling movie rights is the growth of a new B-picture market. Few big-budget blockbusters are financed by pre-sales but hundreds of marginal low-budget pictures are. These are films that would not be made if they had to depend on their survival at the box office. In fact, many of them are never shown in theaters; instead, they are filmed for video or pay TV markets. HBO, for example, purchases many made-for-cable movies each year to fill its 24-hour-a-day needs.

The difference between an independent film and one financed by a studio is in the budget. A studio-financed film averages about $40 million, ranging upward of $100 million for an expected blockbuster, while an independent film usually costs only a few million to produce. The major differences are found in the stars and the special effects. Depending on the budget, the quality of the filming and editing equipment may also be evident between studio films and those made by independents, although the advent of high-quality digital equipment is fast making this difference less obvious.

The exhibition market was changed most in the last three decades by the growing popularity and economic advantages of the multiplex. The number of screens has grown from nearly 13,000 in the early 1960s to 24,000 in 1990, to 35,280 in 2002. The advantages of the multiplex include economies of scale—one ticket booth and one concession stand for multiple screens; diversification, five or six different movies on different screens appealing to a variety of audiences; and the ability to run multiple screens of a popular movie at staggered starting times by cycling one copy of the film back and forth—reel by reel. By the 1980s, the exhibition market had become concentrated into a few national chains which dominated the market. United Artist Theaters, Cineplex Odeon, General Cinema, and American Multi-Cinemas controlled one-third of the screens, but they accounted for almost 90 percent of the total box office. As in the days of the vertically integrated studio, the control of the market lay in the control of the major market theaters.

The rise of the importance of the theater has drawn the studios back into the exhibition arena. Studios began to move back into the exhibition business in the late 1980s and early 1990s. MCA made the first major move in this direction when it purchased a 49 percent share of Cineplex Odeon's nearly 2,000 screens in 1989. This was followed by major theater acquisitions by Columbia and Paramount.

MOVIES AND TV

The arrival of television was at first thought to be the death knell for the movie industry. Television was seen as a substitute for the movies, and since it was much cheaper and more convenient, it seemed that TV would completely displace movies. Television was a substitute in some ways, but not completely. In many ways it has served as a complement to the movie industry. Network and cable television have become havens for recycled older movies. Pay-per-view and movie channels (HBO, Showtime, etc.) have become alternate outlets for movies just off the theater circuit. While there is a segment of the market for which television and the theater are close substitutes, there are always people who are not willing to wait and will go to the theater, in large part because the movie theater is part of a social experience and an evening of entertainment.

Because of its fear of being replaced, the movie industry withheld its films from television until 1955. That year RKO got out of the movie production business and sold its assets to General Teleradio. This marked the first time a major studio's film library was owned by a broadcaster. General Teleradio used the films for its own stations and licensed them for use by stations outside of its own markets. Since it only owned and operated five stations, most of the audience exposure to these pictures was via licensing. One year later, Warner Brothers sold its old films for $21 million. Paramount sold its pre-1948 film library to MCA in 1958 for $50 million. Television stations either purchased films outright, as was the case with the RKO and Warner libraries, or leased specific films, or groups of films, for a set period of time during which they broadcast them a set number of times for a fixed fee. Studios that retained their film libraries, such as MGM and Columbia, set up separate departments to handle the leasing of their old films to television.

The licensing of films to television was the first step in an increasingly cooperative relationship between Hollywood and TV. The next step was the production of original programming for TV. As technology made the taping of shows for rebroadcast feasible, the popularity of live television waned and gave way to the filmed broadcast. Hollywood studios began to produce filmed product for broadcast on television. Much of this market was filled by independent producers who leased studio space from the majors for the purpose of creating television programs. By 1955, Hollywood produced about 20 percent of prime-time television programs and 40 percent of the average television station's fare. By 1960, Hollywood earned nearly one-third of its income from television production and was filming about ten hours of television for every hour of theater film.

The rise of the video and pay cable industry and the changing attitude of the major networks has altered the role of networks toward films. They no longer spend as much money buying theatrical releases for broadcast on network TV. In fact, that segment of the market has been in decline for thirty years. By 1974, the networks began to spend more money to produce original, made-for-television movies than they did for rights to theatrical films. Now the four major networks finance the production of more original movies each year than all the studios combined. Despite this large number of films, the impact on the movie industry is negligible. The only sources of release for these films are domestic and foreign television, the least profitable of the venues for feature films. So while they dominate the industry in sheer quantity, their quality does not rival that of feature films and their financial impact is minimal.

CONCLUSION

The motion picture industry has matured from a fledgling storefront curiosity to a multibillion dollar entertainment industry over the course of the twentieth century. In the process, it has embedded itself into the culture and fabric of American life. Movies are no longer the sole source of filmed entertainment. They are not even the primary source of such entertainment. Over the course of roughly one hundred years technology has changed the movie industry, and the movie industry has changed American culture. The industry has survived the Great Depression, two world wars, and the technological revolutions of sound, color, television, and the computer. Each has only added an outlet to the industry and strengthened it, rather than diminished it. The movies are an everyday part of our lives and are likely to continue as such, adapting to future technological changes as readily as they have in the past.

—5—

The Radio Revolutionizes Entertainment

INTRODUCTION

Radio changed America in the twentieth century the way the computer has revolutionized it today. It brought an immediacy to the news that had heretofore not existed. The telegraph wire reduced the time it took for news to travel from point to point, but it still had to be gathered by newspapers and converted to print before being distributed to the general public. Radio brought the initial news directly into the homes of listeners, who could sit by their radios and hear the live broadcast of the explosion of the Hindenburg as it happened. Or listen directly to the response of the president to the attack on Pearl Harbor, or hear the Yankees win the World Series.

Three men are largely responsible for the development of the radio industry. Two inventors, Lee de Forest and Howard Armstrong, along with David Sarnoff, an RCA executive. De Forest invented the audion tube, which made radio transmission possible. Armstrong invented the superheterodyne, which increased the amplitude of the broadcasts and turned AM broadcasts into a national industry. Armstrong also invented FM radio, although he never lived to see its commercial success. While Sarnoff did not invent any hardware, he essentially invented the industry. He was responsible for organizing and marketing the radio and television industries, from the construction and sale of sets to the broadcast of programs and the invention of improvements. Even though he was not an engineer, Sarnoff was arguably the most influential man in the radio industry.

The other individual who was key to the evolution of radio was Guglielmo Marconi. He immigrated to the United States in 1899, bringing his invention of wireless telegraph with him. This invention, when coupled with de Forest's audion tube, became the radio. Marconi's invention revolutionized the communication industry by dramatically lowering the cost and time of sending messages. Prior to the advent of his wireless method of communication, it was a cumbersome and expensive process to spread news. The cost of transmitting a message using the speediest available system, the hard-wired telegraph, was primarily associated with the construction and maintenance of telegraph lines—the most impressive of which was the underwater cable that crossed the Atlantic, linking North America with Europe. At the time Marconi arrived in America, a telegram sent this way cost 25 cents a word. Sending one across the American continent from New York to San Francisco cost 10 cents a word. Letters were cheaper, only a nickel for a half-ounce letter to London and 2 cents to San Francisco, but much slower. It took a week to transport mail across the continent and ten or more days across the Atlantic. Marconi's invention eliminated the need for wires, thus lowering the cost of transmitting messages and establishing contact points. However, he never considered the possibility of sending human voices through the airwaves. This was the contribution of de Forest and Armstrong.

The advantage of wireless communication was the ability to bypass wires. The drawback was that it was not completely private, because anyone with a receiver tuned in to the specific frequency of the transmission could receive it. The inventions of de Forest, Armstrong, and others exploited this drawback and created the concept of "broadcasting" a signal to as wide an audience as possible. From this concept evolved the word radio, signifying the radiation of waves from a transmitter. A new era, and a new social construct were soon to be born. Radio would revolutionize the world.

THE AGE OF INVENTION

The key patent for the radio was de Forest's audion tube, which enabled radios to receive signals from great distances. This invention was arguably more important to radio than Marconi's contribution. Marconi, however, is the more famous of the two. De Forest sold his patent to AT&T, while Marconi stayed in the public eye by starting his own company, American Marconi. In 1899 Marconi was granted the first patent related to wireless communication. In 1910 alone, 270 separate patents were granted in this area, and in 1912 an additional 350 were granted. Clearly wireless communication, of which radio was to become the most profitable part, was a burgeoning field.

Armstrong and de Forest were antagonists. While both of their inventions were necessary for the development of wireless communication, and radio in particular, and the inventions were co-dependant, neither man liked the other. They spent most of their lives and much of their fortunes in court fighting over patents. The patent battle between Lee de Forest and Howard Armstrong over who had actually discovered regeneration would become one of the longest-lasting and most bitter patent fights in the industry. For twenty years, beginning in 1914, the two were in court over the issue. By the time the Supreme Court finally found in favor of de Forest, much to the incredulity of the scientific community, the patents had long expired, and both men had exhausted huge amounts of money. Essentially, they never profited from the invention; instead RCA reaped the profits because they shrewdly played both sides in the patent fights, acquiring the licenses to the competing claims. By the time the fight ended, de Forest was ruined financially and Armstrong was ruined emotionally. Armstrong would commit suicide twenty years later after losing another patent case, this one to RCA. The two cases were unrelated except for the intensity displayed by Armstrong. That intensity served him well in the laboratory, but led to his downfall in the courts. He was unable to back away from the situation and make a business decision separate from his emotional attachment to the inventions he felt were being stolen from him.

The Marconi invention made possible wireless transmission in the form of distinguishable interruptions of the transmission, much like the telegraph was used to send and receive signals. The interruptions were deliberately spaced, using Morse code to interpret them.

De Forest contributed the audion, which permitted the transmission of a continuous electromagnetic wave, allowing for the transmission of human voices and sounds through the air. Prior to this, wireless communication was possible only through the use of code.

Morse code, named after inventor Samuel Morse, inventor of the telegraph, was a series of short (dots) and long (dashes) interruptions in the transmission of a signal over wires. These dots and dashes were combined to create an alphabet, which skilled telegraph operators could send and receive rapidly in order to relay messages.

Armstrong discovered the principle of regeneration, which built upon de Forest's principle and amplified the sounds. This led to the evolution of the loud speaker instead of headphones to hear the broadcast signals. Armstrong's principle of regeneration allowed for louder, clearer sounds. Further inventions led to the ability to transmit broadcasts thousands of miles through the air, bypassing the need to relay signals over expensive phone line connections.

Howard Armstrong and Lee de Forest invented the physical properties that made radio possible, while David Sarnoff pioneered the commercial exploitation of those inventions into an industry that changed the world. Sarnoff rose from a messenger boy in the American Marconi wireless company to become president and CEO of RCA. He recognized the potential of these inventions and exploited them.

Armstrong's final contribution to radio was the discovery of the concept of "multiplexing." In 1953 he announced this discovery, which would once again have great impact on the broadcasting field by allowing a single station to transmit simultaneous signals over the same FM wave. This led to stereo broadcasting, which Armstrong would not live to see.

Incidentally, the first recognized radio broadcast involved none of these three radio pioneers. It took place on Christmas Eve in 1906 when inventor Reginald Fessenden demonstrated his improvement on the de Forest audion tube with a broadcast of recorded music. It hardly resembled today's industry in that only a select few listeners, gathered together and each wearing headsets, were able to pick up the signal broadcast from Fessenden's nearby laboratory.

THE RADIO CORPORATION OF AMERICA

David Sarnoff was a visionary. He seized upon these inventions, correctly predicting the revolutionary potential of radio. He foresaw the radio as a household utility and urged the Marconi company to adopt that view. The ultimate result was the creation of the Radio Corporation of America (RCA). David Sarnoff built RCA into the dominant firm in the radio industry by purchasing all of the important patents. Some have likened Sarnoff to a self-aggrandizing thief, but he did oversee the most powerful media company in the first half of the century, and pioneered its growth from a small participant in the electronics industry to become the industry giant, and a dominant monopolist. By the early 1920s RCA controlled the radio industry, holding more than 2,000 key patents. No radio could be made or sold in the United States without using RCA technology. In fact, over 90 percent of the world's radios were sold under license to RCA. Besides radio, RCA would eventually play a leading role in television and the movies, launching the National Broadcasting Corporation (NBC) as one of its many progenies.

With no competition in sight and a radio revolution about to hit America, RCA was a virtual money machine. Sarnoff is credited with the idea of licensing RCA's radio patents to its foes instead of spending a fortune in litigation against them. He struck deals with most of RCA's big rivals, including Zenith and Philco, two of the largest manufacturers of radios in the United States, and soon 90 percent of the world's radios were being manufactured under license agreement with RCA. Without having to construct a single set, RCA was receiving 7.5 percent of the gross radio sale proceeds around the world. Money was flowing in so quickly and freely that the license fee was eventually reduced to only 5 percent in order to spur the sale of more sets.

Not only did the licensing plan bring in money, but it freed RCA from constant litigation and softened their public image as a greedy bully. This also transformed the basic business of RCA from manufacturing to inventing. Instead of assembling radios, the firm was focusing on perfecting their operation, and eventually, on developing a workable television system. Because the licensing agreements brought in cash, RCA could devote more resources to perfecting the radio. Of course, RCA needed to follow this path, since its patents would only last seventeen years. After they expired, no licenses were necessary to use the ideas, therefore the RCA license system would only last as long as the patents, unless the patents kept changing, necessitating continued purchase of the license. This, of course, would only happen if new innovations were discovered, improving the quality of the radio by applying new patents, and thus requiring a renewal of the licenses in order to have access to the latest radio innovation.

Sarnoff established one of the first great research laboratories. He hired the best engineers, paid them a competitive, steady wage, gave them state-of-the-art facilities and equipment, the chance to work with the best and brightest in their field, and the opportunity to work on the cutting edge of their field. In return, all patents belonged to RCA. The scientist's name would appear on the patent but always in conjunction with RCA. The scientist could claim credit for his invention, as long as the profits went to the corporation. RCA paid a token $1 to the scientist whose name appeared on the patent. This was not the first arrangement of its kind. Sarnoff modeled it after the General Electric (GE) laboratory.

The RCA and GE research labs were among the first in a new era of inventive activity—the corporate research laboratory. By the 1920s it largely replaced the individual inventor model of research that is associated with great American inventors prior to the twentieth century. Thomas Edison is perhaps the most famous example of the individual inventor. The benefits to the individual of joining a research lab have been noted. The costs were the loss of independence, fame, and fortune. However, since the last two were never certain, it was an attractive possibility too good to pass up for all but the most doggedly independent few. And as history has demonstrated, the deck was stacked against independents. When it came to legal wrangling over patents, the giant corporate research labs held a huge advantage.

They could tie up an individual inventor in court for years, using their tremendous legal and financial advantage to wear the inventor down until they prevailed, developed their own invention which skirted existing patents, or delayed long enough so that the patent expired.

As early as 1922, David Sarnoff recognized that the future of radio was in entertainment. He correctly predicted that the novelty of merely hearing human voices over the airwaves would soon wear off and that the public would look for something more. Sarnoff sought to provide that in the form of entertainment. He set up a separate division within RCA to handle this, calling on specialists in talent and public taste, since the engineers, inventors, and businessmen were not qualified for the job. The separate company he organized for this purpose was called the National Broadcasting Company (NBC).

After World War I, business executives worked behind the scenes to create one of the greatest monopolies in American history. Negotiations with the U.S. government resulted in the creation of an American corporation to replace the Marconi corporation as the dominant radio firm. The issue of foreign control of the industry had originally motivated the navy to consider overseeing the industry it had virtually taken over during the war. However, there was opposition to the idea of a government monopoly in Congress, and the RCA pitch looked like an attractive alternative. RCA would become the American leader, holding the patents in the navy's possession, along with its own and those of General Electric.

On October 17, 1919, the Radio Corporation of America was incorporated. RCA was born out of a merger between General Electric and Marconi Wireless, with the aid of the navy patents. The resulting company resembled Marconi Wireless in its executive offices, including the future president, David Sarnoff, who began his RCA career as commercial manager. The difference was that by corporate charter the company must always remain American. No more than 20 percent of its stock could be held by foreigners and its executives had to be U.S. citizens.

In 1920 David Sarnoff proved prescient when he predicted that RCA could sell a million "radio music boxes" within three years to meet the expected demand for what he saw as a revolutionary new product—the demand by people to listen to classical music and speeches in their homes. These cultural and educational broadcasts would be sponsored by radio manufacturers, who would pay part of their proceeds from selling radios to cover the costs. Of course, Sarnoff was correct in some ways. By 1923 over 600,000 radio sets would be sold, though nearly all by competitors of RCA. Most of these manufacturers had licensed the rights to produce radios from RCA. Radio would soon become the predominant form of entertainment for the American family. However, Sarnoff's vision of radio as a means of spreading culture to the hinterlands and bringing great orchestras and teachers into the average American home was not accurate. While this does describe public radio, that took a long time to develop, and still only serves a fraction of the radio audience. During the heyday of radio, it was not culture, but comedy and soap operas that sold. And it was not radio manufacturers who underwrote the shows, but the selling of commercial airtime.

The prototype for the radio music box was created by Dr. Alfred Goldsmith, a professor at City College of New York, for David Sarnoff and RCA. Goldsmith's "radiola" was a small box with a loudspeaker and a knob for tuning to the desired frequency. The innards consisted of the de Forest and Armstrong components that made the broadcasting and receiving of human voices over the air possible.

RCA bought the patent rights to certain key components from AT&T. Indeed, this would be their pattern. They would either purchase outright the rights to key patents, and then lease them to manufacturers of radios, or they would impinge on patents. This meant tying up small inventors in court for years, draining their resources until RCA emerged victorious, invented their own part that avoided the patented one, or watched the patent expire.

RCA moved quickly, and in March of 1921 they signed an agreement with Westinghouse, whereby RCA acquired all of Westinghouse's patents in turn for 40 percent of RCA's manufacturing orders and a 20 percent share of RCA stock. Once again, RCA eliminated its chief competitor. RCA was moving toward acquiring patents from any source in order to completely dominate the radio industry. One of the more unlikely sources turned out to be the United Fruit Company, which held a key patent on a loop antenna that RCA thought might be valuable. By the time they were finished, RCA controlled approximately 2,000 radio patents, and earned a royalty on almost every radio set sold in the world. In 1922 radio sales totaled $60 million. This rose to $136 million the following year and $358 million in 1924. The Federal Trade Commission (FTC) estimated about 75 percent of RCA's total revenue during these years had come from radio sales, none of which they manufactured.

The agreements that formed RCA authorized AT&T to manufacture transmitting stations and authorized Westinghouse and GE to manufacture radios. RCA held the patents and licensed them, receiving a dividend on each set sold. By 1921 AT&T had grown weary of the agreement, since they were making little money in the deal. Only about 5 percent of all broadcast transmitters were paying royalties to AT&T, the rest were violating patents. AT&T responded under the leadership of Walter Gifford by selling its RCA stock, rescinding its agreement to lease its telephone lines, initiating the manufacture of radio sets that skirted the RCA patents, and resigning from the RCA board. The two companies were destined to become great rivals, but in an area quite different from the manufacture of radios and receivers.

Relations between AT&T and RCA never returned to what they were during their agreement. However, the two corporate giants quit feuding long enough in 1926 to strike a business agreement profitable to both of them. AT&T got out of the radio manufacturing and broadcasting business altogether, selling its stations to RCA. They also agreed to resume the lease of telephone lines to RCA. RCA remained in the radio business, while AT&T concentrated on telephones.

RCA became the dominant firm in the radio industry during the 1920s. Not only did NBC become a successful revenue-generating arm of the company, but under the leadership of David Sarnoff RCA pioneered car radios, sound movies, and combination radio-phonograph sets. During the decade Sarnoff abandoned his ideal dream of radio as purely a source of cultural entertainment and turned NBC into a self-supporting additional source of revenue through a total commitment to commercially sponsored radio broadcasts. He also struck deals with General Motors to manufacture car radios, and merged with the Keith-Albee-Orpheum theater circuit, installing sound systems in their theaters. This ultimately resulted in a motion picture studio, Radio Keith Orpheum (RKO). The merger with the Victor phonograph company gave RCA control of the largest manufacturing operation in the industry.

The expropriation of patents by RCA and other corporate giants was not unusual behavior in this era. This was a period when the lone inventor had to contend with massive corporate legal resources. A corporation like RCA could violate a patent and then tie up a lone inventor in court for years. During the legal wrangling, the corporation continued with its business. The inventor, however, was forced to spend time on legal matters at the expense of laboratory time, and saw his income dwindle. Financial ruin was often the result, whether he ultimately proved victorious or not, because a legal fight lasting several years took valuable time during which the patent was in force. RCA's typical pattern was to purchase exclusive rights to a patent, or in the rare case it had to license a patent, to do so with an exclusive license. The only exception RCA ever made to this policy was with Philo Farnsworth, the inventor of the image dissector, a critical component in the television camera. RCA lost in patent court to Farnsworth, who then refused to sell his invention to RCA or grant an exclusive license.

COMMERCIALIZATION

Radio as we know it, the broadcasting of music, news, and sports events, began as early as 1914. One of the first acknowledged "broadcasts" was made by "Doc" Herrold, an amateur wireless operator from San Jose who began broadcasting music and advertising in California by illegally hooking into the Santa Fe Railway streetcar lines to boost the power of his broadcasts to a radius of about 50 miles.

Doc was not the only one to foresee the possibility of the radio. Lee de Forest broadcast nightly concerts from his Highbridge factory beginning in 1915. In 1916 he broadcast the first sporting event, the Yale-Harvard football game, and on election night, he became the first broadcaster to incorrectly predict a presidential race, when he signed off at 11 p.m. and declared Charles Evans Hughes the winner over Woodrow Wilson.

The concept of broadcasting to a large, invisible, and largely anonymous audience was ahead of its time. True success in the field awaited technical inventions that would permit broadcasting over larger areas. Advances in circuitry and tube technology made during the First World War allowed for clearer broadcasts over greater distances, just what was needed to give commercial radio a boost. Though these innovations were not readily available, well-connected radio enthusiasts would eventually find a way to get them. Frank Conrad, acknowledged as the first true broadcaster, found a way.

Conrad, an engineer at Westinghouse and a lifelong amateur radio enthusiast, constructed a transmitter after the war using the new equipment, and began playing musical concerts on Saturday nights from his station 8XK in Pittsburgh. Requests from listeners soon led to nightly broadcasts, including live musical performances. When the Pittsburgh newspapers began to report on his broadcasts, the audience swelled even further. Now that listeners could hear actual music and conversation, not just dots and dashes that had to be decoded, the airwaves were opened to everyone, not just skilled Morse code interpreters. A vast new market was opening, and riches awaited those in a position to exploit it.

The first to do so was the Joseph Horne department store in Pittsburgh. Capitalizing on the publicity about the Conrad broadcasts generated by the newspapers, the store began running ads in the Pittsburgh papers touting its receiving sets as the ideal way to listen in on the Conrad musical concerts. Soon the big companies were picking up on the action. When a Westinghouse executive saw the ad, it occurred to him that the future of radio lay in these mass broadcasts, not person-to-person communication. It changed the nature of the industry permanently. Westinghouse built a more powerful transmitter for Conrad at its plant and encouraged him to broadcast more frequently. This, of course, was in order to stimulate sales of receiving sets manufactured by Westinghouse. On November 2, 1920, the first licensed commercial radio broadcasting station, KDKA, began operating in Pittsburgh, Pennsylvania.

The Westinghouse business plan was simple: Create a demand for the radios it was manufacturing by broadcasting entertainment. It did exactly that, though the original broadcasting was limited to only an hour of music each evening. The broadcasting was soon expanded to include sports, church services, news; eventually original comedy and drama shows would dominate the airwaves and broadcasts would continue around the clock. The Pittsburgh station proved so successful that Westinghouse followed it with stations in Newark, East Springfield, Massachusetts, and Chicago.

The radio craze swept America; soon stations were popping up all over the country and sets were being manufactured by everyone from furniture makers and engineers to back-room tinkerers with simple crystal components. Within two years, over 550 stations were broadcasting across the country. Some of the receivers were elegant pieces of furniture that were more beautiful than practical, while others were crude crystal receiver kits that required assembly and a set of earphones to hear the signal. One hundred thousand radios were produced in 1922 and more than half a million sets were sold the following year.

The greatest change from the perspective of the average American was the creation of the broadcasting networks. They changed the way Americans entertained themselves, they changed the makeup of the family home, and they impacted the dynamics of the average day. Gathering around the radio for a scheduled broadcast of a favorite show became an accepted practice in the American family. The room fell silent as everyone gathered around the radio to hear the broadcast. The radio became a central piece of furniture in many households, and it grew from a luxury to a common piece of furniture to a household necessity. The television occupies the same status today, and we are seeing the invasion of the personal computer in much the same way.

The radio allowed Americans access to news and entertainment from the privacy of their living rooms. No longer was it necessary to go out to the crowds or travel great distances (made greater by the primitive transportation and more rural population of 1920s America) to be entertained. Now it was available from home, and at no cost beyond that of the initial price of the radio. Commercial broadcasting was a liberating innovation for millions of Americans, and it changed the pattern of life. At once, the radio made it possible to unify the country as a whole as well as emphasize its differences. This was accomplished when the population listened to the same things. Much of the country listened to *Amos and Andy* together at the same time each week. On the other end of the spectrum, cultural differences became popularized. Bluegrass music, for example, moved out of Kentucky to the rest of the country via radio broadcasts. Idealists saw the radio as the great equalizing medium. It would allow for the education of the masses via the broadcast of cultural events such as lectures, operas, and classical concerts to those previously unable to gain access to them.

In 1933 there were 605 radio stations in the United States. New York had the most, 48, and every state had at least two, except Wyoming, which brought up the rear with a lone station. Depending on the quality of your radio set and atmospheric conditions, some of these stations could be picked up thousands of miles away. Despite the troubled times of the Great Depression, when unemployment was rampant, corporate America was reeling, and banks were closing, radio survived. Indeed, Americans continued to consider the radio one of their most important and necessary possessions. During these rough times, it was the escape provided by radio that helped many persevere the tough years of the Depression.

Beginning in 1913 under Woodrow Wilson, the U.S. government sought to wrest control of the airwaves. This began through the efforts of the U.S. navy, which sought domination of the airwaves, particularly at the expense of foreign companies on American soil, like Marconi Wireless. It used its power as a large customer to dictate its terms, awarding huge contracts to preferred companies, giants like American Telephone and Telegraph and smaller companies like De Forest Radio Telephone and Telegraph. The power of huge customers with influence on the market meant the large corporations that were in a position to deliver to these customers would get the contracts, the profits, and the future growth. It marked the end of the line for small inventors, who would struggle to make ends meet in the face of corporate inventive activity financed by federal government contracts. By the time the United States entered the war, they were essentially the only customer for wireless communications. The army and navy both ordered the installation of radios as the standard means of communication. The orders they made for equipment essentially froze out all other customers.

President Woodrow Wilson, in a speech broadcast via radio from Des Moines, Iowa, on September 6, 1919, was prophetic in his pronouncements about the advantages and disadvantages of radio. He said, "All the impulses of mankind are thrown out upon the air and reach to the ends of the earth; quietly upon steamships, silently under the cover of the Postal Service, with the tongue of the wireless and the tongue of the telegraph, all the suggestions of disorder are spread through the world." The radio would become a great tool, neither good nor evil in its own sense, but able to magnify the good or evil of those who used it.

AT&T president Walter Gifford initiated the concept of commercial radio when he announced that AT&T's station WEAF in New York would begin selling commercial airtime. Gifford referred to this as "toll broadcasting." It was the opposite of the concept foreseen by Sarnoff and Lee de Forest, in which corporations would underwrite commercial-free radio, which would concentrate on bringing culture to all Americans.

Under the leadership of Walter Gifford, AT&T, in an effort to establish a foothold in the broadcasting business, used its considerable telephone muscle to do so. They first established a high-watt radio station, WEAF in New York, and then used their telephone model to finance it. When you used a telephone, you paid for the time you used the wire, and AT&T applied the same model for use of the radio waves. AT&T set up their station and invited any and all to come and rent airtime, to say what they wanted during a broadcast that would reach hundreds of thousands of potential listeners. Customers flocked to the idea, among them Macy's and Gimbel's department stores. In order to fill the empty time between paid broadcasts, Gifford hired people to sing, play piano, lecture, and otherwise entertain. The model for radio, and eventually television broadcasting, was set: scheduled interruptions of paid advertisements.

On August 28, 1922, the first commercial was aired on the radio. The Queensboro Corporation paid $50 to air a commercial advertising a new apartment complex they were leasing. The ability to reach millions of people simultaneously via radio ads proved appealing and quickly became popular. At first, WEAF had strict guidelines which would assure the quality of the radio airwaves. For example, no prices could be mentioned and blatant product description was not allowed. These standards would ultimately slip, but the concept of sponsor-financed broadcasting was here to stay.

Perhaps the greatest impact that radio had was to increase experiences among Americans. Radio, especially network radio, allowed Americans across the country to experience the same event at the same time. Major sporting contests and political events, major news items, and entertainment in the form of music, comedy, and drama were now shared in common from New York to Alabama and from South Carolina to California. Radio generated a common national social fabric that knit the country together. Regional differences, while they still existed, were substantially weakened, as radio made it possible–even necessary–to reach a broad segment of the population. The successful national shows had to appeal to the broadest possible audience.

Radio also had a major impact on politics, much the same way television does today. The whistle-stop, cross-country meet-and-greet campaigns gave way to sound-bite campaigning designed to make an emotional appeal (as opposed to long speeches created to appeal to the intellect) using radio as a medium to reach the broadest possible audience at once. Of course, in order to appeal to a broad audience instead of a smaller concentration of localized audiences, politicians changed the nature of their campaign messages. Radio had permeated the country deeply enough by 1928 that this became the first election truly dominated by the radio.

Radio, like the television and the computer to follow, had the impact of reducing the average attention span of Americans. Politics were one example, as were news items. Instead of long public speeches, short radio speeches prevailed. Instead of lengthy, detailed newspaper articles, Americans increasingly gathered their news from short radio newscasts, in which the basic details were provided on numerous news stories, chosen by the network, not the listener. The role of the sound bite quite naturally extended to television.

Networks

NBC naturally spawned rivals. On October 1, 1928, the Columbia Broadcasting System (CBS) was formed by William S. Paley. He merged two struggling networks, and, despite having no experience in radio, this proved wildly successful. Paley's real gift lay in his ability to identify what the average listener wanted to hear. CBS was continually more successful than NBC in programming. With the most popular comedies, such as *Amos and Andy*, and the biggest stars, like Jack Benny, they were always one step ahead of NBC. While Sarnoff hated to be in second place, he despised the low level of radio programming and especially detested the huge salaries and undue influence acting stars could wield, so he distanced himself from this part of the business as much as possible. Paley represented a different perspective. He was not interested in the manufacturing end of the business, nor even the technicalities of broadcasting. His only interest was in providing entertainment and he excelled at this. By 1930 it was evident that CBS was here to stay. While NBC concentrated on more sophisticated broadcasting, such as classical music and lectures (think PBS and NPR), CBS aimed for the lowest common denominator and featured popular music, comedies, and soap operas.

The concept of networking was slightly ahead of the technology necessary to fully exploit it. As AT&T increased its broadcast business by adding more stations, they pioneered another innovation: the synchronized broadcasting of programming over multiple stations. The technology for relaying signals through the airwaves had not yet been perfected, but AT&T overcame this problem by sending the signal over its phone lines where the stations picked them up for broadcast locally. In this way, the first true network was born. As technology improved, the phone lines were ultimately rendered obsolete, and synchronized broadcasting through the airwaves became the norm.

The battle for radio supremacy ended behind closed doors. RCA and AT&T, through some of their patent agreements, had a clause in their contract to settle any differences via binding arbitration. RCA did not want to sue AT&T, which they accused of illegally using their telephone monopoly to create a broadcasting monopoly, because of the cost and potential reputation damage they might bring upon themselves. After all, RCA monopolized the radio industry to the same extent that AT&T did the phone industry. Instead, the two sides went to binding arbitration, where RCA won, forcing AT&T to negotiate. In the end, AT&T bowed out of the broadcast business, selling its flagship WEAF station to RCA for $1 million and licensing use of its phone lines to RCA for broadcast purposes.

REGULATION

The United States was a relative latecomer to regulating the radio industry. Initially, the use of "wireless communication" was in the form of communication between individuals, similar to today's use of short-wave radio. Government oversight of the airwaves began before the commercialization of the medium into the broadcasting industry we know today. Even so, government regulation of the airwaves came to Europe far earlier. The first international treaty was signed by European nations in 1903. The United States did not consider such regulation necessary and refused to sign the treaty. Politicians were too concerned with weightier regulatory matters in the first decade of the twentieth century, including child labor and meat packing, to give wireless communication much thought. In addition, the wireless industry was in flux, with seemingly continual groundbreaking inventions coming forth. It was possible technology might solve the problem for the politicians. Moreover, a thorny issue was raised: how does one regulate and assign property rights to airwaves?

The push to regulate the airwaves finally succeeded, but on a tragic note. The primary players in the battle were the military, the amateur wireless operators, and the companies manufacturing the hardware for communication. The primary issue at hand was interference from overuse of common wavelengths. This was a particular problem aboard ships. The usefulness of wireless communication as a safety device aboard ships was limited by the ability to get a distress signal through the cacophony that sometimes existed on a particular wavelength. The closer to shore, the more likely this problem was to exist. A rash of ship accidents in the latter part of the first decade and early part of the second decade of the century, culminating with the *Titanic* disaster, finally spurred Congress to action.

The first government involvement came about two years before the sinking of the *Titanic*. On June 24, 1910, the Wireless Ship Act was passed. It required that any ship carrying 50 or more passengers sailing to or from a U.S. port and sailing more than 200 miles between ports be equipped with radio communication equipment of a minimum strength. The law did not prevent the *Titanic* from sinking, nor did noncompliance cause the disaster. Yet the government used the disaster as a catalyst to move into the radio business. Within four months of the sinking the government moved to take over the airwaves. What had once been considered a right now became a privilege: access to the airwaves.

The Radio Act of 1912 required that all operators of radio equipment be licensed, wavelength access be allocated between users, distress calls be given preferential treatment, and the secretaries of commerce and labor be empowered to grant licenses and make other necessary regulations as they saw fit. Amateur radio operators were allowed to listen in on any frequency but could only broadcast on the lowest wavelengths, heretofore considered useless.

The government involvement determined the direction radio would take. The allocation of airwave space clearly favored the military and the commercial interests over those of amateurs. Amateurs were allocated the least desirable wavelengths and forced to share them among the great number of operators in existence at the time. Thus, the allotted amateur band was overcrowded. The next step was to allocate power maximums. In 1923 Congress divided radio stations into three classes: high, medium, and low power. The high power stations went to the major corporations for their broadcasts. These were the most desirable and least congested and consequently became the dominant stations. AT&T, GE, and Westinghouse, not surprisingly, benefited the most from this allocation. This pattern of regulation perpetuated by the regulated continued with future legislation, which inevitably benefited the large commercial broadcasters to the detriment of the small broadcasters. The nature of the history of radio broadcasting was thus largely determined by the large corporations. This was the result of the tendency of the government to consult closely with the experts in the field when making regulatory decisions, and those experts invariably included the leaders of the most prominent firms in the radio industry. As a result, the likes of David Sarnoff played an important part in determining the regulations under which RCA was governed.

The problem with this type of control of the media, which still exists today, is swept away with the argument that the listener has the power to change the dial, turn the channel, or quit listening altogether. To the extent that this is the primary source of our news and entertainment, however, this choice becomes less realistic, and the increasing monopolization of the airwaves more a concern.

Antitrust Action

The government began antitrust proceedings against RCA in May of 1930, and the case concluded in November of 1932 with the forced cancellation of the RCA-GE-Westinghouse agreements that Sarnoff had authored approximately a decade earlier, ending the radio monopoly that had brought riches to RCA and Sarnoff. Now, however, the ties were becoming a hindrance to Sarnoff in his efforts to win control of television; the settlement kept RCA out of federal court, and was exactly what Sarnoff had hoped and planned for.

The federal government's antitrust actions against RCA, which began under Hoover in 1932 and ended within days of the election of Franklin D. Roosevelt in November of that year, were largely favorable to RCA. The biggest winner was David Sarnoff. RCA was forced to divest itself of its ties with AT&T, GE, and Westinghouse, but was left with its broadcast networks and its patents. Its management underwent dramatic changes, all in Sarnoff's favor. The size of the board shrank, and he controlled its membership. He had nearly total control of the largest and most important firm in the broadcasting industry.

RADIO SHOWS

Broadcasting had changed to conform to popular tastes, not the cultural edification that inventor de Forest and industry tycoon Sarnoff had envisioned. While there were broadcasts of a cultural nature, most of the airtime was filled with popular music, such as country and jazz, soap operas, comedies, and radio vaudeville shows. Some were so popular that people planned their daily schedule around broadcasts of their favorite shows.

Amos and Andy was one such hit show. Charles Correl and Freeman Gosden played Amos and Andy in a popular comedy. They were white men depicting black men in a form called blackface, and they were quite successful at it. In 1933 the duo was earning $100,000 annually from NBC as the stars of the most successful radio show on the air. They were heard at 7:00 each weekday evening in New York. Theirs was the first show to be syndicated and the first to be serialized, setting standards for the radio and television industry that still persist to this day.

By the onset of the Depression, the format for radio had evolved into what we are familiar with today in the television industry. The primary fare was popular shows, consisting mostly of popular music, soap operas, and situation comedies. The shows were financed by the sale of commercial airtime to sponsors. Eventually, the format evolved from a sponsor paying for an individual show, to the show selling a variety of sponsorship spots to different sponsors. There are few shows today, on either radio or television that are sponsored by a single company. Rather, networks purchase or produce a show and sell advertising to pay for it. Depending on the show, the products would be pitched at the expected audience—household products, such as laundry soap and flour, during the daytime soap operas; breakfast cereal during the children's shows; and cigarettes, coffee, and automobiles during evening broadcasts. Radio had become an advertising medium with entertainment scheduled around many short sales pitches.

The highly popular and profitable entertainment on commercial radio relegated the classical fare and public service aspects of the medium as envisioned by Sarnoff and de Forest, to the figurative and literal fringes of the industry. Stations with little popular appeal were allocated less desirable frequencies at the lower and upper end of the range, and had fewer sponsors, fewer stations, and less influence in the industry. None of that has changed over the past seventy-five years.

FM RADIO

Interestingly, radio's three primary inventors became disenchanted with the medium. While de Forest and Sarnoff were disappointed that radio largely churned out lowbrow fare, Armstrong was disinterested in the broadcasting because he did not like the fidelity of the music. He would ultimately address this point by inventing FM broadcasting. At any rate, he seldom listened because he was more often occupied in his lab.

Howard Armstrong discovered an improved method of transmitting radio waves, and filed patents between 1930 and 1933. His inventions focused on wideband frequency modulations and became known as FM. While we are quite familiar with FM today, Armstrong never lived to see its commercial success. He spent the waning days of his life in a court battle with RCA over the rights to the patents. The radio industry resisted the new technology because of the cost of creating new radios to receive the transmissions and the duplication of transmission—although when Sarnoff first saw a demonstration of FM, he declared it a revolution. At the time, however, he was more involved in what he considered an even more important new technology—television—that he wrongly guessed would spell the end of radio.

The invention of FM was an effort to eliminate static, the primary problem with AM broadcasts. Armstrong viewed his FM invention as an opportunity to regain his image as a leading inventor. His reputation had been tarnished, more in his mind than in fact, by his court losses to de Forest. But this was not to be. He soon found himself in court again over FM patents.

His first foray into FM radio was encouraging. When he began experimental broadcasts in 1938, rivals of RCA were quite interested, in part because RCA was against it. If RCA was not going to pursue FM, it left the field wide open for competition. The military became the primary customer for FM. They used it exclusively as a short-range communication method in the field between tanks and jeeps. Gradually, it became the standard for all branches of the military. Armstrong was ahead of his time with the invention of FM. It would prove to be of vast importance in regard to transistors, communication with spacecraft, stereo, and digital storage. All of this, however, would come long after his death.

FM made no commercial progress or impact until after World War II, when it grabbed worldwide headlines in January of 1946 after the U.S. armed forces conducted an experiment in which they successfully bounced an FM signal off the moon. Technologically, FM was far superior to AM, with its static-free, finer quality sound. As a result, Armstrong and other technicians assumed that after the war, there would be a rush to FM. Consumers would purchase new radios, with both AM and FM bands. However, science and business did not marry well in this instance. While FM was undoubtedly superior, broadcasters did not rush to broadcast over FM. They were not as interested in undertaking large expenditures for little gain. It did not seem that they would profit by installing expensive new equipment so that they could simply replace or duplicate their current broadcasts. And manufacturers, particularly RCA, were more concerned with television than better radio. Sarnoff expected television to replace radio anyway, so there seemed little sense in investing in it.

The technicians and scientists never got a chance to prove themselves in the market, since the broadcasters and manufacturers used the FCC to shut them out. They convinced the FCC that FM would interfere with the development of television by using up valuable bandwidth space. Many an FCC appointee had previously worked in the broadcasting industry and, even more importantly, could look forward to a lucrative career in the industry after finishing a few "good" years in the government. Ultimately, FM was scuttled by the FCC when it decided to use the lower bandwidths for television and force FM to higher bandwidths. While this is not a problem today, it did slow down the introduction of FM for years, as engineers had to redesign and recalibrate their work to the higher frequency.

Another blow to FM came through the FCC ruling that FM broadcasters would be restricted to broadcasting their signal to a single market. FM was a clearer signal, and as the armed forces had aptly demonstrated, it could be broadcast over great distance with impressive results. The static-free broadcast could render AM obsolete. This, of course, was the crux of the problem and the reason the broadcasters and manufacturers resisted it.

The biggest blow to FM broadcasting came from the networks. They did not want to compete with the independent FM stations that were cropping up. The superior quality of FM transmission meant the signals could be broadcast with greater clarity over greater distances than AM signals. The FCC, however, set a maximum power limit of 1.2 kilowatts for FM stations, essentially making them local stations. The broadcasters claimed this was a democratic way of introducing FM to the larger U.S. population—far better, they argued, than a situation where some FM stations could totally dominate others because they entered the market early and established such a strong signal that they controlled distant markets. With limits on FM power, the FCC essentially turned all FM stations into unprofitable local stations. This was a death knell for the independent stations, but beneficial for the networks that used their profitable AM stations to subsidize their FM stations while they developed greater control over the technology.

To further handicap FM, the networks won permission from the FCC to duplicate their programming from AM to be broadcast over FM. The argument was that the listening public would be better served by having access to the same high quality in their AM broadcasts as their FM signals, especially for those folks who were unable to receive a clear AM signal. This essentially made it impossible for independent FM operators to attract advertising. Because the AM broadcasts were duplicated over FM, an advertiser on AM was essentially getting two broadcast markets for the price of one.

Armstrong's work in FM had far greater consequences than just static-free radio broadcasts. It ultimately led to the development of the early warning radar system and microwave relay systems for transmitting telephone and television signals over immense distances. Howard Armstrong was as confident and competent in the laboratory as he was frustrated and overmatched in the political and legal arena. Despite his amazing discoveries, all of which play an important and prominent part in today's technology, he was shut out and trumped by corporate politics at every turn. His superior FM technology was neutered to fit the political will of the networks. He became similarly frustrated by the legal and business world due to his loss to de Forest in court. This round of frustration would have a tragic end. Burned out by his frustrations and repeated setbacks in the courts, even though it seemed obvious to him and the rest of the independent scientific community that he was right, Armstrong committed suicide on January 31, 1954. Ironically, it wasn't until after his death that he proved victorious in court. His widow oversaw victories in his outstanding patent suits against RCA.

THE MODERN ERA

The economic value of a radio station, as with a TV station, is a function of the available technology and regulations. Of course, the market in which the station is located is also a factor, but the other two factors can change over time, whereas the location does not.

The FCC restricts most AM stations from broadcasting at full power at night in order to cut down on interference. Because AM signals bounce off the ionosphere at night, they can interfere with one another over distances thousands of miles away. As a result, most small stations are restricted in the power at which they may transmit after dark. Some stations, designated clear-channel stations, may broadcast at full power (up to 50,000 watts). As a result, these channels can be received over vast distances, especially after sunset. Obviously, these stations are worth more because they reach a broader audience.

FM radio is a different type of technology. Even though the signal is superior in quality to AM, it cannot be broadcast over the same distance. Power limitations make it essentially a local medium, because the signal usually cannot be broadcast beyond about 60 miles. This is being challenged by the growth in the last decade of Web radio, which of course allows a radio signal to be broadcast worldwide over the Internet. As computers become more common transmitters of radio broadcasts, the relative value of AM and FM stations is likely to adjust.

The value of a radio station is closely tied to the number of listeners. The more listeners (especially in a specific demographic) the more advertising revenue is generated, and the more valuable the station. As with television the measure of a listening audience is made in ratings points and audience share. A ratings point is the percentage of all households tuned in to the station, while a share point is the percentage of all radios in use that are tuned in to the station. Thus, the share will always be greater than or equal to the rating. The quarterly measures of ratings determine the advertising rates for the next quarter.

Local radio stations are often affiliated with one of the three major radio networks: NBC, CBS, or ABC. FCC regulations limit the number and location of stations that a single owner may purchase. Currently the limit is 12 FM and 12 AM stations along with 12 television stations. There is also a limit on the size of the television audience, which was increased from 25 percent to 35 percent with the passage of the 1996 Telecommunications Act. The purpose of these limits has been to restrict the ability of any owner from monopolizing broadcasting power. With the rise of the Internet, cable, and satellite as potential competitors to over-the-air broadcasters, these fears have been diminished. As a result, the FCC is currently considering relaxing these ownership restrictions even further.

FM and AM radio stations have carved out market niches. Radio broadcasting on FM is dominated by the broadcast of music, while AM is more likely to broadcast talk shows. In part, this is because of the superior quality of FM broadcasts. Stations typically focus on a particular format in an attempt to appeal to a certain audience niche, and then sell to advertisers based on the demographics of the population listening in. For example, a station devoted to popular hit music is more likely to be listened to by a younger audience than is a golden-oldies station. At the other end of the spectrum are public radio stations, tending to specialize in classical music or news programs. Like public television, public radio does not sell advertising, but relies on listener contributions and government subsidies to pay the bills.

FM Radio stations rely more heavily on local content than do television stations and some AM stations. They may only broadcast network news updates on the hour, otherwise relying totally on local programming. AM stations are more likely to rely on network programming for nationally syndicated talk shows. During the last few years political talk shows and sports talk shows have gained popularity to the extent that many mid- and large-size markets have dedicated sports talk stations.

CONCLUSION

The radio industry changed the way Americans communicated, relaxed, received their news, and ultimately lived. It has survived changing lifestyles and revolutionary technology and still thrives today. Nearly $8 billion is spent on radio advertising each year on approximately 10,000 stations broadcasting over the airwaves and computers. It appears that reports of its demise in the face of modern technology are greatly exaggerated.

—6—

Television: The New Vaudeville

According to a 1996 survey conducted by the Leisure Trends Group, 21 percent of Americans named watching television as their favorite leisure time activity. This was second only to those who listed reading as their favorite and just ahead of time with family and friends. Since regular broadcasting began during the 1939 World's Fair in New York, television has entertained, enthralled, and occupied the time of Americans of all ages. The average American household watches fifty-three hours of television each week. More than $40 billion are spent each year on television advertising on the 1,600 network and independent television stations in the United States, which reach into nearly 100 million homes. This does not include the hundreds of public television or cable television stations. Certain mega events, such as the Olympic Games, draw considerable attention. NBC agreed to a $793 million dollar payout for the 2004 games in Athens and $894 million for the 2008 games—before they even knew where they would be located.

Television is ubiquitous. It shapes our lives: whether it is influencing the outcome of elections, bringing the horror of catastrophe into our living rooms, entertaining, or educating us. It has made an indelible mark on American society.

Television has permanently and drastically changed the nature of leisure in America. Never before have Americans been exposed to so much entertainment, available so many hours per day, and at such a low cost, as they have been by the evolution of television. Television changed the concept and availability of entertainment. We can sit at home and choose from hundreds of different television shows, not to mention the recent Hollywood movies that are available on pay-per-view or subscription channels, 24 hours per day, 7 days a week, 365 days a year.

INVENTION

The term "television" first appeared in a 1908 article in *Scientific American* that speculated about future technological possibilities. Television became a technological possibility as early as the 1920s. However, it wasn't until the consumer goods explosion following World War II that it became a commercial success. As consumption-starved Americans celebrated the return of prosperity to their country after nearly two decades of depression and then war, the purchase of new cars, suburban homes, and television sets marked the following decade as one of great social change. The impact on the entertainment industry was mammoth. For a short while, Hollywood believed that television would spell the end of the movie industry. Indeed, television's ascendancy did seem to come at the expense of the movies. Inflation-adjusted box-office receipts fell from an all-time high of $8 billion in 1945 to less than half that total by 1960, where it finally leveled off.

The invention of television essentially turned out to be a two-man race between Philo Farnsworth and Vladimir Zworykin. Philo T. Farnsworth, working with a small staff in a ramshackle laboratory in San Francisco, received the first patent in 1927 for electronic television, which would eventually become the industry standard. At the same time, scores of other inventors and corporate research teams were trying to develop a television device. Most of them, however, were pursuing a mechanical approach, as opposed to the Farnsworth electronic system. None of them were to prove workable, though some interesting solutions resulted. An inventor named Charles Jenkins demonstrated a very crude mechanical television system that he patented and marketed in 1925. The system produced outlines of images that were barely recognizable. In hindsight, the system was doomed, because the technical limitations made it unworkable. However, Jenkins was a marketing genius, and while he lost thousands selling his Radiovisors, he turned the excitement over its future potential into a stock market bonanza, creating a company which sold $10 million in stock based only on hope, not on any existing product.

The other major player was the Radio Corporation of America (RCA). Their television research team was headed by Vladimir

Zworykin, a Russian immigrant and a scientific genius. Farnsworth and Zworykin spent nearly two decades in a technological race to perfect television. It was a classic match up, pitting the underdog Farnsworth, a self-taught tinkerer, against Zworykin, the well-financed corporate researcher, a model of twentieth-century corporate research. While Farnsworth would ultimately come to be recognized as the "Father of Television," this outcome was far from certain at the time. He overcame RCA in the laboratory by developing a workable television and battled them in the courtroom over the rights to the patents covering his inventions.

In 1935 Farnsworth scored his biggest legal victory when he successfully sued RCA for patent infringement. In July of that year the patent courts sided with him, proclaiming him the true inventor of television, acknowledging that his patents superseded those of Vladimir Zworykin and RCA. This victory acknowledged the accomplishments of Farnsworth, but did not stop RCA's commercialization plans.

RCA introduced television at the 1939 World's Fair in New York City, attracting the attention of the press and fair-goers. It was a spectacular showing and convinced one and all that television was a reality just around the corner. Unfortunately for RCA, the product they previewed was stolen from Farnsworth, infringing egregiously on his patents. David Sarnoff, president of RCA, was well aware of the patent infringement, and with this successful showing, he forced himself into finally negotiating in good faith with Farnsworth. In September of 1939, RCA and Farnsworth came to an agreement. RCA paid Farnsworth $1 million plus royalties on every television set it sold. For the first time in its history, RCA was now buying, instead of selling, the right to license patents. Furthermore, the agreement was nonexclusive. Thus Farnsworth was free to license his patents to other manufacturers as well.

With the World's Fair, RCA's broadcast corporation, National Broadcasting Company, began the first regularly scheduled television broadcasts. Though the original broadcasts reached only about 2,000 sets in the immediate New York City area, the impact was felt around the world. Television had arrived, and only a world war delayed its spread.

In 1947 Farnsworth's most valuable patents expired, and his ability to receive royalties from them disappeared as well. He still held over a hundred television-related patents, but none as valuable as his original patents, which were now in the public domain. His chance at cashing in on untold riches from his invention expired just as the television craze was about to begin.

Color Television

Color television broadcasting was technically possible as early as 1939, though a commercially feasible system was not ready until 1947. It would not debut, however, because of a legal fight between its innovator, CBS, and RCA. RCA occupied CBS in court for four years, preventing them from beginning to broadcast in color. The legal maneuvering was designed to buy time for RCA, which was working on a color broadcasting system of its own. Their system could only be viewed on RCA sets, which, with each passing year, were showing up in more and more American households. The RCA system was different than that of CBS, and the CBS system could only be viewed on RCA sets with the purchase of an expensive adapter. RCA's delay tactics worked, and in 1953 its system was accepted as the industry standard by the FCC.

RCA continued its development of color television in the early 1950s, but the cost and commercial problems made it a poor seller. Sarnoff had already poured $130 million into its development and was predicting that it would catch on like radio. He said in 1953 that within five years there would be 10 million color sets on the market. In reality, there were less than 400,000 by 1958. The high cost (over $1,000 a set in 1954) and the necessity of a $120 per year service contract, plus the low quality and high maintenance cost kept color television out of the market as a serious alternative until the 1970s. In addition, broadcasters were not willing to undertake the expense of broadcasting in color until they were sure the consumers demanded it. Early color broadcasts were almost exclusively on NBC and were limited to a few hours per week.

Color television brought RCA serious legal difficulties. The antitrust division of the U.S. Department of Justice charged them with monopoly practices. Sarnoff settled with the antitrust authorities by agreeing to add all of its color television patents to a common pool for free usage. Freed from the necessity of having to pay their rival to make color sets, manufacturers jumped on the bandwagon, and color television ultimately took over the market. Like radio and black-and-white television before it, color television became a major achievement for David Sarnoff. It was his last major accomplishment before his death on December 12, 1971.

With the passing of Sarnoff came the end of RCA. RCA had been formed as a separate division of GE in 1919 and was spun off by Sarnoff as an independent corporation in 1933. His vision and willingness to bear risk and forsake present profits for future investment had made RCA the leader first in radio, then in television, and finally in color television. After Sarnoff's death, the company slowly declined until December 1985 when it was sold back to GE and its independent existence came to an end.

THE EARLY YEARS

Both NBC and CBS began regularly scheduled commercial broadcasts on July 1, 1941, and it appeared the television industry was set to take off. However, it ground to a halt with the bombing of Pearl Harbor and was mothballed until after the war as the government suspended most television broadcasting in the spring of 1942.

The first television sets only vaguely resembled today's version. There were no flat screens, plasma TVs, or large screens. There was no cable, satellite, or 24-hour programming. In the first years of viable commercial television, the late 1940s and early 1950s, programming was confined to a few hours in a day, usually during what we now refer to as "prime time," 8–11 p.m. EST. Television broadcasts were local, with networking still on the horizon. Television sets were in their infancy. The 7-inch screen was the industry standard, for which you could expect to pay about $180 in 1950. This sounds reasonable until you consider that the average annual wage in 1950 was only $3200.

In the beginning, before technology allowed the simultaneous broadcast of shows coast-to-coast, networks shared their programs with their affiliates across the country by means of filmed kinescope—a photo of the show taken directly off the television cathode tube. The quality and durability of these images were poor. An unfortunate result is that few of the early television shows survive for us to view today.

An example of the television lineup on the DuMont network, WABD Channel 5 in New York City, on a typical day in 1948 began in the evening:

6:05	The Weather Report
6:15	Small Fry Club
6:45	News from Washington
7:00	Doorway to Fame
7:30	Camera Headlines
7:45	Film Shorts
8:15	Magic Carpet
8:30	Swing into Sports
9:00	Sport Names to Remember
9:05	Boxing, Jamaica Arena

A similar lineup appeared on the NBC station. On this particular night, CBS decided not to broadcast at all for lack of programming.

In the fall of 1950, *The Ford Television Theater* on CBS became one of the first successful weekly broadcasts. The show was quickly imitated by rival networks with shows such as *Studio One* and *Philco Playhouse*. Studio One concentrated on original drama, written specially for television. The other two broadcast a different play or short novel, adapted for television, each week. All of these broadcasts were live.

In the early years of television, production was concentrated in New York. Hollywood was still primarily focused on movies. In fact, the predominant attitude at the movie studios was that TV was a fad that would soon go away. Little if any television production took place in Hollywood, and few movie actors crossed over to television. Movie theaters neither cooperated with TV stations, nor did business with them. They viewed television as a potential competitor, but not a serious one likely to last long.

The growth of original programming was due in part to the lawsuits threatened by movie studios. They prevented networks from rebroadcasting original films on television and distributing kinescope copies to affiliates. The result was the growth of original dramatic programming on the television networks. With a need for programming, the networks clamored to hire writers, creating an entire new industry niche for television writers, one that would eventually flourish into a specialty of its own.

More so than the movies, it was television which sent vaudeville revues to their grave. Prior to television, the revue was where the public could find a variety of entertainment brought together. Vaudeville promised two hours of variety entertainment, well-rehearsed and, on Broadway at least, the best available talent. Television wiped that out by providing the same thing, but on a weekly basis.

Besides the dramatic theater written for television, the other logical type of programming was the variety show. The transfer of vaudeville acts to television, centering around an MC who would introduce the acts, was a popular theme. Unfortunately, the medium of television was much more exhausting for stage performers than it first appeared. A successful vaudeville act was usually perfected over months or even years of performing on the small-town circuit, before moving to the big stage for extended runs. This allowed the performer to perfect an act and then repeat it, refine it, and run it again for months or even years. In contrast, television, because it played to much larger audiences, used up a year or more of material in one shot. Thus, a weekly show required a performer to come up with a new set of material on a weekly basis and required the maintenance of quality on that heretofore unheard of pace. The successful shows, such as *Your Show of Shows*, *Texaco Star Theater*, and *The Ed Sullivan Show* are legendary. The pressure resulted in scores of failed attempts launched by highly successful vaudeville and movie talents who simply could not stand the pace. Many successful performers, seeing what happened to their colleagues, avoided television altogether, even refusing to appear as a guest on a variety show or for a one-time appearance in a drama. Television tended instead to create its own stars, independent of the movies: Lucille Ball, Jackie Gleason, and Ed Sullivan are among the most famous early examples.

Early shows tended to be supported by a sponsor in their entirety, rather than selling commercial time piecemeal. Westinghouse, for example, was the sponsor of the weekly drama *Studio One*. It paid $8,100 per episode when it debuted in 1948. The series was not a financial success in the beginning, since it cost CBS about $12,000 per week to air. The investment in technical and organizational capital would prove invaluable for the networks however, so the investment was worthwhile.

The first successful situation comedy (sitcom) was *Mama*, airing on CBS for eight years beginning in 1949. The show was adapted from the bestseller *Mama's Bank Account* by Kathryn Forbes. Before becoming a successful television show, it was a hit on Broadway and in the movie theater as *I Remember Mama*. The show was sponsored by Maxwell House Coffee, and as was so common in those pioneering days of television, the show sponsor had more control over the content of the show than did the network brass. *Mama* was also unique in that it did not feature any commercial interruptions. Maxwell House broadcast their commercials only at the beginning and end of the show.

Television Newscasts

Another standard of television is the newscast. The first major political event covered by the networks was the 1948 Republican National Convention. This coverage also was a first in the technology it employed, a precursor to satellite transmission. The convention was held in Philadelphia, and the proceedings were broadcast to the surrounding nine-state area by means of "stratovision." The signal was transmitted to a plane flying above and then relayed to television stations on the ground.

In 1949 the first regular newscast was launched. *The Camel News Caravan*, anchored by John Cameron Swayze, began its nightly fifteen-minute broadcasts from New York, still the center of network news broadcasts.

Along with the growth of television newscasts came the growth of live news events. It is difficult to imagine, in this day of 24-hour news networks and on-the-spot reporting, that live coverage of major events was ever novel for television. However, only in 1951 did the first live coverage of a Congressional hearing take place, when cameras were allowed in the Senate chambers for the first time to televise Senator Estes Kefauver chairing the committee investigating organized crime. Even more dramatic, in 1954 the same cameras elevated Senator Joseph McCarthy to national celebrity in his crusade to oust communists from America. The power of television to make and break celebrities virtually overnight is commonplace today, but it was a new and powerful force in its infancy, one that was only beginning to be understood.

The Eisenhower administration realized the vast potential for television to aid the president in communicating his message to the American public. The first live press conference by a president was held by Eisenhower in 1956 in San Francisco where he announced he would run for reelection later that year. While the power of television was understood, it was not yet mastered. Perhaps the most famous example of the power of television in a political race is the 1960 presidential debates between John F. Kennedy and Richard Nixon. Kennedy used the medium well, while Nixon did not, and the difference has often been cited as an important factor in the close Kennedy victory.

Politicians were not the only ones who could be turned into instant stars. Before television, an entertainer had to work his or her way up from the bottom, working local circuits and vacation resorts before eventually landing a spot in the big vaudeville revues. By the time the top was reached, the act was practiced and refined, and the entertainer was a veteran of the circuit. With television, all that changed. Now a green performer, thrust onto television in the *Ed Sullivan Show* or the *Amateur Hour* could suddenly capture the attention of the nation in one brief moment. Careers could now be launched with one good appearance, where the performer would command a larger audience than a lifetime of vaudeville circuits could ever provide. The meteoric rise and decline of stars became commonplace. Some, like Elvis Presley, would rise and stay at the top. Others, like Julius La Rosa, a young Brooklyn singer who rocketed to fame on *Arthur Godfrey and His Friends*, burned brightly and briefly before fading into obscurity. The brief celebrity status enjoyed by participants on today's reality shows, such as *Survivor* and *The Bachelor*, carry on this trend.

The Move to Videotape

The late 1950s were a period of change for television on two fronts. The industry moved West, from New York to California, and moved into posterity, taking advantage of advances in technology which allowed for the recording of shows on tape for later broadcast. While little remains of the fragile kinescopes of the earliest broadcasts, videotape has preserved virtually everything since. Lucille Ball and Desi Arnaz were pioneers in this medium. They started their own company, DesiLu, when CBS turned down their plan to record a weekly show on film in a California studio instead of moving to New York to do the weekly show live. The transformation to film was quick because sponsors jumped on the television bandwagon, recognizing its ability as a sales medium. Without the sponsors, there would be no sustainable network.

In the 1950s, industry pundits believed that viewers preferred live broadcasts, similar to live stage shows. They believed taped broadcasts would leave the viewers feeling cheated somehow. As a result, the taping of broadcasts was rare. When networks and critics realized that it was quality programming, not live programming, that appealed to audiences, live broadcasts quickly faded in favor of videotape. In 1953 more than 80 percent of all television broadcasts were live. By 1965 only 25 percent of broadcasts were live, and these were dominated by newscasts. By 1974, 90 percent of all prime-time television viewing originated on video. Aside from sports and news programs, video is the industry standard today, though the computer will eventually render video obsolete. This will change the method of storage, but not the fact that little on television is broadcast live anymore.

Another change brought about by the transformation to videotape was the creation of reruns. By the beginning of the 1960s, summer reruns, as we know them today, were the norm. While regular programs today are rebroadcast during the "summer rerun period," that was not originally the case. During the summer break, replacement shows were offered instead of reruns of the season originals.

Interestingly, early critics and network executives were convinced that television was different than radio and the movies in its attractiveness to audiences. They were sure that its success lay not in imitating radio, with regular weekly shows centered around the same theme, setting, or characters as radio had done, but rather with live, spectacular shows, more like vaudeville or a concert. This "big events" philosophy was perceived to be the key that would sustain television.

Innovation is important in any industry, and television is certainly no exception. Not all executives thought this way, and it was CBS, behind its president Frank Stanton, that first pioneered the regular weekly broadcast. Stanton correctly predicted that regular broadcasts of the same show on the same day and time each week would become events around which people would plan their entertainment schedules. This was not exactly a novel idea, as it had been the format successfully used by the radio networks (owned by the same companies). For nearly twenty years, *The Jack Benny Show* had been a staple on Sunday night. It led all other radio shows in the ratings in the postwar years until Benny eventually moved to television, where he proved a success as well.

THE NETWORKS

Networks were established in the 1920s for radio, and were transformed into television networks in the 1940s and 1950s. Each of the three major networks had about 200 affiliates by the end of the century. The relatively newer Fox and WB network have about half as many. The networks no longer dominate the industry. Their share of the audience has decreased from over 90 percent as recently as 1980 to less than 35 percent by the end of the century.

Bill Paley, the first president of CBS, invented the affiliate system that now prevails in both the radio and television industry. The early model, pioneered by NBC, was for the network to charge affiliates to receive its programming. The affiliates could then air popular shows produced by the network, attract listeners, and sell local advertising. Paley took the opposite approach. He attracted greater numbers of stations to the CBS network by paying the affiliates to receive broadcasting exclusively from CBS. Paley then sold national advertising to national brands, which were able to reach vast audiences provided by the large numbers of local stations that Paley attracted. The local stations also set aside time to sell their own advertising. The system was carried over to television when it was commercialized and prevails to this day.

While RCA and its NBC subsidiary often led the technological side of television, it was CBS that set the industry programming standard, signing the biggest radio stars and turning them into television stars. In addition, they created a new breed of celebrity, the television star, with such personae as Lucille Ball and Jackie Gleason vaulting to the top of what would become the industry master—the Nielsen ratings.

American Broadcasting Corporation was formed by a divestiture of the NBC radio network, when RCA was forced by the FCC in 1941 to divest itself of one of its two networks. Edward J. Noble, CEO of Beech-Nut Life Savers, Inc., branched into broadcasting with the purchase of the network, which he named ABC in 1943.

DuMont joined NBC and CBS in 1945 as the third major television network. DuMont was a firm which manufactured cathode ray oscilloscopes and televisions. It was a relative newcomer to the industry, having been founded only in 1931. When the FCC began accepting applications for television broadcast licenses, DuMont diversified into the broadcasting business.

DuMont and latecomer ABC fought for the dubious distinction of being the third viable weak sister in the network scheme. ABC gained a better position when they merged with United Paramount Theaters, the chain of theaters sold off by Paramount during the divestiture move of the late 1940s. DuMont, which didn't have the radio relationships the other three networks used to sign up affiliates, finally folded in 1955, leaving the television landscape settled for the next generation, until the technology of cable and satellite created the next upheaval.

Even after the departure of DuMont, ABC was the weakest network because of its latecomer status. It was forced to sign up UHF stations as its affiliates in many top markets, thus it reached fewer homes and garnered less advertising dollars. Without the financial resources of NBC and CBS, ABC turned to an alternative form of broadcasting. Instead of producing its own shows, it licensed material from independent producers. It financed the production of pilots and series in return for a share of the profits, their big breakthrough coming in 1954 with the signing of Walt Disney to produce a weekly series revolving around the successful Disneyland theme park. The success of the ABC–Disney partnership changed the way studios viewed the broadcasting industry and convinced the major studios that television could be a profitable venue for movies, not necessarily a competitor to be feared.

CABLE AND SATELLITE

Cable Television

Cable television's roots go back to the 1940s, when it served as a means for communities in geographically remote areas to receive a better signal. Television signals do not travel very far, and they cannot go through mountains. This created problems for reception in certain areas. The solution was a signal delivered through a cable instead of over-the-air.

The earliest cable systems were created in towns where the geographic terrain made over-the-air reception difficult or impossible. Early cable bore little resemblance to today's multichannel offerings. It offered little more than a retransmission of over-the-air network broadcasts, with the occasional addition of a local access channel and perhaps a text channel, such as the AP scroll or an early weather channel which broadcast pressure and temperature and wind gauges for current local conditions. They remained small and insignificant for a number of years. The total number of cable TV subscribers did not reach 1 million until 1963. Intense lobbying from the networks kept cable a small and unimportant player in the market through various FCC regulations which, for example, restricted the distance that signals could be transmitted for relay over cable systems and prohibited carrying movies less than a decade old or sporting events that had been broadcast by the networks in the previous five years.

In 1970, Ted Turner introduced the concept of the Super station, when he convinced cable systems outside of Atlanta to carry his independent Atlanta station, WTCG (Watch This Channel Grow). He felt a larger audience would make it easier to sell advertising. Distant cable systems took interest in his channel, because they had excess capacity to carry additional broadcasts. The appeal of his station was that he carried the rights to broadcast the Atlanta Braves baseball games. Imitating the success of Turner, who ultimately renamed the station WTBS (Turner Broadcasting System), were WGN (World's Greatest Newspaper) of Chicago, owned by the Chicago Tribune newspaper, and then the ultimate cable innovation, HBO (Home Box Office), which for the first time sold premium television subscription to movies and other broadcasting offered without commercial interruption.

The distribution of signals to the local cable operators by microwave was neither high quality nor reliable. Poor weather interrupted signals and the construction of microwave towers was expensive, requiring the purchase of real estate. Maintenance was also a problem, and the towers required FCC licenses. This meant that cable operators were eager to move into the newest technology: satellite distribution. Each satellite contains several transponders, each of which can transmit a different signal. Hence several cable networks can broadcast from the same satellite. Since few cable channels could afford to launch their own satellite, this allowed a greater number to survive by leasing transponder space.

Local cable systems function like local stations in that they provide access to the signal. A local cable system makes the physical hookup to the household and delivers a digital signal to the household. The household then receives a variety of cable network programming, as well as digital versions of broadcast network shows.

The first satellite transmission of a cable program was the HBO transmission of the Muhammad Ali vs. Joe Frazier heavyweight title fight from Manila on September 30, 1975. Turner's channel was the next to be broadcast over satellite, and by 1980 nearly every cable network was being distributed by satellite, leading to rapid growth of cable into a national industry during the early 1980s. Cable evolved as a local monopoly because most municipalities did not want competing cable systems to duplicate overhead wires or tear up streets on multiple occasions so that each could lay its own cable. Instead, most cities granted a local monopoly to one cable system. In return, the local government received some concessions, such as a percentage of the gross revenues and local access channels.

Cable began hitting with niche markets, or narrowcasting, to identifiable market segments. ESPN, Nickelodeon, and MTV are obvious examples. The Weather Channel was one of the earliest specialty channels. This type of specialized targeting of audiences had always been the potential of cable television but was not exploited until the 1980s.

Since it was a government-granted monopoly, the cable system was heavily regulated. Subscription rates, access, quality, and quantity of service, and channel authorization were all subject to government oversight. In 1984, cable companies lodged a protest against what they claimed was unfair regulation. They cited the increased competition in the television industry from other technologies, such as microwave broadcasts, television signals carried by telephone companies, over-the-air broadcast networks, and home satellite systems. At this time, the broadcast networks still dominated the airwaves. ABC, CBS, and NBC together had more than 73 percent of the market, in part because cable was not available in about half the country, including several of the largest cities where over-the-air broadcasts were easily available.

By the mid-1970s, FCC restrictions on cable's ability to retransmit signals slackened and cable grew in prominence, primarily on the strength of so-called "Super stations" like WGN and WTBS. These were local stations that programmed for a national cable audience. Perhaps even more important was the rise of premium channels like HBO and Showtime, which for the first time made pay television a national broadcast reality. Pay-per-view service technology was previously available on smaller scales in terms of geography and event. By the mid-1980s, after the passage of the Cable Communications Policy Act of 1984, which deregulated service pricing, the cable industry was the dominant television provider in America, with over half of all television homes subscribing to some sort of cable service. Subscription fees represent 80 percent of cable's revenue, with only 20 percent coming from advertising. In recent years satellite television has begun to grow to a point where it now controls about a quarter of the market.

The most popular cable networks charge local operators a fee to carry their signal. In the early days of the industry, this was rare. In 1981, only ESPN, CNN, and USA were able to get fees for their signal. This was an advantage for them, because it removed advertising as the sole source of income. The opposite was the case for networks, which usually pay their affiliates for carrying their signal. It was not unusual for an upstart cable network to offer to pay cable systems to carry their signal early in their lifespan in an effort to grab a foothold in the market. Some cable companies explained their rate practice as an economic necessity. They correctly pointed out that popular cable networks could exploit their position by demanding high fees from the cable providers for the right to carry their signal, so the most popular networks, such as ESPN and CNN, were also the most expensive. It made sense, therefore, to charge more for these channels. The fact that consumers readily purchased them suggested they were willing to pay the price.

Complicating this pricing logic was the fact that consumers were not able to make straightforward choices. Since the channels were packaged, not purchased individually, it was difficult to determine exactly how valuable a particular channel was to a consumer. Consumers were forced to purchase a package of channels to get the one or two they might want. In this way the cable provider could point to decreasing per channel subscription prices, while at the same time consumers complained about increasing cable rates. Of course consumers are not necessarily interested in the quantity of channels, but the quality—that is, what content it delivered. Cable companies subsidize the expensive channels by forcing consumers to buy less expensive channels at the same time. The system is a bit like the block booking process Hollywood once used to guarantee an outlet for its lower quality movies.

In 1987 the cable companies received the deregulation they requested. The FCC ruled that any city where three or more over-the-air broadcast stations could be received was sufficiently competitive to allow for deregulation. This described 97 percent of households. After deregulation, consumer complaints rose. Cable revenue more than doubled, as did rates. Less than 1 percent of households are located in a market with competing cable systems. The most feared competitor has not been over-the-air broadcasters, who now account for less than a third of the market, but satellite dish systems, which captured 15 percent of the market by 2000.

Deregulation of the cable industry has not been all bad. While rates skyrocketed, so did the number of available channels. The average cable system increased its offerings from 27 to more than 200. The per channel cost of subscription has actually decreased slightly when adjusted for inflation. On the downside, several of the new channels in any system are purely advertising, or infomercial channels, like the Home Shopping Network and QVC. Many subscribers do not consider such channels as positive additions to their packages.

Competition does work. In those markets with competing cable systems, the cost of subscribing is just over half that found in the systems with no competition. The number of subscribers to satellite systems has also increased dramatically, tripling between 1995 and 2000. Satellite systems still reach less than a quarter of the market, but their future potential impact on the industry is great, especially in light of the recent FCC ruling allowing satellite systems to relay local signals.

Regulation returned to the cable industry in 1992. Exclusive contracts between cable companies and cable networks were prohibited. In addition, the definition of the competition, needed to avoid reregulation, was changed from three over-the-air broadcast stations to six, significant competition from another television provider, such as satellite or cable—or "good behavior" by the cable company. Cable companies responded to rate regulation by offering tiered service as a way around it. The basic cable package they offered, which included the over-the-air networks and a small selection of less popular cable stations, was regulated, while the tiered packages of "extras" generally escaped regulation. These tiers included the most popular cable networks, such as CNN, ESPN, and TBS, not to mention the numerous specialty networks like the History Channel, Food TV, and MTV.

Satellite Systems

A satellite system is a small satellite dish, about the size of a large pizza, mounted on a house, and aimed at a dedicated satellite that relays television signals provided by a satellite broadcast company, such as DirecTV or Dish Network. Larger satellite dishes that picked up the actual transmissions from satellites to transmission towers were the first type of satellite television. While they still exist, the satellite industry is now dominated by the satellite broadcast companies. The satellite companies had one distinct disadvantage relative to cable companies. That is, in most markets they did not have the right to relay local station signals. Under a complicated ruling, cable and networks worked out an agreement whereby cable networks would carry local stations without requiring the stations to pay fees for the privilege (as the cable networks wanted) or the cable networks paying fees for the privilege (as the local stations wanted). This type of agreement between local channels and satellite companies was forbidden under FCC rules, and was gradually relaxed. Only recently could satellite systems broadcast a local station's signal. Initially they were allowed to do so only if the signal could not be adequately reached by the local community. This is much the same situation in which cable companies started: providing a signal to a community that was geographically isolated from local signals. Eventually cable systems added over-the-air broadcast stations to their packages, as did satellite companies.

The rise of cable television and its penetration in the U.S. market, has eroded the market share of the four major networks (three between 1960, when the DuMont Network folded, and 1986, when Fox became a network), which has steadily declined from 95 percent of the television audience in 1980 to just over one-third by the turn of the millennium. Cable television and satellite have penetrated the American market so that three out of four households now receive one or the other, typically featuring access between 30 and 230 channels.

THE TECHNOLOGY

As technology evolves, television broadcasting will evolve as well. Internet television and pay-per-view are the next revolutions. Internet television is on the horizon. Pay-per-view is here, but its market penetration still is not high enough (33 percent of households in 2000) to make it a major factor in the market. It is likely to become more important as a source of income for the release of feature movies. Industry analysts suggest the potential exists for the theater to become the second window for the release of movies when pay-per-view capability reaches enough homes.

As technology changes, so does the value of a television station. There are three different types of over-the-air broadcast technologies: very high frequency (VHF), ultra high frequency (UHF), and low power television (LPTV). In addition, there are cable broadcasters whose signal is delivered by satellite transmission. There are approximately 650 VHF stations, 750 UHF, and 600 LPTV stations. VHF is a local signal. It does not transmit much more than about 60 miles. The signal must be boosted by relay stations to travel further. UHF signals travel even shorter distances, and it requires significantly greater power to produce. Because of the expense of transmitting a UHF signal, it was commercialized after VHF. LPTV is a strictly local medium, commercialized in the 1980s. It is characterized by low-budget, local broadcasts. The signal requires only a one kilowatt transmitter compared to a UHF station, which requires a megawatt (1,000,000 watts). The LPTV signal carries less than 20 miles and requires a high-gain antenna to receive the signal. A UHF signal is broadcast in the range 300 to 3,000 megahertz, and these channels are numbered 14 through 83 (channels are numbered differently on satellite systems). A VHF signal is in the range of 30 to 300 megahertz, and occupies channels 2 through 13.

Interestingly enough, because of its forerunner status in television technology, the United States now has the most outdated television technology in the world. The U.S. broadcast standard is called NTSC (National Television Systems Committee) and features a 525-line scan at a rate of 30 frames per second. The TV picture is composed of 525 lines scrolling across the screen. The more lines there are, the higher quality the picture. Most countries in the world use a higher line scan system called SECAM (sequential color and memory) or PAL (phase-alternation line). This quality issue is currently being addressed in the United States with the requirement that new televisions be capable of receiving HDTV (high definition television) signals, even though few if any broadcasts are made in HDTV. The United States is implementing this standard by requiring all manufacturers to produce suitable equipment, and eventually all broadcasters will be required to broadcast their signals in HDTV as well. The change is expected to be fully implemented by 2008.

Videotape is a standard in the television industry. Little that is broadcast on television is "live" broadcasting. Beyond newscasts, almost all shows are recorded and then rebroadcast at a later time or date. This was not always the case, however. In fact, it wasn't until the 1957 inauguration of Dwight Eisenhower, which was taped and rebroadcast, that the practice became common. Taped broadcasts of East Coast newscasts for later broadcast to the West Coast had been used by networks prior to this time, but they were clandestine events. The West Coast viewers were not told of the taping, as the belief at the time was that prerecorded shows would have no appeal. The great success and praise of the inauguration broadcast, however, ushered in a new era of television—the standard use of taped broadcasts. This had major impacts on the primetime lineups of the networks, which could now tape shows in quantity in a compressed time period, saving money. For example, a whole season's worth of a series could be taped over a short time period and broadcast at later dates. This also allowed for the rebroadcast of episodes during the "off season," and summer reruns were born.

REGULATION

In 1912 the federal government got involved in the broadcast industry by nationalizing the broadcast spectrum. This would impact the television industry, still more than a generation away. The spectrum is allocated to allow for a variety of uses by numerous companies and individuals with maximum efficiency. The broadcast spectrum is a common pool asset, something that is available to anyone to use, but decreases in usefulness if too many people try to use it. The regulation of the spectrum not only controls the quantity of users, but the particular space they use as well.

There is a finite amount of space for broadcasting certain types of signals, and if broadcasters crowd the space, they will interfere with one another and ruin each other's signal and ability to broadcast. The FCC allocates the available space on the broadcast spectrum so that broadcasters do not interfere with one another's signals. That space is divided among many uses, including radio, cellular telephones, military use, microwave systems, satellites, and television broadcasters. The privilege to claim a space on the spectrum as your broadcast space requires only a license. A license is granted for five years and is renewable. With limited space available, competition for broadcast licenses is intense. The result in the American market has been that significant funds are usually spent lobbying for the right to purchase a license, and less money spent on new technology to improve the quality of the broadcast signal.

During the summer of 1940 the FCC set about to standardize television broadcasts, much as it had done for radio a generation earlier. The broadcast of television and radio signals was a clear case of a public good that would require government oversight. Broadcasters would have to agree on specific frequencies they would use, so as not to interfere with one another. They also had to agree upon a standard image quality for their broadcasts, that is, how many lines of each image were to be displayed on each screen. This was important because the television sets were constructed to receive a certain transmission standard, and if all broadcasters did not use the same standard, or changed the standard over time, television sets would be rendered obsolete. In order to make the sets more attractive to consumers, they had to be able to receive all the broadcasts and receive them over the long run. This is where the FCC came in. They forced the interested parties to negotiate and come up with a standard that was then enforced by the FCC.

The other standard set by the FCC that gave a boost to set sales was one that put color out of the market pending future research. This settled the question of how pictures would be broadcast. They chose the standard developed by RCA over its rival system developed by CBS, but since color broadcasts took three times as much bandwidth as black-and-white, they elected in 1947 not to allocate any stations for the transmission of color, putting off a decision until the technology was further refined. This set the industry up for a black-and-white standard that would continue to exist for many years and would lead to an explosion in the sale of sets so that consumers could be certain that the set they purchased would be able to receive the signals that were broadcast. Sales of television sets grew from 14,000 in 1947 to 32 million in 1954. By 1955 over 50 percent of American households had a television.

The number of local stations available in any broadcast area is restricted by the FCC. This is due to a set of preferences on their part. The decision was made long ago to maximize the quality of local broadcasts by limiting the number of licenses in an area. In this way, the licensees were granted positions on the spectrum which are far enough away from one another so that they will not interfere with each other's transmission. The effective maximum number of television signals in a geographic area was three. Hence, three networks ultimately evolved. Over time, as technology changed, particularly the dominance of cable and the popularity of home television satellite receivers, the number of locally viable, high-quality signals increased, and so did the number of networks. Not long ago there were three networks: ABC, NBC, and CBS. Now Fox, Viacom (UPN), and WB have joined the group. UPN and WB merged as CW in 2006, while Fox has established itself as a major player in the television market. In addition, there are scores of cable networks, each filling a specialized niche.

It did not take the FCC long to realize they had overallocated frequency space. With only 50 stations in existence in 1948, they discovered they were placed too close together, both on the bandwidth and geographically, and interference was commonplace. In an effort to sort out the problem, they placed a freeze on new licenses in late 1948, effectively giving all the existing stations a huge leg up on any future competition. It was not until 1952 that a new allocation plan was released. For four years, the 50 existing stations, and an additional 58 that had been under construction at the time of the freeze, had the television airwaves all to themselves. Most of the stations were affiliated with either NBC or CBS. They served 63 markets, 40 of which had only one station, 11 had two stations, and the remaining 12 had three or more.

The FCC decision in 1952 was no solution to the domination problem that had developed in the lull. Instead of moving all television to the broader UHF spectrum, which would have rendered all television sets obsolete, they decided to intermix VHF and UHF, allocating new stations to the UHF bandwidth. The problem with this, of course, was that no existing sets could receive these signals without a converter. It wasn't until 1964 that the FCC required all sets to be constructed with UHF receivers. In the meantime, the FCC "solved" the problem of interference by allocating three VHF stations each to the twenty largest markets and a mix of UHF and VHF stations to the next thirty largest markets. Another disadvantage faced by those stations allocated UHF bandwidth was that the signal was weaker, thus UHF stations were unable to broadcast as far or reach as many homes, and were ignored by the networks as they created their affiliations.

Without network affiliation, their ability to sell advertising was stunted.

The new FCC plan provided for 1,300 UHF stations. However, by 1956 only 400 applications had been received for these stations, and fewer than 300 ever went on the air. As a result, the three-network system was created. NBC and CBS had the lions share of the VHF stations; a third network could survive on the scraps, but for decades it would be a weak sister, until technology caught up with regulation. At first it was the DuMont network, but ultimately ABC would emerge as the third network. As satellite and cable technology changed the landscape, other networks would emerge.

When the FCC began issuing television broadcasting licenses, they claimed that they did not want the television industry to evolve as a national network. Instead, they emphasized the importance of local programming and public service responsibility. Licenses would be granted to local stations that could promise they would devote an average of eight hours a day to local programming. This was very much the environment in the early days of television station growth, primarily the period from the early 1950s through the mid-1960s, when the nation was saturated with stations.

During the Reagan administration there was a broad movement toward deregulation of industries. The airline, trucking, and banking industries have been deregulated in a series of bills passed since the 1980s. Deregulation in the television industry has been slower to arrive, though movement has occurred. In 1976 satellite dishes were allowed, opening a new sector of the television industry that has grown rapidly. The number of households with satellite dishes is still small, numbering only 9.6 million in 2000, but that number has tripled since 1995. Another burgeoning market is the home computer market. As of 2000, two-thirds of American homes had a computer and more than half of all households had Internet access. While the market to receive television signals over the computer is small, its potential impact is enormous.

Another factor in the deregulation history of television was the 1977 Supreme Court decision which prohibited the FCC from barring pay cable channels from cable systems. Premium movie channels and pay-per-view have grown in popularity since. Two years later most of the restrictions that prevented cable broadcasters from competing with over-the-air broadcasters were eliminated. The commission decided to regulate cable systems. In 1966 the FCC took ancillary jurisdiction over all cable systems, claiming that if it was allowed to grow in an unregulated environment it would degrade local broadcast service. In the interest of protecting local service, the FCC prohibited systems in major markets from bringing in over-the-air broadcast signals unless they could show that such service would serve the public interest. Moreover, in 1984 station ownership restrictions were loosened. Prior to that time, the maximum number of stations that could be held by one owner was seven each of (AM and FM) radio and television. Now the new maximum is twelve of each and 25 percent of total U.S. audience. Pending legislation may ultimately reduce these restrictions further. Opponents cite the potential of a few giant media conglomerates to dominate the industry.

The deregulation trend in the mid-1980s resulted in a major reorganization of the television industry. The major networks became part of large conglomerates, serving as another piece of a diversified portfolio. It was during this era that ABC was acquired by Capital Cities Communications, which was subsequently purchased by Disney. At one time this conglomerate also included ESPN, the California Angels major league baseball team, the Anaheim Mighty Ducks NHL franchise, and Disneyland and Disneyworld theme parks, among its vast holdings of entertainment-related assets. NBC was purchased by General Electric, and CBS by Viacom in 2000 after several failed takeover attempts over the course of the previous decade. The merger of Twentieth Century Fox and Metromedia created a corporation with the financial might to launch a fourth network. Fox has established itself as a major network, the first to do so since ABC in the 1960s. With the ability to produce and market their own shows, other entertainment conglomerates—Warner Brothers(WB) and Viacom (UPN)—also launched networks. They did not achieve the same level of success as Fox, and merged in 2006. The financial realities of cable competition, smaller audience shares, and more entertainment options have meant that vertical integration in the industry has become the norm, with production and broadcast facilities merged.

THE INDUSTRIAL ORGANIZATION OF THE INDUSTRY

The television industry mirrors the movie industry in some ways. There are five basic levels to the industry: producers, broadcasters, local stations, advertisers, and exhibitors.

The producers play the equivalent role to the movie producers; they "manufacture" television shows. Though the more artistically inclined among them would chafe at the use of that word, in essence, that is what they do. They then sell these shows to networks and independent stations. First-run series, shows like *Friends* and *Boston Legal*, for example, are usually sold to networks, who then provide them to their affiliates. Independent stations more commonly purchase from syndicators. Their typical fare includes game shows, talk shows, lower budget sitcoms, and reruns. Network affiliates get about two-thirds of their programming from the network. The rest they either produce themselves (local news and sports, or specials, e.g., coverage of a parade) or purchase through syndicators. These affiliates will purchase the same kind of fare that they produce.

Broadcasters purchase shows from producers and produce an audience for advertisers, to whom they sell airtime during broadcasts. The airtime will sell for varying amounts, depending on how many people are watching and their demographic makeup. Prices increase with the size and homogeneity of the viewing audience. A local audience will be at the bottom of the price range; a large national audience, say for the Super Bowl, will be at the top. In between is a vast range of prices, determined in large part by the Nielsen ratings of the television viewing public.

Broadcasters are the retailers in the television market. They buy the programs from producers and provide them to their affiliated stations. They produce some of their own material, particularly news programs and live event coverage, mostly sporting events and political events. The broadcasters are not a necessary component in the TV industry, but they do promote efficiency by way of economies of scale.

Broadcasters are commonly allied in networks, which decrease transaction costs, that is, the cost of doing business. There are fewer contracts to negotiate when a producer sells a show to one network rather than 100 independent stations. Economies of scale also exist in putting together a television schedule. It is much easier to put together one schedule and pass it on to 100 affiliated stations than to try and build schedules for each of the 100 stations. Also, a network can broadcast one copy of a show by satellite for its independent stations to download, and it will be aired at the same time in every market (though in practice, western markets are usually aired at a separate time due to the three-hour time difference between the coasts). If there were no networks, separate copies of the show would have to be produced for each independent station, since they may each be airing the show at a different time or day.

Broadcasters also offer advertisers an efficient way to distribute their ad budget over multiple programs. They can benefit from scheduling shows together to get viewers. For example, new shows are usually paired with popular mainstays in order to get a carryover audience.

Cable systems and local stations can be compared to retailers and networks (broadcast and cable) and syndicators to wholesalers. Both get their products from program producers. Program producers include major studios, such as Fox and Disney, as well as independent producers.

The production of an audience is measured in quantity of people per unit of time. Sometimes that measure is refined to qualify the viewers, most commonly by gender and age, as well as geographic location and income. Snow blowers, for example, are not marketed to national audiences for obvious reasons. This is valuable information for potential advertisers who want to be able to deliver their message to the largest audience of potential buyers possible. Note that this does not say the "largest audience possible." The word potential is critical here. An advertiser may be more interested in a smaller, more homogenous audience than a larger, diversified one. For example, marketers of pickup trucks are more likely to purchase, or pay more for, an audience of men ages 24–48 than they are for a larger audience composed of males and females ages 6–66.

The last link in the chain is the exhibition level. In the movie industry this is the theater. In the TV industry it is the manufacturer of the television set. They provide the hardware required to receive the signal which is broadcast over-the-air or sent via cable or satellite. Viewers are the consumers, and they demand a range of products, from small simple sets to large flat-screen systems. The quality and size of the image are what differs here, as well as the presence the set makes in the room in which it will be located.

There are two types of local stations. Either a local station is an independent station, or it is affiliated with one of the major networks: ABC, NBC, CBS, or Fox. In 2000, just over 86 percent of the 1393 local stations were affiliated with a network.

Networks themselves own very few stations. Law prohibits anyone from owning more than 12 stations, which may not reach more than 25 percent of the total market. Instead of owning stations, networks get local stations to sign on as affiliates. In return for affiliating with a network, a local station gets network programming to air during certain hours of the day. They also receive a payment from the network for airing these shows. Although this may sound like a good deal, it is advertising which pays the freight in the television industry. While the networks supply prime-time programming and a payment to the local station for carrying it, they keep most of the commercial airtime for sale to national sponsors. This is why they sign up local stations and pay them in the first place. The more stations and the greater the geographic spread, the greater the potential audience for advertising purposes.

The local stations benefit from this arrangement because they do not have to produce twenty-four hours of programming and they receive relatively high-quality shows from the network during which they can sell limited amounts of commercial time. Commercial time is very valuable for some shows, and translates into a financial windfall for the station if the show is a popular one.

Independent stations and affiliated stations must also buy or produce their own programming. Affiliated stations carry network productions only during certain hours of the day, prime-time, morning, and afternoon-shows such as *Good Morning America*, *Oprah*, and *The Young and the Restless*. With about two-thirds of the programming of an affiliated station provided by the network, the rest is up to the station. While they produce some of their own shows they also purchase some shows from syndicators.

Though some of these syndicated shows are original programming, many are reruns of popular shows. In reality, popularity has little more to do with the desirability of a show for reruns than does the number of episodes available. Of course, the two are related, since an unpopular show will not last long enough to generate a sufficient number of episodes for reruns. The rule of thumb is that about three season's worth of original programming is needed to make syndication as a rerun viable.

THE SUPPLY OF PROGRAMMING

Out of the hundreds of ideas proposed for television series each year, only about a dozen will actually make it to air, and only about two of these will be successful enough to make it to a second or third season. Since it takes approximately sixty total episodes to be a viable candidate for the rerun circuit, this is critical, because it is only in syndication that most programs will finally turn a profit for the network. The typical show loses money its first few years and, ironically, a highly successful show may never make money on its original run if the costs of keeping the stars on board rise enough. For example, the sitcom *Friends* was a costly show due to the high salaries earned by its six principal cast members.

When a show concept is purchased by a network, it initially commits to produce a pilot episode which it will eventually air to gauge audience reaction. Only about half of the pilot episodes will ever be accepted for regular broadcast. Accepting a show for regular broadcast typically means committing to a thirteen-episode run. If the initial season is successful, then additional runs will be produced. The commitment to produce the original thirteen episodes comes with a contract option on the part of the network for future renewals for a predetermined number of years, with a fixed fee increase each year for the rights to the show. The original fee increases are modest, usually in the range of 3–8 percent per year.

The original broadcast of a show is usually not profitable for the producers. Network fees do not typically cover all of the cost of producing a series, but rather, often cover only about 80 percent of the cost. Accounting practices also result in losses due to the way in which studio overhead expenses are budgeted. Thus, it is common for a hit show to lose money until it has stockpiled enough episodes to be sold into the lucrative syndication market where it can potentially earn returns for years to come.

Syndication rights are sold to stations with a geographic exclusivity clause, assuring that no competing station in the area will be airing the same show. Of course, the shows will be sold to other stations in other markets at the same time, allowing for a hugely profitable second-run (i.e., rerun) market. The syndicated episodes of a television show are broadcast during non-prime-time hours for affiliated stations and are restricted by syndication agreement with independent stations so that they cannot compete with original broadcasts of the same show. The most successful shows will be sold into syndication while they are still running new episodes in prime time. A classic show, like *I Love Lucy* or *Cheers*, will have a life well beyond the airing of its original episodes.

The appearance of cable networks like TV Land and Nickelodeon has given many old television shows a new venue for rebroadcast. A syndication agreement will generally give a station the right to rebroadcast each episode up to six times over three to five years. The shows may be rebroadcast at multiple times during the day, subject to the noncompetition clause. Typically, networks will air these shows during the late afternoon and early evening time period or after the evening news at the end of the prime-time schedule.

The proliferation of cable networks in the last two decades has spawned a new source of material for networks and their affiliates—the production of first-run syndicated shows. These include game shows, talk shows, tabloid news shows, and reality type shows that are cheap to produce and can thus be profitably aired without having to rely on a lengthy network run before they can become profitable. By their nature, there is not much demand for these shows in the second-run (rerun) syndication market. Many of these shows skip the networks altogether and debut directly on local affiliates or cable networks.

Long-running series can pose a challenge for the networks for many reasons. The challenge of coming up with fresh storylines for the series can be daunting, as can the financial demands. On the one hand, the cost of a long-running series decreases as the cost of fixed props and sets is amortized over a longer run, and the successful reputation of the show makes it easier to sell sponsor time at a higher cost. However, the success of a show often leads to greater salary demands for the stars. Some shows meet the demands. *Seinfeld*, for example, was paying its stars multimillion-dollar salaries by the time it ceased production. Other shows do not meet the demands of stars, leading to plot lines which remove characters from the show. While these episodes tend to be heavily watched, resulting in a ratings bonanza, they do come at the cost of losing popular characters from the show. Thus, a long-running show may see main characters come and go over the length of its runs, both to keep the story fresh and to keep it affordable. It is a delicate balancing act to keep a show together for a long time, especially if the stars are children, who age much more noticeably and change the very nature of the show as they do. In some long-running shows the characters will literally grow up with the television audience. Early hit shows such as *I Remember Mama* (1949–1957) and *Father Knows Best* (1954–1963), and later hits such as *The Waltons* (1972–1982), *The Brady Bunch* (1969–1974), and *The Cosby Show* (1984–1992), all featured television families whose children grew up on screen. Each of these series required plot changes and in some instances major character changes to remain viable over their long-running success.

Types of Programming

Television programming takes different forms. There are entertainment shows produced for television, like *Friends*, *NYPD Blue*, *Sesame Street*, and *Survivor*. There are news programs, which are essentially live broadcasts; there are live sports shows; and there are movies, both those produced directly for television and those produced originally for the theater. Besides the initial broadcast of each of these, there are the rebroadcasts, or reruns, of these shows. Reruns have value and compete with original broadcasts.

Programs are supplied in a format that maximizes the revenue from their broadcast. This is particularly true of movies originally released for the theater. The theater is the first place they are shown, because it is the venue in which they can return the greatest amount of revenue in the shortest amount of time. From the domestic theater, they move to foreign theater, home and then foreign video, cable television such as HBO or Cinemax, network television, a second cable run, most likely on a nonpremium channel, and then syndication for local stations. Each of these has a window of time for its appearance after initial release.

Competition is great among producers of television shows. They compete with one another to sell the programs they produce, as well as to attract the talent to make the programs. Producers only indirectly compete for a viewing audience. While they actually create the shows, not the audiences, the audience is attracted by the quality of the program. So the higher the quality of the show the producer creates, the greater the interest in it from competing networks who can then attract a greater audience and a better price for advertising.

Producers of television shows also compete with themselves due to the nature of the rerun market. Hit shows from the past, or even shows with marginal success, are rebroadcast as syndicated shows on local stations as well as specialized cable networks. For example, recent or current shows, especially sitcoms like *Frasier*, *Friends*, or *Will and Grace* air on local stations during off-network hours. Older shows, such as *Gilligan's Island* and *Cheers*, air on cable networks like TV Land and Nickelodeon.

A venue for a program is known as a window. For example, the first window that a motion picture usually plays in is the domestic movie theater. Multiple windows affect production. There are a number of shows, for example, that are released directly to a window lower on the chain. Television shows, of course, are released to cable or network television, not the theater, but they may now cross over to video as well. Some popular shows are released in packages on video. For example, the season series of *The Sopranos* or *Sex in the City* is available on video at the conclusion of the season. Videos of classic TV programs are also available. For example, *The Honeymooners* and *Star Trek* episodes can be found in video packages.

In 2001 the average cost of a one hour dramatic television program was $1 million, while a documentary cost half that much, and a "reality" show, such as *American Idol* or *Survivor*, could be produced for about $300,000 an hour. Of course, the most successful television series are much more expensive than the average ones.

The cost of distributing television shows is similar to distributing movies. Prints must be made and distributed or broadcast via satellite. In addition, residual payments are often owed to actors, directors, and producers of the show each time it is aired. However, in the old system, nothing was owed, or could be paid, to the network that originally purchased and financed the show. For foreign markets, dubbing or retitling into a different language had to take place. Before satellite technology began to dominate the market, multiple copies of films had to be made so that they could be sold to multiple stations. This price was held down by bicycling the shows, that is, trading different episodes among nearby stations.

The Financial Interest Rule

The biggest change in the network/production relationship and distribution practices came in the 1990s, when the government repealed its long-standing restriction prohibiting television networks from having an ownership stake in the syndication interests of any shows they broadcast and placed a limit on the number of hours of their own programming that they could produce for themselves. This rule opened the profitable syndication market to the networks as another source of income. The changes also led to the merger of studios and broadcast networks.

The Syndication Rule prohibited the networks from syndicating off-network shows. These rules restricted the ability of the networks to operate in the market and dampened their control of the prime-time television market. This benefited the studios and independent producers who could develop and produce television shows without fear of competition from well-heeled networks.

In 1995 the FCC repealed the ban and allowed networks to produce and own television programs. In part, this change was brought about by the change in industry structure. By 1995, three networks were owned by production studios that had long been producing television shows. The three were all fledgling networks, but Fox eventually gained status as the fourth major network. The other two were still in the infant stage as networks, but have long been major players in the production market: Warner Brothers (WB network) and United Paramount Network—a 50/50 partnership between Viacom and Paramount. WB and UPN merged in 2006.

Since 1995, networks have produced some of their own shows and been allowed to own those that they do not produce themselves. The result has been a change in the way series are funded. Now they can be sold outright to the networks, who can then sell them into syndication and share in this profitable market. On the other hand, they now bear the cost of unprofitable shows in the early stages of their television life. The network production of shows for their own use caught on quickly. In the first year, CBS was producing nearly 20 percent of its own prime-time schedule. This does not include news and sportscasts, which had always been produced and owned by the networks.

Each network spends in excess of $40 million a year buying pilots and developing scripts, and roughly a billion dollars each year for prime-time series that make it past the development stage. As mentioned, it is unusual for the network fees to cover the cost of production. The network hopes the show will last long enough to enter the lucrative syndication market so that a profit is earned. "Reality" shows are an exception. They can be profitable from the beginning, because they are not using professional actors. Consequently labor costs are much lower. On the other hand, however, there is no obvious syndication market for some of these shows since they are based on a surprise ending. For example, who will survive on *Survivor*, and which bride will be chosen by the dating reality shows?

Newscasts

The major networks have nightly national newscasts, and hundreds of local stations have local newscasts, sometimes up to three a night, plus a morning show. In addition, there are the "news magazine" shows, such as *20/20*, *60 Minutes*, and *Crossfire*.

The national newscasts are expensive propositions to put on and often lose money for a network. The most interesting aspect, however, may be their impact on what Americans perceive as important and newsworthy. Networks cover what they believe viewers will watch and hence what advertisers will sponsor. For this reason, they select only a few of the multitude of possible stories they can cover each day. They are even more selective about international coverage. Covering an international event requires sending crews and equipment to remote locations for uncertain lengths of time. This is expensive, and if the American audience isn't particularly interested in the news item, it can be a huge money loser. Gauging potential interest in a particular news story is a major task for the producers of the newscasts. It is why only a select number of international stories are covered: they don't always pay. Most conflicts and wars around the world are given little or no coverage by the American newscasts because it doesn't pay to cover them. While the newscasts don't necessarily try to tell viewers what to think about, they do reflect what they believe will interest the audience.

Television news is also affected by the availability of visual images. Since television is a visual medium, the newsworthiness of some items is a function of the pictures available. A protest with screaming, potentially violent mobs makes for much better television than does a shot of delegates arriving in cars to make important decisions behind closed doors. For this reason, war is a better ratings story than diplomacy. Shots of rumbling tanks and exploding missiles are much more dramatic than diplomats shaking hands.

This method of providing news—thirty-minute broadcasts to cover the world's events (and then only those with potential audience appeal)—is not an unbiased nor a representative view of the world. Yet it is the way many Americans stay informed. The focus on bad news is a function of the economic decision of what to cover. Only so many stories can be covered, the expense of covering them is great, and the ratings pay the bills. In addition there is the difficulty of providing both sides of a story, which is what responsible reporting is all about. Particularly in war situations, this is often impossible. The American government, for example, is not interested in a balanced report of a conflict involving American troops; therefore allowing access for reporters to the war zone is often accompanied by a restriction on the news available for reporting, news that is understandably biased toward the side providing the access.

Dedicated news coverage, such as CNN and Headline news, have increased the amount of news coverage available to viewers. But satellite and cable television have helped balance news coverage by providing access to a diverse range of news programs from around the world, such as the BBC (British Broadcasting Corporation).

THE ECONOMICS OF TV

As a science, television is complex. As a business enterprise it is rather straightforward; it is an advertising mechanism. Networks and local stations sell airtime to national and local advertisers and in return deliver viewers. Nielsen, the television ratings service, measures the number and demographic detail of the viewers. Arbitron also provided television ratings services until 1993, when they quit to concentrate solely on radio. While the average viewer may think this measurement takes place to determine which shows are most popular and should remain on the air, the real reason is to determine not just how many, but exactly who the viewers for each show are and how much the commercial airtime is worth for each show. Ultimately, television programming is little more than scheduled interruptions of advertising messages, rather than the other way around.

Ratings

The value to an advertiser of a particular television show is measured by Nielsen. The measure of the number of viewers a show attracts is called either a rating or a share. The former is the percentage of all households that own a television that are tuned in to a particular show. The latter is the percentage of all sets that are turned on and also tuned in to a particular show. For example, if there are a hundred television-set-owning households in a market, and ten of them are tuned in to the local news, then the local news has a rating of 10. If only twenty of the households have their TV sets turned on during the local news, and ten of them are watching it, the show has a share of 50. That is 10 percent of the televisions in the market are tuned in to the show, but 50 percent of the televisions in use are tuned in to the show.

The ratings services do not monitor every household, instead they attempt to randomly sample viewers by taking a selection of households that represent the total number of households. The average characteristics of a good random sample are similar to the average characteristics of the whole population, therefore reasonable predictions can be made about the behavior of the whole by studying the behavior of a subset. These conditions are not always met in television rating, and hence the validity of the ratings has often been called into question. Nevertheless, because we have no other system in place, the Nielsen ratings system is relied upon to paint a picture of television viewing in the United States.

The ratings are used to determine who is watching what show. This information is then used to determine advertising rates for shows. Indirectly, of course, it is also used to determine what shows will be produced and aired. Television, like the movies, is a great imitator. A successful formula will quickly be copied by competitors. Take the rash of "reality TV" shows that have sprung up since the success of *Survivor* a few years ago. New reality shows followed, such as *The Amazing Race, Big Brother*, and *American Idol*.

Television ratings are estimated four times per year, during the months of November, February, May, and July. These are known in the trade as "sweeps months." Viewers know them as the times of year when they are most likely to see new episodes of their favorite series, first-time showings of hit movies, and highly touted made-for-TV specials. The more highly rated a show, the higher priced will be its advertising rates. If a show is too poorly rated, it is likely to be canceled and replaced with something else. Stations are continually changing their lineups—whether it is new shows or old shows in different time slots—in order to maximize ratings, and hence advertising revenue. Keep in mind that it is not necessarily the largest ratings they are after, but in some cases the largest ratings for a certain demographic.

Advertisers

Ad rates are determined by the ratings. The terms used by advertisers are "reach," "frequency," and "gross ratings points." The reach of an ad is the percentage of households (or the target audience, e.g., teenagers or men 20–40 years old) exposed to an ad at least once over a predetermined time span. This is equivalent to a ratings point. The frequency is the number of times the ad is run over the time period in question, and a gross rating point is the reach times the frequency. For example, if Ford runs a national ad twice during the broadcast of an NFL football game on a Sunday afternoon, the frequency is two. If 100 million households are able to receive the broadcast and 10 million tune in, then the rating (or reach) is 10 and the gross rating point for the ad is 2 × 10, or 20.

The price for advertising on television shows is quoted in dollars per viewers per unit of time. The time blocks for advertising are most commonly thirty seconds, though fifteen- and sixty-second blocks can be purchased. The only reason to purchase these blocks is to sell a product or deliver a message. Television is only one of many ways that advertisers can deliver their messages. They can (and do) also rely on radio, print, and billboard advertising. In 2002, the leading source of advertising expenditures was television ($58 billion), followed closely by magazines and newspapers ($55 billion), with radio ($19 billion) and billboards ($5.3 billion) far behind.

The viewer that advertisers truly covet is the one who is willing to pay to receive their messages. These people reveal their preference for the product, and thus make the advertisers job much easier and increase the likelihood of a successful sale. Examples of such advertising includes ads in specialty magazines or dedicated topic shows or networks, such as the audience watching *ESPN Sports Center*. The same can be said for viewers of the Food TV Network, Nickelodeon Jr., Golf Channel, Eternal World Network, and MTV. All these stations deliver an audience that appeals to producers of certain goods, and all are specialty cable stations that must be purchased through subscription.

Super Bowl ads are usually the most expensive of the year, though other major events, such as the Olympics, can also command premium prices. Ad industry estimates put the cost of a single, 30-second spot at upwards of two million dollars for prime-time viewing during the first and second quarters of the Super Bowl.

There are three types of ads on television: national, regional, and local. National ads are usually purchased through advertising agencies, which represent several customers, designing, producing, and selling the ads. National spot ads, or regional ads, are national in scope, but target certain regions. Snow blowers, for example, are not going to be marketed in the South, but they are likely to be marketed across the entire North and upper Midwest from coast to coast. They are typically sold by specialized ad representatives who specialize in certain regions of the country. Local ads are marketed only in the immediate listening area of each station. The local stations sell their own ads, usually through representatives of the individual companies.

Prior to 1981, six minutes per hour was the maximum amount of time that could be used for commercials (seven minutes during movies, sporting events, and specials). These were voluntary limits observed in response to unofficial guidelines of the National Association of Broadcasters (NAB). After the adherence was found to violate antitrust laws, the number of minutes of commercial time sold has increased and varied. For the typical network program, ten minutes per hour are set aside for commercials during prime-time showings. Of this amount, two-and-a-half minutes are allocated to affiliates, normally one minute at the beginning and end of each hour, and thirty seconds in between. Thirty seconds are normally used each hour for station promos, teasers, identification, and program titles and credits. Other than prime time, sixteen minutes per hour are used for commercials, with affiliates retaining four to twelve minutes, depending on the show and time of day. On the weekends, the minimum for affiliates rises to seven minutes per hour.

Despite the rather scanty portion of commercial time, network offerings are still attractive to affiliates because they are profitable to air. The commercial time can be sold locally for higher prices, and the network pays the affiliates to carry its offerings. With no cost of production for the affiliates, network offerings can be very profitable.

The most profitable regular broadcast for networks is daytime television. Program costs are relatively low—on average $150,000 to produce a one hour soap opera and only about $50–75,000 to produce a game show or talk show. In addition, there are more minutes for commercials in nonprime-time. The typical one-hour soap opera generates $1 million per day in revenue. For local stations, local news accounts for 35–40 percent of the advertising base, thus it is the largest single source of revenue for most affiliates.

Costs

Costs are slightly more complicated and vary greatly between affiliated and independent stations. An affiliate station will spend most of its budget—about one-third—on general and administrative expenses, that is, basic overhead costs of running the station. Producing local programming and acquiring syndicated programming accounts for about 25 percent, engineering 11 percent, news production 13 percent, and sales 12 percent. An independent station will spend a far greater amount on producing and acquiring programming—up to half its total expenditures and about half as much on producing newscasts.

TELEVISION AND THE MOVIES

The movie and television industries are mutually dependant. The movie industry supplies much of the talent and facilities used to produce television shows, and television serves as an important ancillary market for the movie industry. Movies are shown on television as pay-per-view, pay cable, cable, and network broadcasts at various times in the lifecycle of a motion picture.

It was not always such a comfortable relationship, however. The movie industry originally saw television as a competitor that would drain viewers away from theaters. Indeed, the growth of the television industry was a major cause of the decrease in movie theater attendance from a high point of 4 billion in annual attendance in 1946 to 1 billion in the early 1960s.

Studios also exhibit their feature films on television after they have played in the more profitable domestic and foreign theater and pay TV windows. The peak of this activity for broadcast television was the 1970s, before the advent of pay cable networks like HBO and Cinemax. A typical arrangement was for a network to pay a studio an average of $20 million for the right to air a hit movie five times over a specified time period. Prices have actually dropped in real terms since then, because by the time a movie reaches one of the networks, it has pretty well saturated the market. The penetration of videocassette players (present in 85 percent of households in 1998 and 91 percent in 2002), DVD players, and pay cable (over one-third of households) into the American market has depressed the market for network broadcasts of feature films.

Although they do compete with one another for the leisure time of consumers and the advertising dollars of firms, they are also complementary in many ways. Studios lease their soundstages to television producers to make films. In some cases (e.g., Fox), they own television networks themselves. Motion pictures are also made directly for television or cable. Many stars successfully cross over from television to movie success and back again, as do writers, directors, and other off-screen talent. Of course, television also serves as a handy advertising medium for the movies.

CONCLUSION

Many studies have been done on television viewership. One of the most revealing was performed by Glick and Levy in 1962. They discovered that the quantity of television watched is not a function of the quality of the programming. People tend to turn on the TV and watch whatever is on. With hundreds of options now available through cable and satellite systems, this is likely more true now than it was in 1962, when the average household had access to three or four stations. Now with hundreds, it might take a viewer half an hour just to figure out that there is nothing on that appeals to them. Moreover, by the time half an hour is up, many shows have changed, so it will take another half hour to revisit the new possibilities.

Television competes with other leisure time activities for entertainment dollars, advertising dollars, and time. Because of the convenience of being located in the consumer's home, it enjoys the advantage of easy accessibility and monopolizes the time period during which movie theaters are closed, outdoor activities are restricted because of inclement weather, and consumers are tired, sick, or not in the mood to go out. In addition, the marginal cost of watching television is just equal to the opportunity cost of the time spent sitting in front of the TV. In some cases it is even less, since it is possible, and not uncommon, for people to multitask while the television is on. Reading, laundry, cooking, cleaning, and many other chores can be done simultaneously while watching television. The downfall of TV is that it does not provide an opportunity to get out of the house and break from the daily routine. For that reason it never displaced the movie theater as a source of motion pictures as the industry initially feared it would. In the future, television and the movies will both face a challenge from the personal computer. It remains to be seen how future generations will spend their limited leisure hours given the ever-growing number of possible diversions.

—7—

Spectator Sports and the Viewing American Public

INTRODUCTION

On November 6, 1999, 111,794 screaming fans jammed the Michigan Stadium to see the University of Michigan football team defeat the visiting Northwestern University football team. It was the largest crowd to attend a sporting event in the United States. Several million more football fans watched the game on television. As impressive as it was, the television audience did not even crack the top fifty all-time sports events for television audiences.

Sports are big business. From the payroll to the ticket sales, they bring in billions of dollars a year and entertain millions of fans, most of whom never make it to the stadium, but follow their favorite team on television, radio, newsprint, and more recently, over the Internet. Spectator sports are a popular form of entertainment that use several of the media discussed earlier in this book to deliver their product.

As the size of the Michigan crowd suggests, professional sports do not have a stranglehold on this financial largesse. Amateur sports are also big business in America, especially college sports. The most popular among them are the NCAA football and basketball programs. On a local level, high school sports are also popular.

The demand for spectator sports has grown tremendously. Since 1920 Americans have increased their expenditures on spectator sports by a factor of nearly 400. The demand has been especially dramatic in the last quarter century. From 1920, when the census bureau first began tracking spending on spectator sports, until 1930, spending doubled from $30 to $65 million. Despite a decade of depression, spending increased another $30 million by 1940, and then doubled to just over $200 million by 1950. It took two more decades to double again. Throughout the 1970s and 1980s spending increased by a factor of nearly ten, and then doubled once more from $5 billion to more than $11 billion during the 1990s.

As impressive as this growth is, when put in perspective, it is not quite so spectacular. Americans spent nearly 10 percent of their income, approximately $500 billion, on recreation in the year 2000. Of this amount, less than 2 percent was on spectator sports. While Americans spent more on spectator sports than the movies or theater, they spent nearly twice as much on their flower gardens, three times as much on books, and $7 on radios and televisions for every one they spent on spectator sports.

For the purposes of this chapter, most of the focus will be on those spectator sports that are run purely as a business: professional sports. We will touch on big time collegiate sports, because they are, after all, spectator sports. In fact, almost 40 million people attended college football games alone in 1999, twice as many as attended NFL games.

ORIGIN OF SPORTS

The origin of most sports is shrouded in the uncertain mists of history. Anthropologists know that the Olympic Games date back to at least 776 BC, representing the oldest known form of organized sport. The only major sport with a known date of origin is basketball, invented by Dr. James Naismith in the fall of 1891 in Springfield, Massachusetts.

In general, all sports followed a similar pattern in their development. They began as childhood games, evolved first into accepted leisure time activities for adults, and then industries employing professional athletes. At each juncture, their role and acceptance in society expanded across age groups and income classes. Sports today are enjoyed on two levels: as a participatory activity and as a spectator sport, competing with many other forms of entertainment for leisure expenditures.

The acceptance of sports by adults has its roots in two distinct classes: the wealthy and the working class. The wealthy began participating in sports as a means of leisure activity. Among the earliest known sports in which this occurred are tennis, lawn bowling, and golf. As a spectator activity, the wealthy also were drawn to sports early on. Horse racing, on which wagers could be placed, is an early example of a spectator sport. Boxing matches and wrestling, pitting humans, instead of animals, against one another were additional forms of early spectator sports which gained popularity among the upper classes. These latter sports were derivations of gladiator matches contested in the ancient Roman Empire.

The working class was also drawn to sport, in some cases for the wagering excitement, in others for the ability to participate in a form of leisurely physical activity. These workers would gather to play their games, often representing town, company, or church teams. The pride of winning the contest was sometimes represented by a trophy or cash prize put up by the participants. As the stakes grew, so did the degree to which teams were willing to go to win the contests. The evolution of professional team sports has its roots in these early town contests.

The first professional athletes were individuals hired by teams bent on gaining an advantage in the match with a rival. The use of an individual or two eventually led to whole teams being paid to perform. As the best players were gathered together the level of play was elevated. Once the athletes began to earn a salary, the teams needed a method of recouping the costs of these salaries, and charging admission became a permanent fixture on the sports landscape. The willingness to pay to watch sports is closely related to the higher quality of play exhibited by the professional athletes.

The rise of spectator sports as an important form of entertainment begins in the twentieth century. Like other forms of entertainment discussed earlier, the rapid rise in the twentieth century is closely related to the increase in living standards and income and the decrease in the average length of the workweek. Unlike those other forms of entertainment, spectator sports did not rely as much on changes of technology for its development. That is not to say that they had no impact, however. Television, for example, while not changing the basic concept of spectator sports, would dramatically change the way most spectators consumed sports, and the vast amount of money produced by television would change the structure of organized sports leagues. The automobile also had an important impact on sports, in particular on the construction and location of stadiums. As travelers to the ballpark changed from mass transit to private car, the need for parking, and hence the impracticality of inner city locations for ballparks moved them to the suburbs. Changing perceptions of the role of sports teams to a city have subsequently moved those stadiums back into the center city in the modern era of "retro" ballpark construction. A different set of circumstances and feelings now exists. Municipalities have come to believe that sports teams are an important and desired element in their economy, so they have used their powers of eminent domain, bond-issuing capacity, and taxation policy to secure sufficient land for stadiums and parking in the inner city and construct grand new cathedrals dedicated to sports. This is usually done in the name of urban renewal and economic development, despite the lack of evidence that the latter occurs and that the former is done efficiently.

EARLY PROFESSIONAL SPORTS

While professional sports, and spectator sports in general, flourished in the twentieth century, they originated earlier than that. As mentioned, the roots of professional team sports are the town and company competitions of the nineteenth century. The first professional team sport to formally organize was baseball. The first all professional team, the Cincinnati Red Stockings, was founded in 1869. The first professional league, the National League, was formed in 1876. Professional hockey, basketball, and football did not debut for another half century, but those sports were already being played in front of cheering spectators in the nineteenth century. The first college football game, pitting Rutgers against Princeton, took place in November of 1869. It hardly resembled the game today, with Rutgers winning 6-4, but it is forever marked as the birth of one of the most popular sports in America.

Boxing is an example of an individual sport that attracted professionals at an early stage. Early boxing matches in America were popular as a means of wagering. These matches often pitted slaves against each other, with hefty wagers on the outcome. Because of its brutality it was eventually outlawed and its popularity among spectators decreased when allegations of match fixing cropped up.

Boxing regained its popularity in the late nineteenth century. John L. Sullivan is credited with saving the sport and boosting its global popularity. Sullivan became the first individual athlete to tour and exhibit his skills. English cricket teams pioneered the athletic team tour, but Sullivan became the first individual to do so. His tour was significant for many other reasons as well. While the concept of touring was popularized by vaudeville acts and politicians, Sullivan toured longer and covered a greater distance than anyone before. He blazed the endorsement trail for modern-day athletes as well, signing endorsement deals and making personal appearances as well as opening a popular saloon that banked on his name.

The first professional organization of team sports in America was the formation of a professional baseball league in 1876. Ultimately it served as the model for all professional sports league in the United States. The league underwent some structural changes, including competition from competing leagues, until adopting its current format in 1901, the American League and the National League joined under the structure of Major League Baseball. The game itself has changed little, and the business format has basically remained unchanged as well. As with all professional sports leagues, the league cooperates on the field by offering teams to compete against one another, and it cooperates off the field in its attempt to maximize revenues. Recently there has been an increase in off-field competition among teams in labor and advertising markets, to the protest of some team owners, but it has not hurt the overall financial stability or performance of the leagues, which have mushroomed into a multibillion dollar industry, thanks to the largesse of television.

AMATEUR VS. PROFESSIONAL

Tension between amateur and professional athletes has been a recurring problem in sports. In individual sports, such as golf and tennis, the distinction between amateur and professional was sometimes not clear. The Olympic Games are the most famous example of amateur athletics, and they were the last major sporting event to openly allow professional athletes to participate. It was the nineteenth-century British aristocracy, not the ancient Greeks, who invented the concept of athletic amateurism. The aristocracy was interested in promoting amateur status for athletes as a means of preventing the rougher, lower class participants from competing in the same games.

The struggle between amateur and professional athletes has its origins in the nineteenth century, when the presence of professional athletes began to emerge. In some sports it ended quickly and gave way to professionals at the highest levels. This was most apparent in team sports, where professional leagues were formed featuring entire rosters of paid players, while amateur leagues, separate in organization and competitors, survived on a lesser, more often local scale. The difference quickly became one of business. Professional athletes were hired as performers by entrepreneurs who sought to earn money by providing spectator sports as a form of entertainment.

Amateur sports, on the other hand, followed two different paths. On the one hand they served primarily as a vehicle for participation with no focus on selling tickets and turning a profit. Ticket sales, if they existed, were primarily aimed at covering costs. Some amateur athletic contests, however, are big business. The Olympics, until they ratified the participation of professionals in 1981, are the most obvious example of amateur athletics becoming big business. Big-time college athletics are another example.

Unlike other sports, the Olympics have no permanent home—they change venues every two years, alternating between winter and summer games. The preparation necessary to host the Olympic Games is so large that the site is chosen several years in advance. A city hosting the games must provide venues for all the events, adequate housing for the athletes, media, and hordes of spectators, and establish an infrastructure capable of handling millions of tourists.

The perceived benefits of hosting the games are high enough to warrant such expenditures. In fact, hosting the games is in such demand that cities compete against one another for the privilege. Sometimes the competition gets out of hand, as it did when Salt Lake City was chosen to host the Winter Games in 2002. Several Olympic officials were found guilty of accepting bribes in return for their vote for Salt Lake City in the competition leading to the awarding of the games.

The potential financial benefits to hosting the Olympics come primarily from the tourism generated by the games. These funds seldom cover the costs of attracting them. Additional funds are needed to justify the expenditures, and these sources, while acknowledged, are harder to measure, thus it is not clear whether hosting the Olympic Games is a financial benefit to a city.

The gains beyond tourist dollars can be seen in the example of Atlanta, which hosted the summer games in 1996. The city gained a brand new state-of-the-art baseball stadium, now occupied by the Atlanta Braves, new dormitories for Georgia State University (the Olympic village), an improved public image, and improvements in the local transportation network—none of which would have been likely had they not hosted the Olympics. The dollar value of some of these things is difficult if not impossible to measure.

In the early days of tennis and golf, professionals were distinct from amateurs in that they earned their living from the game. Their primary source of income was as a club pro—teaching golf lessons and managing a golf course, since few professional tournaments existed. It was not until 1968 that professionals were first allowed to play in the major tennis tournaments. Wimbledon was the first major tournament to invite professionals to compete against amateurs. The other major tournaments immediately followed suit, and the positive market reaction to the higher caliber of play soon led to a series of tournaments for professionals. In golf, the professional tournaments came earlier, though the prize money was not significant enough to allow for more than a few of the best players to earn a living as a touring professional.

Television played a major role in promoting golf and tennis tournaments around the world, paying sponsorship fees which increased the size of the purse, thus attracting more and better players. The sale of sponsorships for individual tournaments, such as The Chrysler Classic, the Sony Open, and the Buick Invitational further increased the cash prizes, increasing the level of play and fan interest, leading to further increases in sponsorship and television money in an upward spiral that continues into the twenty-first century. The concept has spread. In college football, for example, the season-ending bowl games are almost all sold to sponsors. What used to be the Orange Bowl, Sugar Bowl, and Cotton Bowl are now the Fedex Orange Bowl, Nokia Sugar Bowl, and AT&T Cotton Bowl. The money paid by the sponsors, when combined with the television rights fees and ticket sales has made the major bowl games at the end of the season multimillion dollar paydays for the teams which share in the revenues.

Athletes become professional when it is the best way for them to earn a living. This requires that they be talented enough to be able to convince someone to pay to see them perform, and that the supply of similarly talented athletes is small enough so that they can command a wage high enough to cover their opportunity cost. That is, a high enough salary to make it worthwhile to pursue a career in athletics instead of advertising or construction, for example.

The higher the demand for athletics by spectators and the smaller the supply of talented athletes, the higher the wages they can earn. Of course, it isn't quite that simple. For the first three quarters of the twentieth century the demand for spectator sports grew, generating billions of dollars in revenue. Only a small percentage of this went to the athletes though, for two reasons. First, professional leagues were successful monopolists and monopsonists, thus they successfully held down wages. Second, some very financially successful leagues did, and still do, use only amateur athletes.

The NCAA is an example of the latter case. College athletics are lucrative sources of revenue, particularly men's basketball and football, with no labor costs for the actual performers (athletes). In some cases, the athletes are reimbursed in kind with a free college education. For the best among them, these college sports serve as a training ground for professional sports. For most college athletes however, playing sports is a way for them to finance their education. They perform for the fans, whose ticket purchases cover the cost of their education— and then some.

While the potential for revenue was a major factor in leading to the professionalization of sports, it would be wrong to view it as a necessary chain of events. NCAA football, with its 100+ division IA schools, is a much larger organization than the NFL. In 1998 the NFL played before approximately 20 million fans and earned $2 billion in television revenue. That same year the NCAA entertained almost 40 million fans but took in a mere $214 million from its several television contracts.

The largest sports stadiums in the country are not home to professional teams, but college football teams. The largest professional stadium, The Meadowlands, home to the NFL's New York Jets and

Giants, holds 80,000 spectators. That is not large enough to crack the top 20 largest college football stadiums. Four state universities (Michigan, Penn State, Tennessee, and Ohio State) have football stadiums with capacities of over 100,000.

From a consumer's point of view, is there really any difference between professional and amateur? There is certainly a perceived difference on the part of the producers, or there would not be professional athletes. Theory suggests consumers will pay the highest prices for the highest quality products. In the case of spectator sports, that is the best performers, or the best athletes. While it is not true that simply paying an athlete will make him or her better, it does stand to reason that money will attract the best athletes. Professional athletics are more likely to attract the best athletes because they pay them the best salaries. Athletes who are paid to do nothing but play and practice their sports to perfection are much more likely to perform at a higher level than someone who is participating in the sport as an unpaid amateur. In that case, they are less likely to have the desire, drive, or ability to put in the same amount of time and effort and thus get the same level of output. For example, if an athlete is a professional, he or she can devote the off-season for the sport to training. If an athlete is not a professional, then he or she must use that time to earn a living instead. In addition, opportunity cost is an issue. If an athlete can earn a better living as an accountant, for example, she is less likely to pursue athletics. Professional athletes are paid, so they can be compensated for any opportunity cost. In fact, professional athletes in America are paid quite handsomely. The minimum wage for a professional MLB player, for example, is nearly ten times what the average American earns. The average wage of an athlete, which is well over $2 million per year, dwarfs the average wage to an even greater extent.

COMMERCIAL SUCCESS OF SPORTS

Sports that have succeeded commercially are recognized as businesses in the entertainment industry. The supply of spectator sports has grown to match the demand. In the twentieth-century football, men's and women's basketball, soccer, men's and women's tennis, hockey, indoor (arena) football, men's and women's golf, and even for a short period, track spawned professional leagues and organizations, joining baseball, boxing, and horse racing as professional sports.

As spectator sports increased in popularity, complementary markets evolved. Brewers were early ancillary participants in sporting matches, providing liquid refreshments for patrons. Sports trading cards (originally packaged in tobacco), souvenir sales, and specialty magazine and even television networks (e.g., ESPN and FoxSports) are other examples.

Sometimes an ancillary group benefits so much from sports that they create a league as a marketing vehicle for their own product. In 1946 a group of American arena owners, seeking tenants, formed a professional basketball league, the BAA, to compete with the existing National Basketball League (NBL). The two leagues competed to sign the best players, driving up salaries and decreasing profits until they ultimately merged, forming the NBA in 1949.

Municipally funded sports stadiums are an example of the commercialization of sports and the perceived economic benefits to a city of hosting big-time sports. Most professional sports stadiums in the United States have been constructed primarily with public monies. The usual argument is that the teams provide economic benefits to the community as a whole, therefore it should be up to the community to provide the stadium, which, as teams argue, they themselves cannot afford to provide. Communities build these stadiums because they do not want to lose the team to another city. The professional sports leagues have closely controlled monopoly power of their leagues. Like any good monopolist, they restrict the supply of their product. Besides maximizing profits in the traditional sense, this also assures that there are more cities who could serve as potential hosts of a professional team than there are teams in the league. That way pressure can be exerted on municipalities for financial gains. Stadium construction is a perfect example. The cost of construction is borne by the city, but the revenues from the stadium are typically controlled by the team. The city gets the benefit of having the team in town, including the dubious economic benefits, while the team gets the additional revenue associated with a new stadium, including the sale of luxury boxes, advertising, and stadium naming rights. In addition, the team does not have to tie up $300–500 million in capital to build a stadium.

Research suggests that there are few if any tangible economic benefits to a city of hosting a professional team. Most of the benefits accrue to the owners and players. Most of the money that is spent on a professional team leaves a local community, so it provides no benefits to the city. For example, players often do not live in the city where they play, so they take their considerable salaries—which amount to as much as 70 percent of total revenues— to their hometown with them. The owners, who are multimillionaires, and may live in town, usually have their income invested in worldwide financial markets, so most of the revenue they take out of the team is sent elsewhere. Finally, the revenues used to purchase the souvenirs and the food sold at the stadium only stay locally if they are actually produced locally.

Most of the spending at sports venues is local spending anyway. The majority of the fans attending a game are from the area, so the spending they do at the game has no greater impact on the local community than if the team was not there. For example, if the team was not in town, then those entertainment dollars would have been spent elsewhere, at the local bowling alley or movie theater, for example. The money spent at the restaurants and bars would have been spent there anyway by the local citizens. Perhaps it would have been spent at a different bar or restaurant, in a different part of town, instead of across the street from the stadium, but that does not affect the overall economy.

The only funds that actually add to the local economy are those spent by tourists who come in from different communities and spend their money at the stadium and in local establishments. The only new economic impact on the community comes from tourist spending on things like restaurants, hotels, and shops. This is a fraction of the total amount spent because of the team, since most of the spending is by locals. In addition, not all of the tourist spending is due to the team. Some of the tourist spending at a stadium is done by tourists who are in town for another reason, and would have spent their money elsewhere if the team was not in town. A business traveler who takes in a game the night after closing a deal would likely have gone to a restaurant or theater instead if the team was not there, and spent the same funds elsewhere.

The final possible economic impact of a stadium is in the area of employment. Sports teams employ hundreds of workers. However, except for the players, almost all of the workers are part-time seasonal employees paid an hourly wage. Sports teams hire only a few full-time employees in their management level executive positions, such as marketing, ticket sales, and management. The vast majority of the employees are ticket takers, vendors, and ushers who work only when the team is in town. At best, this is about 80–90 days per year for baseball. On the low end, it is 10–12 days per year for a pro-football team. During the off season these workers are unemployed, and either must find other jobs or collect unemployment benefits, which is a drain on the local economy.

The economic impact of a team on a city is little if anything. As mentioned, most of the revenues either leave the city or are local funds anyway. In addition, even if they were all new funds brought in from outside the city, and they all stayed locally, the magnitude of professional sports revenue is trivial as a percentage of total economic activity in a city, representing just over one-tenth of 1 percent of total GDP. As an employer, professional sports have an only slightly greater impact. In 2000 there were 200,000 professional athletes, umpires, coaches, and related employees in the United States, representing just 0.15 percent of the workforce, about one-third the number of hairdressers and one-tenth the number of grade school teachers.

SPORTS AND THE MEDIA

A symbiotic relationship has evolved between sports and the media. As newspapers proliferated in the nineteen century, sports matches were reported more frequently. The reporting of sports events was a way to attract the lower classes to reading papers. In post-bellum America increasing literacy and leisure time brought the American public to newsprint as never before.

Games in progress were broadcast by telegraph to saloons as early as the 1890s. In 1897 the first sale of broadcast rights took place. Each team in the National League of Professional Baseball Teams received $300 in free telegrams as part of a leaguewide contract to transmit game play by play accounts over the telegraph wire. In 1913 Western Union paid each MLB team $17,000 per year over five years for the rights to broadcast the games. The movie industry purchased the rights to film and show the highlights of the 1910 World Series for $500. In 1911 the owners managed to increase that rights fee to $3,500.

Television has had an enormous impact on sports in the last half of the twentieth century. The financial success of sports is due to its exposure on television. The most successful sports leagues, such as the NFL, MLB, and the NCAA, generate more money from television rights fees than they do from live attendance. Golf and tennis owe their large purses to the growth of television fees in the last two decades. The less successful professional team sports, such as hockey and basketball, have improved their status greatly with television packages, but are still not on the same par as the aforementioned sports.

Sports dominate the All-Time Top-Rated TV Programs in America, and NFL Football dominates television sports with 22 Super Bowls and the 1981 NFC Championship Game making the list of the top fifty most popular broadcasts. Super Bowl broadcasts hold four of the top ten and ten of the top twenty spots. Sports include five of the top ten, with the women's figure skating finals at the 1994 Winter Olympics included with the Super Bowls.

Television has not always had a positive impact on sports. While it created a vast audience for sports in the 1950s, it drastically reduced attendance in small towns for minor league ball clubs and local boxing clubs, leading to their dissolution. By 1959 TV did not need boxing anymore. The medium had grown up and moved on to other forms of entertainment and cut back on boxing telecasts. By this time, however, overexposure had seriously damaged the sport. The arrival of Muhammad Ali, then known as Cassius Clay, on the scene in the early 1960s gave a much-needed boost to a sport that had lost its allure. He resurrected boxing in the twentieth century much as John L. Sullivan had in the previous century.

The National Football League began its Monday Night Football broadcasts in 1970. This meant that the NFL was broadcast on all three national networks, risking the same overexposure that killed boxing. The league was willing to undertake this risk for rights fees totaling more than $150 million over three years. Today those same revenues are worth more than $2 billion each year. Television rights fees have since become the primary source of revenue, displacing live attendance.

It is hard to imagine that sports teams once saw the media as a threat to the value of their franchises. But originally, they resisted putting their games on the radio for fear that customers would stay home and listen to the game for free rather than come to the park. They soon discovered that radio (and eventually television) was a source of income and free advertising, helping to attract even more fans as well as serving as an additional source of revenue.

Eventually teams realized the broadcasting of their games was free publicity, and charged little or nothing for the rights. The Chicago Cubs was the first team to regularly broadcast its home games, giving them away to local radio in 1925. It would be another fourteen years, however, before every team began regular radio broadcasts of their games. In 1946 the New York Yankees became the first team with a local television contract when they sold the rights to their games for $75,000. By the end of the century they sold those same rights for $52 million per season. The NFL pioneered the national television contract in the 1960s. What was unique about this contract was that it shared all the revenues equally among teams despite market size and number of games broadcast for each team. This contract forbad teams from negotiating local television contracts on their own.

As the importance of local media contracts grew for professional baseball teams, so did the problems associated with them. As cable and pay-per-view television became more popular, teams found them attractive sources of revenue. A fledgling cable channel could make its reputation by carrying the local ball team. In a large enough market, this could result in substantial payments to the local team. These local contracts did not pay all teams, only the home team. The problem from MLB's point of view was not the income, but the variance in that income. That variance has increased over time, and is the primary source of the gap in payrolls, which is linked to the gap in quality, which is cited as the "competitive balance problem." The argument suggests that the wealthiest teams will buy the best players and win most of the games. In 1962 the MLB average for local media income was $640,000 ranging from a low of $300,000 (Washington) to a high of $1.2 million (New York Yankees). In 2000, the average team garnered $19 million from local radio and television contracts, but the gap between the bottom and top had widened to a whopping $51.5 million. The Montreal Expos received $536,000 for their local broadcast rights while the New York Yankees received more than $52 million for theirs. A form of revenue sharing has resulted in a redistribution of some of these funds from the wealthiest to the poorest teams, but the impact of this on the competitive balance problem remains to be seen.

This is a problem unique to MLB because the other leagues all have "socialized" television contracts, allowing the league to act as sole negotiator for all TV contracts, which are then shared equally among teams. This is not the case any longer for the NCAA, which was successfully sued by a subset of big-time NCAA football programs in 1984. Teams and conferences are free to negotiate their own television packages. This, along with the explosion of the number of cable channels, has greatly increased the number of games broadcast. It has not caused competitive balance problems because none of the proceeds may be used to entice players to college teams, as all are amateurs.

Athletic endorsements grew in size and stature as television exposure increased the visibility of athletes. In some cases, they earn more from endorsements than from their sport. In 1990, fourteen-year-old Jennifer Capriati received $5 million in endorsement contracts before playing her first professional match. Golfer Tiger Woods took endorsements to a whole new level when he signed deals with Nike and American Express upon turning professional in 1996. The endorsements were multiyear hundred-million-dollar deals; eclipsing any amount of money he is likely to earn actually playing golf over his lifetime.

Sponsorships are another source of revenue for sports, dating back to 1887, when the French magazine Velocipede sponsored the first automobile sporting event. Kodak was a sponsor at the first modern Olympic Games in 1896. The most recent role of sponsors has been in the purchase of the naming rights for public arenas and stadiums.

SPORTS AND RACE IN AMERICA

Unfortunately, sports shares the same checkered past as the rest of the country in race relations. African Americans were either explicitly or quietly discriminated against in professional sports. Usually this took the form of prohibiting them from employment in the industry, not so much as refusing them entrance as spectators. As a result, separate leagues evolved for whites and blacks. This was most obvious in baseball, as it was the first of the major team sports to organize. It was less of an issue in other sports, which did not gain the same popularity until after civil rights had progressed further.

Separate professional leagues for African Americans existed, since they were excluded from participating in MLB until 1947 when Jackie Robinson broke the color barrier. The first was formed in 1920, and the last survived until 1960, though their future was doomed by the integration of MLB.

There was a silver lining in this cloud, and that was the opportunity created for African Americans to own, manage, and promote their own teams. In the Negro Leagues several teams were created, mostly owned by African Americans, and some quite financially successful. While the segregation of black baseball players from the white leagues cost the players in terms of potential salary, it did provide earning opportunities for other African Americans that would not have been possible otherwise.

The segregation was nearly complete. While no black players were allowed in MLB, there were also no black executives, managers, or front office workers. There were some black hourly employees, such as ushers and vendors, and a minority of the fans at MLB games were black.

In the Negro Leagues, all the players were black, and the vast majority of the employees were also black. Some teams had white executives, and a minority of the fans were white. Otherwise, baseball existed in a parallel universe divided by race.

The other professional sports were not as bad, primarily because they did not start out as early as baseball. The allure of the big dollar is evidenced by the fact that once MLB integrated, the Negro Leagues began an inexorable slide into oblivion. The best players were attracted to MLB, as were, ultimately, the best executives—though it took much longer for professional sports to integrate the front office.

WOMEN IN SPORTS

The role of women in sports has grown over time. Although there were female competitors in the Olympics as early as 1900, the IOC did not regard their presence as official until 1912, when women's swimming events were sanctioned. Until 1960 women were prohibited from running distances in excess of 200 meters.

Arguably the greatest impact on women's sports came in the person of Babe Didrickson Zaharias, the first female superstar athlete. She excelled at everything she did, from collegiate track star to 1932 Olympic champion to professional golfer. Shortly after her Olympic triumphs she hit the touring circuit, displaying her incredible athletic talents to admiring audiences across the country, promoting the idea that women could also be athletes. She eventually turned to golf and was responsible for the creation and early survival of the Ladies Professional Golf Association (LPGA).

Team sports have not had as much success for women. Professional women's baseball and basketball leagues have started and failed, beginning with the All American Girls Professional Baseball League during the Second World War, to the recent collapse of one of two competing professional basketball leagues. The second survives on subsidies from the NBA.

Women have enjoyed their greatest financial success in individual sports, such as tennis, golf, and figure skating. The 1994 Women's Olympic Figure skating finals is the only sport other than football to crack the top fifty television shows in America. Women's professional tennis got a boost in 1973 when Bobby Riggs challenged Billie Jean King to a match and lost. The gimmick attracted a huge television audience and captured a new audience for women's tennis. It began to appear regularly on TV and prize money increased as did sponsorships for players.

Recognition has not led to financial equality, however. As the purses grew, so did the disparity between prizes for men and women. Gladys Heldman, founder of World Tennis magazine, led the revolt of women who split away from mixed tournaments and started their own tour in 1970, originally sponsored by Virginia Slims. The women's tours in both golf and tennis still pay significantly less than their male counterparts.

On the collegiate level some movement was made in rectifying the imbalance with the passage of Title IX, a federal requirement that colleges equalize the playing field between male and female athletes. Title IX is complicated, but basically requires equal opportunity and financing for male and female athletes. This has been controversial, as many schools addressed the issue not by expanding women's sports, but by eliminating men's sports. They claimed they could not afford to add more sports, especially since the majority of them, including all women's sports, are not revenue positive. They lose money, so only a limited number can be afforded. The tremendous revenues generated by men's basketball and football cannot cover the losses of an infinite number of sports.

THE STRUCTURE OF SPORTS LEAGUES

Big time sports leagues have all evolved in a monopoly framework, seeking to control the competition, the consumer base, and the labor pool, to varying degrees of success. In team sports, the owners formed cartels. Organizers of individual sports, like tennis and golf attempted to control the tournaments, while boxing was monopolized in the 1940s by the mob, which controlled the television rights and the heavyweight championship fights. Without fail, the most financially successful sports leagues have been cartels that grew and thrived on the back of exploited labor and monopolized geographic areas for teams. In the United States, competing leagues arose to cash in on the monopoly profits in football, hockey, basketball, and baseball, and in every case they were either bankrupted or merged into the established league. As a result, despite a century of monopoly profits, each of these sports still enjoys monopoly status.

The market structure of team sports in general can be understood by using professional baseball as an example. MLB is a highly successful oligopoly of professional baseball teams. The teams have successfully protected themselves against competition from other leagues for more than 125 years. The closest call came when two rival leagues merged in 1903 to form the structure that exists to this day. The league lost some of its power in 1976 when it lost its monopsonistic control over the player labor market, but it retains its monopolistic hold on the number and location of franchises. Now the franchise owners must share a greater percentage of their revenue with the hired help, whereas prior to 1976 they controlled how much of the revenue to divert to the players.

The owners of professional baseball teams have acted in unison since the very beginning. They conspired to hold down the salaries of players with a secret reserve agreement in 1878. This created a monopsony whereby a player could only bargain with the team that originally signed him. This stranglehold on the labor market would last a century.

The baseball labor market is one of extremes. Baseball players began their labor history as amateurs. The skills of the best of them quickly became highly demanded. For some, this translated into a career. Ultimately, all players became victims of a well-organized and obstinate cartel. Players lost their ability to bargain and offer their services competitively for a century. Despite several attempts to organize and a few attempts to create additional demand for their services from outside sources, they failed to win the right to sell their labor to employers in a competitive market until 1976.

The location and number of franchises has been a tightly controlled issue for teams since leagues were first organized. Though franchise movements were not rare in the early days of the league, they have always been under the control of the league, not the individual franchise owners. An owner is accepted into the league, but may not change the location of his or her franchise without the approval of the other members of the league. In addition, moving the location of a franchise within the vicinity of another franchise requires the permission of the affected franchise. As a result, MLB franchises have been very stable over time in regard to location. The size of the league has also been stable. From the merger of the AL and NL in 1903 until 1961, the league retained the same sixteen teams. Since that time, expansion has occurred fairly regularly, increasing to its present size of 30 teams with the latest round of expansion in 1998.

The first attack on the organizational structure of the major leagues to reach the U.S. Supreme Court occurred when the shunned owner of the Baltimore club of the Federal League, a failed competitor to MLB in 1914 and 1915, sued major league baseball for violation of antitrust law. *Federal Baseball Club of Baltimore v. the National League* eventually reached the Supreme Court, where in 1922 the famous decision that baseball was not interstate commerce, and therefore was exempt from antitrust laws was rendered. Baseball alone enjoys this exemption, but the basic league structure is the same for all team sports.

Off the field, teams have cooperated for many years in their efforts to control the market for their sport in order to maximize profits. These efforts have taken place in two primary ways: monopolization of the franchises and monopsonization of the labor markets. The franchises have established local monopolies to minimize competition among themselves. At the same time, all professional sports leagues originally used a form of labor contract that restricted the ability of workers to move to other teams and thus held down their wages. This combination of restrictions allowed teams to maximize their profits by increasing ticket revenue and lowering player salaries (the largest source of expenses for a professional sports team) beyond the levels that would be possible in competitive markets.

Monopoly control of franchises is the backbone of any sports league. Sports leagues serve to control schedules and maintain the quality of play on the field. But even more importantly, they serve to maximize profits for the teams. This is done in a number of ways, beginning with attempts to corner the market on playing talent, desirable markets, and television income. Leagues do this by signing the best available players, and then tying up the next tier of talent at minor league levels. This prepares them for the major leagues as well as keeps them away from potential competitor leagues.

Leagues also attempt to control the best markets. They locate teams in the largest markets in an effort to make it more difficult for a competitor to start up. At the same time, leagues limit the number of franchises to less than the market will bear. This insures that they can exploit monopoly profits by limiting the output of their product. This is most obvious in the use of relocation of franchises as a threat to get stadiums built and season tickets sold.

These attempts have not always resulted in the absence of competition. In all major team sports the lure of monopoly level profits caused competing leagues to form. In every case, however, the leagues either failed or were eventually merged into the existing leagues. Baseball has done the best job of maintaining its monopoly. The NL and AL merged in 1901, held off the competing Federal League in 1914–1915, and have not been challenged since. In the other three major team sports competition has been more recent. The NFL merged with the AFL in 1967, and together they held off competing leagues on two occasions. Both professional hockey and basketball have similar stories of merging with competing leagues in the last thirty years.

Beginning in the mid-1970s, teams lost the ability to suppress player wages, but because of the original Supreme Court ruling baseball still has the right to artificially restrict the location of teams, preserving the local monopoly each team has on their home market. Restrictions on television broadcasts also restrict the ability of teams to broadcast their games into other team's television markets.

The other major team sports do not have this unusual antitrust immunity, and the result has been obvious. There have been many more franchise relocations, as owners of teams seek the best markets in which to sell their product. From 1970 through the end of the century, one MLB team moved (the Washington Senators became the Texas Rangers in 1972). In that same period of time twenty-two teams in the other three leagues moved. During that time, however, expansion was taking place. MLB added six teams, while the other leagues added a total of thirty-seven franchises.

Despite all of the attention sports receive from the media, it is really a rather trivial portion of the economy. The media attention it receives is grossly disproportionate to its economic importance.

The current status of sports is decried by many as having become too commercialized. However, sports have been commercial enterprises since the nineteenth century. The only real change is the reporting of the financial dealings. As players gained the right to negotiate with competitors, their salaries increased dramatically and financial stories about sports began to creep into the news along with the reporting of the games on the field.

FRANCHISE VALUES

Sports has been about profits since the first admission fee was charged. The first professional league, the National Association of Professional Baseball Clubs, founded in 1871, charged a $10 franchise fee. The latest teams to join MLB paid $130 million apiece for the privilege in 1998.

The value of franchises has mushroomed over time. In the early part of the twentieth century, owning a sports franchise was a career choice for a wealthy sportsman. In some instances, it was a natural choice for someone with a financial interest in a related business, such as a brewery, that provided complementary goods. More commonly, the operation of a sports team was a full time occupation of the owner, who was usually an individual, occasionally a partnership, but never a corporation. In 1915 the New York Yankees were sold for $460,000. Today, Forbes magazine estimates the value of the team at about $1 billion.

This model of ownership has since changed. The typical owner of a professional sports team is now either a conglomerate, such as Disney, AOL Time Warner, the Chicago Tribune Company, or a wealthy individual who owns a (sometimes) related business, and operates the team on the side—perhaps as a hobby, or as a complementary business. This transition began to occur when the tax benefits of owning a team became significant enough that they were worth more to a wealthy conglomerate than a family owner. A team that can show a negative bottom line while delivering a positive cash flow can provide significant tax benefits by offsetting income from another business. Another advantage of corporate ownership is the ability to cross-market products. For example, the Tribune Company owns the Chicago Cubs, and is able to use the team as part of its television programming. Disney exploited its ownership of professional sports teams to market movies such as *Angels in the Outfield* and *The Mighty Ducks*. If it is more profitable for the company to show income on the corporate ledger than the sports team ledger, then it decreases the payment made to the team for broadcast rights, or licensing fees, for example. If a team owner does not have another source of income, then the ability to show a loss on a baseball team does not provide a tax break, decreasing the potential value of the team to the individual.

The most significant change in the value of franchises has occurred in the last decade as a function of new stadium construction. The construction of a new stadium creates additional sources of revenue for a team owner, which impacts the value of the franchise. It is the increase in the value of franchises which is the most profitable part of ownership. Sixty-nine new stadiums were constructed between 1991 and 1999 for the 114 top tier professional sports teams located in the United States, with several more in various stages of planning. The average franchise value for the teams in those stadiums increased 20 percent the year the new stadium opened.

The value of professional sports franchises has increased much faster than the rate of inflation, the stock market, or any other financial investment this century. When the fledgling NFL expanded by five franchises in 1925, the New York Giants joined the league for $500. Forbes magazine recently estimated the value of the team at $800 million, barely cracking the top twenty most valuable NFL franchises. The Washington Redskins, with an estimated value of $1.2 billion are the most valuable.

LABOR MARKETS

Labor markets for players have evolved similarly across leagues and national boundaries. In all team sports, the original labor pool was exploited because the league, as a cartel, was a monopsonistic employer. The standard player contract in professional sports leagues had a form of reserve clause, which the teams and leagues instituted under the guise that it was required to keep teams balanced, games competitive, and the league viable. In the name of preservation, the team owners exercised tight control over athletes, exploiting their labor for monopoly profits. Players were signed to contracts which bound them to the signing team indefinitely. The team had the right to renew the player's contract each year, restricting the player's ability to bargain, thus depressing wages.

Players began to level the playing field in the 1970s through a series of legal victories and the growing strength of their unions. The rapid increase in the strength of player unions has evolved such that the Major League Baseball Players Association is considered one of the strongest labor unions in the world. Other employee gains that improved the lot of players included the method by which they were signed to their first professional contracts. In North American team sports, teams were assigned exclusive rights to bargain with newly eligible players. In football and basketball, players were prohibited from the league until they had completed their college eligibility. This created tension for those talented athletes who were not academically inclined. The relaxation of this restriction was won by players in the courts. Now the most talented athletes leave their college teams early, or in some cases are signed after graduating from high school, to pursue a career as a professional athlete.

In all leagues, players eventually won the right to bargain freely with other teams, commonly referred to as "free agency," thus dramatically increasing their wages. Through a series of strikes, players have won the right to bargain with competing teams for contract terms, substantial pension increases, and a host of lesser concessions. The result has been a dramatic increase in the salaries earned by professional athletes. In 1900 the average MLB player earned about five times the average American salary. By the end of the century that multiple had increased to nearly 100.

To date, no original league has failed. The popularity of the sport, the quality of competition at the highest level, the vast amounts of television and sponsorship dollars, and the monopoly status of leagues have generated revenues sufficient to guarantee large paychecks for athletes and profits for owners. The last quarter century in American sports, however, has been marred by labor unrest between athletes and owners. This fighting has centered around the method of splitting the revenues, and has led to work stoppages in all four major team sports.

The first independent organization of professional athletes, the Major League Baseball Players Association, was formed in 1954. It remained in the background, however, until the players hired Marvin Miller in 1966 to head the organization. Hiring Miller, a former negotiator for the U.S. steel workers, turned out to be a stroke of genius. Miller began with a series of small gains for players, including increases in the minimum salary, pension contributions by owners, and limits to the maximum salary reduction owners could impose. The first test of the big item—the reserve clause—reached the Supreme Court in 1972.

FREE AGENCY

Curt Flood, a star player for the St. Louis Cardinals, had been traded to the Philadelphia Phillies in 1970. Flood did not want to move from St. Louis, and informed both teams and the commissioner's office that he did not intend to leave. He would play out his contract in St. Louis. Commissioner Bowie Kuhn ruled that Flood had no right to act in this way, and ordered him to play for Philadelphia, or not play at all. Flood chose the latter, and sued MLB for violation of antitrust laws. The case reached the Supreme Court in 1972, and the court sided with MLB in *Flood v. Kuhn*. The court acknowledged that the 1922 ruling that MLB was exempt from antitrust law was an anomaly and should be overturned, but it refused to overturn the decision itself, arguing instead that if Congress wanted to rectify this anomaly, they should do so. Therefore the court stood pat, and the owners felt the case was settled permanently: the reserve clause had withstood legal challenge. They could not, however, have been more badly mistaken. While the reserve clause never has been overturned in a court of law, it would soon be drastically altered at the bargaining table, and ultimately lead to a revolution in the way talent is dispersed and revenues are shared in the professional sports industry.

Curt Flood lost the legal battle, but the players ultimately won the war, and are no longer restrained by the reserve clause. In a series of labor market victories buoyed by player strikes beginning in the wake of the Flood decision in 1972 and continuing through the rest of the century, players won the right to free agency, individual contract negotiations with agent representation, hearing committees for disciplinary actions, reductions in maximum salary cuts, increases in travel money, and improved travel conditions. Of course the biggest victory was free agency. These rights spread from baseball to other professional team sports. The current generation of professional athletes is among the highest paid workers in the world.

The right to bargain with other teams for their services changed the landscape of the industry dramatically. No longer were players shackled to one team forever, subject to the whims of the owner for their salary and status. Now they were free to bargain with any team. The impact on salaries was incredible. The average salary skyrocketed from $45,000 in 1975 to more than $2 million by the end of the century. Not all of that increase is due to free agency. Revenues increased during this period due to the dramatic increase in television revenue caused by Americans' insatiable appetite for sports. The result is a much larger revenue pie to divide, with the players getting a larger piece of that pie.

Player contracts have changed dramatically since free agency. Players used to be subject to whatever salary the owner offered. The only recourse for a player was to hold out for a better salary. This strategy seldom worked, because the owner had great influence on the media, and usually was able to turn the public against the player, adding another source of pressure on the player to sign for the terms offered by the team. The pressure of no payday—a payday that, while less than the player's value to the team, still exceeded his opportunity cost by a fair amount, was sufficient to minimize the length of most holdouts. The owner influenced the media because the sports reporters were actually paid by the teams in cash or in kind, traveled with them, and enjoyed a relatively luxurious lifestyle for their chosen occupation. This lifestyle could be halted by edict of the team at any time. The team controlled media passes and access and therefore had nearly total control of who covered the team. It was a comfortable lifestyle for a reporter, and spreading owner propaganda on occasion was seldom seen as an unacceptable price to pay.

The major labor issue in the game has shifted from player exploitation, the cry until free agency was granted, to competitive imbalance. Today, critics of the salary structure point to its impact on the competitive balance of the league as a way of criticizing the rising payrolls. Many fans of the game openly pine for a return of "the good old days," when players played for the love of the game. It should be recognized however, that the game has always been a business. All that has changed has been the amount of money at stake and how it is divided among the employers and their employees.

THE DEMAND FOR SPORTS

Americans love their sports. Despite the large amount of media attention, the passion fans display when rooting for the home team, and the importance our society seems to place on sports, the demand for them is still at its base described by the basic laws of supply and demand. The primary determinants of the demand for spectator sports are the same as the primary determinants for any good or service: income, the number of buyers, product quality (usually measured as team winning percentage), and the price and quality of related goods (in this case other entertainment options).

The impact of income and population on the demand for sports is straightforward. Higher incomes allow consumers to purchase more goods. A larger population means a greater potential audience from which to entice customers to the ballpark. It is no surprise therefore that teams located in larger and wealthier metropolitan areas will usually draw larger crowds at the ballpark as well as on television.

Fans like to see their teams succeed, though evidence also suggests that if they succeed too much for too long, interest may be lost. The bottom line, as with any entertainment venue, is that fans like to be entertained. They want to see the best performance possible for the dollar they spend. When they are no longer entertained by the sporting event, they will take their money elsewhere and find a better entertainment deal. In this regard, sports are no different than any other type of entertainment. Teams with losing records tend to draw fewer fans than winning teams—both at the gate and on television. Some teams with perpetually poor records are still able to draw large crowds. The Chicago Cubs baseball team is one example. They are often referred to as the "lovable losers" of the baseball world, yet they consistently fill their ballpark and draw ratings-friendly numbers of viewers to their telecasts. Other losing teams may draw well because of a factor known as the "superstar" effect. In this case fans may turn out or tune in not so much to see the team as to see a particular player on the team, who has risen to the status of "superstar" and is a demand in and of him or herself.

Since spectator sports are in the entertainment industry and are consumed for entertainment purposes, the demand for them is also subject to the quality and price of substitutes. Other spectator sports are an obvious example of a substitute, and large cities may have several professional and college sports for the sports fan to choose among. While sports seasons do not run at the same time, there is overlap between all of the seasons so that there is some head-to-head sports competition for every spectator sport.

It is not just sports that are competitors, however. All forms of entertainment must be considered as potential substitutes for spectator sports. Though they may not be perfect substitutes, they must be considered nonetheless. The greater the number of potential substitutes, the higher their quality, and the lower their price, the more difficult it will be for a sports team to draw an audience.

A live sporting event, like a movie or a stage show, is consumed at the same time as the last stage of production. It is like an airline seat or a hotel room, in that it is a highly perishable good that cannot be inventoried. Once the game is played, unsold tickets cannot be saved and sold at a later date, unlike unsold cars or cans of soup. If the weather is questionable (for outdoor sports) or the timing of the game is bad (the same day as the school Christmas pageant, for example) then the tickets cannot be transferred to another game. Once the game is over, unsold tickets are worthless and represent unrealized potential income to the owners. This situation is ripe for an economic principle known as price discrimination. Price discrimination is the practice of selling the same good to different buyers for different prices. The airline industry practices this routinely. Passengers seated next to one another on a plane may be paying different prices for their tickets depending on when they bought them, what day they are returning, and whether they were willing to waive the ticket exchange fee. Since the earliest days of paid attendance, teams have discriminated based on seat location, sex, and age of the patron. Only recently have sports teams begun to exploit the full potential of price discrimination by varying ticket prices according to the expected quality, date, and time of the game.

Sports have a grip on the American public that is far greater than their economic importance. They are entertaining, the athletes are well paid, and the franchises are quite valuable, but in the end, it is all about entertainment. Sports will continue to be a financial success only as long as it is entertaining. When it ceases to be, then consumers will find entertainment elsewhere.

—8—

A Century of Change and a Springboard to the Future

THE HISTORY OF ENTERTAINMENT: A BRIEF REVIEW

Americans have been entertaining themselves since the Colonists first arrived in the seventeenth century. Before the twentieth century, most of this entertainment was provided in the home. It frequently took the form of games, story-telling, reading, and music making. There were forms of mass entertainment, but they were not very common and tended to be consumed primarily by the upper class. Lower wages, longer work hours, less sophisticated technology, and a predominantly rural population were all contributing factors to the relatively primitive status of the entertainment industry. Until 1920 most Americans lived in rural areas, which meant that venues for mass entertainment were scarce. What little time was available for leisure was likely to be spent at home rather than used to travel to an entertainment venue.

If one wanted to go out to be entertained, the theater was the most likely destination. The choices included ballet, opera, symphony concerts, plays, or vaudeville—all of which might fall under the umbrella title of "stage shows." Although ballet, opera, and symphony are considered to be more refined and "higher class," vaudeville, as essentially a live variety show, was at the other end of the scale. Opera, symphony, ballet, and plays (often referred to as "the legitimate stage," as opposed to vaudeville) were mostly consumed by a small percentage of households. They existed primarily in larger cities, tended to cost more to attend, and, as a result, attracted a disproportionate percentage of their audience from upper income Americans. Vaudeville alone was among the staged shows that were readily accessible to a wide range of Americans. Vaudeville theaters could be found in cities of virtually any size and were attended by a wide cross section of the American public.

Vaudeville served the same purpose that movies would later assume: true mass entertainment. While the movie industry specialized in telling a single story in a ninety-minute time-span, vaudeville was a variety show. This pattern of entertainment was repeated by early radio and then television pioneers who transferred the old vaudeville variety shows to television. *The Milton Berle Show*, one of the pioneers of early television, was just such an example of a variety of acts pulled together for an hour or two of entertainment.

Variety shows still exist, but in a different format—the Internet. While vaudeville is dead and television thrives on reality shows, sitcoms, and dramas, the Internet is perhaps the ultimate example of the variety show. With the click of a mouse, one can move from sports to music to whatever else might be desired. The improvements in computer technology over the past decade have made video and audio streaming commonplace, making the computer a sophisticated and powerful entertainment medium.

TECHNOLOGY AND ENTERTAINMENT

The entertainment industry grew and matured during the twentieth century largely on the back of technological innovation. Even though the movie, radio, television, and computer industries did not even exist at the beginning of the century, all were common parts of our daily life by the end of it. At the beginning of the twenty-first century, nearly two-thirds of American adults attend the movies each year, and more than eight in ten households have a VCR or DVD player. More than 98 percent of households have at least one television, three quarters of which subscribe to cable or satellite. Over 99 percent of American households have at least one radio, and two-thirds of American homes have computers, over 90 percent of which have Internet access.

While it is not the only factor contributing to the growth of the entertainment industry, technology has been the most obvious one. The printing press brought print to the world and to the door of anyone who could afford books. Initially, this was only the wealthy. Newspapers and magazines became low-cost means of reaching the masses, and ultimately brought the world to the door of the average American. These changes took place over centuries. The technological changes discussed in this book took only decades.

Vaudeville, the movies, and sports brought the masses out to gather for their entertainment. Radios and television moved them back into their living rooms. The rise of the Internet and the pervasiveness of the computer is now driving Americans even further inside themselves. Technology has decreased the cost and increased the ease of being entertained. Growing wireless Internet technology leaves us with the possibility that we will all soon be able to be entertained, informed, and educated nonstop from anywhere at anytime.

While the twentieth century saw tremendous growth in the television and movie industries, as we move into the twenty-first century, the newspaper and popular magazine industries are withering. There are only three quarters as many daily newspapers in circulation in the United States today as there were in 1900, and less than half of all American households even subscribe to a daily newspaper. Magazines have proliferated in specialty guise, but the popular press magazines subscribed to by large percentages of the population, which contributed a common base of information, have largely disappeared. And, of course, vaudeville has disappeared entirely. The wave of the entertainment future appears to be the Internet and the computer, a concept which was unimaginable a mere generation ago.

Increasing wealth and innovations in technology led Americans to pursue a variety of different means of entertainment. Still, there are only twenty-four hours in a day, so inevitably one new means of leisure time pursuit came at the expense of another. Radio and phonographs substituted for live music performances, talking films replaced silent films, and television encroached on the movies. Vaudeville could not compete with the movies and Broadway suffered with the rise of movie musicals in the 1930s. The automobile led to an increase in "going out" for entertainment, which in itself did not help the radio and phonograph industry. It was, however, a boon for places like taverns ("speakeasies" during Prohibition), ballparks, and miniature golf courses. Americans were very much into entertaining themselves, but they were not necessarily wedded to one thing. They were willing to try new means of entertainment, or perhaps they became quickly bored with old ones.

Technology has blurred the distinction between entertainment media and caused upheavals in the industry along the way. Movie and television are good examples. The latter is an extension of the technology which created the former. When television first debuted, it was viewed as the eventual successor to the movie theater. Although it came after the movie industry, it is now difficult to tell the difference between the two industries. They share studio space and producers. Actors and directors frequently cross from one medium to the other in an industry that is composed of a shrinking number of companies which produce both television shows and movies. With the growing availability of cable movie channels, on-demand viewing capabilities, and the improvements in television reception promised by high-definition television and large flat-screen televisions, the difference between watching a movie in a movie theater and at home is rapidly diminishing. It may be hard to imagine, but it was only a generation ago that a movie even appeared on television, and then only after it had been out of theaters for several years. Now that same movie may appear on television just a few weeks after closing in theaters.

The same story can be told about the relationships that have developed between radio, television, recorded music, and the movies. Indeed, at one time each of these industries saw one or more of the others as a potential threat to its existence, and instead they have grown to be close complements to one another.

Spectator sports, while initially wary of the growth of radio and television, learned to embrace them and evolve along with them. While technology is not necessary for the production of a sporting event, nor is it needed for the event to be consumed, the two are closely allied. Over time, spectator sports learned not to fear these other forms of entertainment but to exploit them, although it is not really clear whether it is sports which exploits television or vice versa.

THE SPEED OF CHANGE

From its first radio station, licensed to broadcast in 1920 in Pittsburgh, the radio industry exploded across America. A decade later, there were over 600 radio stations, and by the conclusion of WWII, there were nearly 3,000. Not including the burgeoning satellite radio stations, there were more than 10,000 stations by the end of the twentieth century, and radios went from being in less than half of American households in 1930 to more than 99 percent in 2000.

For as quickly as radios exploded into the American home, the arrival of televisions was even more impressive. In 1950, only 8 percent of American homes had a television set. Within a decade, 79 percent had one. Today less than 2 percent of American families do not own at least one television set. In fact, television is such a standard part of the American household that 85 percent of homes have VCRs, three-quarters subscribe to cable, and nearly one-third have DVD players. The number of cable and satellite channels has grown nearly 300 percent in the last decade to 235, not including pay-per-view channels. The number of television broadcast stations has grown from the first one licensed in 1939 in New York City to over 100 a decade later and more than 1,600 today, to say nothing of the vast number of cable and public broadcast stations available.

Not only has technology revolutionized the quality of the entertainment industry, it has led to substantial price decreases as well. Television sets, radios, and music players are all cheaper in actual dollar prices today than when they debuted, and when adjusted for inflation, the price differences are even more dramatic. In addition, the quality has made quantum leaps. Nobody would argue that the first record players can compete with today's iPod or even a run-of-the-mill CD/radio player in terms of quality. And certainly the radios of the 1920s and televisions of the 1950s are no match for today's scts. But what is not as commonly known is how much cheaper these vastly superior pieces of equipment are now than they were originally.

THE COST OF LEISURE

The first Edison phonographs sold in 1880 for upward of $150. Today a portable CD/radio player is widely available for $50. It is a much better piece of equipment that reproduces music of a much higher quality and with infinitely more varieties to choose from. And consider that the $50 cost today is equivalent to about three hours of labor for the average American. In 1880, that phonograph would have taken the average American about ten weeks to earn enough to pay for it.

A standard table-top radio sold for $99 in 1927. Today a portable radio that also plays CDs and cassette tapes can easily be found for under $50. Consider that in 1929 the $99 radio represented 6 percent of the average household annual income. Today, the $50 radio, besides being far superior in quality, represents a fraction of a percent of that same average income. Adjusted for inflation, $99 in 1930 would buy an iPod and a portable satellite radio with a lifetime subscription today.

The price of a television set has dropped even more dramatically than radios. In 1950, an 8-inch black-and-white-screen television with twelve-channel capability (and no remote control!) sold for $190. By the end of the century, a 19-inch color set with remote control and the capacity to receive an unlimited number of satellite or cable-delivered channels regularly sold for $140 and could often be found cheaper than that on sale. And keep in mind that those prices are not adjusted for inflation. When inflation is accounted for, that $190 set in 1950 would cost over $1,300 today—the price of a decent 32-inch, flat screen, high-definition LCD television set.

Ticket prices have remained fairly steady when adjusted for inflation. The fifty cent movie tickets of the 1940s would be the inflation-adjusted equivalent of $6 today, and the standard $1 ticket in the early 1950s would cost just over $10 today. The technical quality of movies today is much higher, though film historians may debate whether the quality of the stories has improved. Color, 70-mm film, special effects, surround sound, and tiered seating have all improved the technical quality of movies, even though the stories may have stagnated.

A theater ticket at the Palace in 1900 was $1.50 for the best seat. As a share of the average wage, that is the equivalent of $150 today, which is not much different than the price of a floor seat at a Broadway show.

A major league baseball game today can cost as little as $5 for a bleacher seat, up to $50 for a reserved field-level box seat, and even more for luxury seating options. In 1910, bleacher seats sold for 25–75 cents, depending on the ballpark, and reserved grandstand seats for about $1.50. That is the equivalent of $4 to $12 for a bleacher seat and about $30 for the reserved grandstand today.

In 2000, the average American household spent almost $6,000 per year on entertainment and recreation—most of it ($1,133) on video and audio products. They spent $83 for movie tickets, $111 on spectator sports, and a little more than $600 each on reading materials, about evenly split between books, magazines, and newspapers. In 1930, the first year for which such data are available, the average household spent $133 on recreation and entertainment ($1,374 adjusted for inflation). Most of it ($31.70) was spent on radios, records, and musical instrument repairs. The second biggest source of entertainment expenditures was movie tickets at $24.48. Spending on theater tickets and spectator sports was at $3.18 and $2.17 respectively. The biggest change in entertainment expenditures over that time period was in the category of gambling, which increased by a factor of more than 200, from less than 25 cents per household in 1930 to just under $50 in 2000.

Overall, American households spent four times more real dollars in 2000 on their entertainment than they did on the cusp of the Great Depression. During that time, real spending in all categories except movies increased. When adjusted for inflation, spending on movie tickets actually decreased by two thirds, from $252 to $84.

WHAT TO EXPECT IN THE FUTURE OF ENTERTAINMENT

Today, technology has redefined all entertainment venues. The computer has altered the way we view movies and listen to music and how we read books, newspapers, and magazines. It has changed how we follow our favorite sports team and will continue to impact the entertainment industry into the future. Will one of the current forms of entertainment become the twenty-first-century vaudeville? How will technology affect what we have now and what might evolve? In particular, how will the copyright and file-sharing problems of today be answered and dealt with? None of these questions has an obvious solution as the twenty-first century begins.

Technology has the potential to turn the television and movie industries on their heads. The ability to record programs and watch them without commercials later on has already sparked debate on the role of viewer ratings and what they mean. Should a show recorded and viewed later be counted by the ratings services? Advertisers are reluctant to use such figures because of the ability of viewers to skip their commercials. With the dawning of super-sized, flat screen, high-definition plasma television screens, and surround sound, the experience of the movie theater can be brought into the home. The popularity of in-home movie systems has further blurred the distinction. This raises questions about the release strategy of movies. How long, if at all, should they play exclusively in a theater? Industry experts believe that the day when major motion picture releases are available on pay-per-view television at the same time as they are on the big screen is in the not too distant future. At the conclusion of the twentieth century, the technology existed to make this possible, but the infrastructure did not. Only one-third of households had access to pay-per-view offerings.

So what does the future hold for the entertainment industry? If we look back at the past century, technology has been the defining characteristic of its evolution. There does not seem to be any reason to think that will change. The advances in the first half of the twentieth century, which saw the electrification of the country and the dawning of recorded sound, movies, radio, and television, were dramatic. But the quantum leap in technology during the past quarter century has been at least as impressive thanks to the personal computer. Technology has transformed the television, record player, and radio, which each once held a conspicuous place in the living room, into a handheld phone, which can also be used to play games, surf the Internet, and even watch movies and television programs.

Television sets used to be the size of ovens, with a screen 8 inches on the diagonal. Today they are available with a 54-inch LCD flat screen. The future holds further improvements for television in the form of better quality, as the FCC has set 2008 as the target date for the transition to high-definition television broadcasts. Early television was restricted to a handful of channels. The eventual arrival of cable and satellite television has increased the number of potential channels into the hundreds. Early television was broadcast in black and white, now television shows are in color and available on computers and cell phones, not just a television set.

The movies and television have metamorphosed from substitute to complementary industries. Mergers at the corporate level have turned television and movie studios into the same companies. Satellite technology has changed the landscape of the material shown on televisions and heard on radios. Since satellite transmissions are not broadcast into the public airwaves, but only to paying subscribers, they are not subject to the regulations of the FCC. This has led to a proliferation of material which would never be allowed over the public airwaves.

The technical quality of entertainment, if not the quality of the product itself, has increased along with the quantity of it consumed. The decadent salaries paid to top entertainers insure that the best and most talented will continue to be attracted to the entertainment industry. Technology has improved the quality of the presentations as well. Today's digital movies are superior to the old silent reels and even cinemascope seems primitive. Today's television offerings are being broadcast in high definition and on flat-screen plasma televisions with screens measured in feet, not inches. Satellite radio has made static and fading signals a thing of the past, and the CD has turned the record into a relic. Now the iPod and computer threaten to eliminate the physical existence of recorded sound altogether, replacing it with digitally stored music in quantities too vast to number.

With almost every household owning a television, radio, and CD player, there is not much to be gained in the way of further market penetration. In terms of the other trends: shorter workweeks, urbanization, and increased incomes, there seem to be limits.

The length of the average workweek fell from 59 hours in 1900 to 38.1 hours on the eve of WWII. Since then, the length has held steady, even increasing slightly to 39.6 hours per week by the end of the century. It does not appear that the trend is toward fewer work hours. That means if there is to be increased time for leisure, it will have to come from savings in time spent on household chores. There is certainly room to maneuver here, as technological advances could continue to allow for reductions in work time spent on these domestic tasks. If technology does not help to reduce the amount of time spent on household chores, changes in other areas may. One that already has for many middle and upper income Americans is hired help. Rising incomes have allowed them to hire others to perform those chores. House cleaners, personal shoppers, yard workers, child care, and personal chefs have all played a part in reducing the amount of time spent on household jobs, thus freeing up leisure time, at least for those who can afford it.

The percentage of the population living in urban areas is already at 79 percent, having nearly doubled since 1900, although most of that increase came in the first half of the twentieth century. By 1950, the total was up to 64 percent, and by 1970, it was over 73 percent. There is less land in America left to urbanize, and the rate of doing so has slowed dramatically.

Since 1960, the share of household expenditures on housing, transportation, food, and clothing have all decreased. Spending on recreation, on the other hand, has increased by 50 percent. Only spending on medical care has outpaced it. Adjusted for inflation, expenditures on recreation and entertainment have increased from $80 million in 1950 to $585 million in 2000, growing by $200 million in the last decade alone. The biggest source of that increase has been expenditures on computer software and games, which have increased by nearly 300 percent since 1990 to just under $50 million.

Increased income and education may lead to a greater diversification of the entertainment industry. As more people can afford to try more varieties of entertainment, the future holds the possibility of an even broader industry with more choices.

By the end of the twentieth century, Americans had fully endorsed the concept of entertainment and recreation. The census breaks down the adult population (age 20 and over) by sex, income, and education level and also by their participation in various leisure activities. Out of a population of 205 million, fully 60 percent attended the movies in 1999 and 35 percent attended at least one sporting event. Watching movies was the most popular form of entertainment for adults, with participatory entertainment in the form of exercise a close second at 55 percent, and playing a sport at 30 percent. As a matter of reference, 29 percent of the adult population reported doing some sort of charity work, and 47 percent reported that they spent part of their leisure time gardening. The results vary somewhat by demographic group. For example, 60 percent of adult males attended the movies while 61 percent of adult females attended the same. By income level, the attendance varied from a low of 39 percent for those earning under $10,000 to 79 percent for those earning over $75,000.

What does the future hold? The past would suggest we should expect more sophisticated forms of entertainment, more time to enjoy it, and a greater number of people being entertained. It is likely that entertainment will continue to be defined by technology, particularly the personal computer, as it finds its way into more American homes and continues to improve in quality. In the end, watching the evolution of the industry in itself should be entertaining. Only time will tell.

—9—

Personalities Who Changed the American Entertainment Landscape

BENJAMIN FRANKLIN KEITH

Benjamin Franklin Keith was known as the father of vaudeville, though he never performed on its stage. Keith assembled the most impressive string of theaters and monopolized the booking of that talent, establishing a near total control over the industry before his death in 1914.

Keith staged his first variety show in a Boston storefront in 1883. It was a financial success. Soon his variety shows became a regular, rotating offering. Each week a different group of acts, all catering to families, was offered. This humble beginning grew into an empire consisting of thousands of theaters, featuring the most famous performers, which dominated the east coast. A parallel network evolved in the west. This duopoly persisted during Keith's lifetime. The two networks eventually merged after his death to create a nationwide monopoly of first-class theaters.

In 1885 Keith took on Edward F. Albee as a partner. Together they built up the premier theater chain in the nation, monopolizing the best theaters in the biggest cities in the east. They also monopolized the acts that appeared on the stage through the United Booking Office, an offshoot of the Association of Vaudeville Managers of the United States, which Keith had formed in 1900 to enhance cooperation and reduce harmful competition among theater owners.

Keith was a business tyrant and he ruled the industry with an iron fist. Since all the best acts booked through the UBO, any theater owner earning Keith's wrath could find himself out of talent. Most of

Keith's influence was east of Chicago. From there west, the Orpheum circuit was in control.

The Orpheum circuit was controlled by Martin Beck. Beck had designs on making inroads into the eastern market, so in 1912 he bought a site in Manhattan and began building what would become the premier theater in all of vaudeville—the Palace. Keith was furious, and in a classic backroom deal, was able to acquire a controlling interest in the property. Thus the Palace became known as Keith's Palace, the crown jewel of the Keith-Albee circuit.

Keith did not settle for simply keeping Beck out of New York. He used him as an example of what happened to men who crossed him. He took over a first-class theater in Chicago, establishing a foothold in what had been Orpheum circuit territory and eventually drove Beck out of town.

Keith made his mark in vaudeville by establishing the continuous performance, a form of variety entertainment that began around noon and played continually until late at night, with the same acts playing several times during the day. Once he established himself in the business he moved away from it and instead focused on the two-a-day format that became the trademark of his high-class theaters.

Keith also made a name for himself by providing a wholesome atmosphere in his theaters. While others before him pioneered the concept of family-friendly acts, it was Keith who brought decorum to the audience. Prior to his efforts, the audience at a vaudeville show was often raucous and offensive. Keith took the stage on numerous occasions to personally persuade the audience to change their behavior, and it worked. Attendance was bolstered after he received the support of church groups who lauded his high standards in the audience and his staunch refusal to allow questionable material on the stage. Thus, vaudeville emerged as family entertainment, suitable for ladies and children.

Keith attributed his virtues to his churchgoing country boyhood and billed his cleanup of the stage as a public service. It may well have been a public service, but it was also true that the clean reputation kept the moral reformers at bay and attracted family audiences. His self-censorship ultimately meant bigger audiences and bigger profits.

Audience decorum was one thing, but Keith's real goal was the economic reorganization of the industry which ultimately gave him wealth and power. During his tenure as "czar" of vaudeville, Keith battled other theater chains and booking agents, fighting challengers with blacklists and buyouts. He also took on the actors union and brought it to its knees.

Together Keith and Albee created a centrally run, scientifically managed industry that would forever alter the field of American leisure consumption. At the time of his death, the Keith-Albee empire was considered by many in the industry to be the greatest consolidation of money and power in the entertainment world.

Born in Hillsboro Bridge, New Hampshire, on January 26, 1846, as one of eight children, Benjamin was sent away by his destitute parents at age 7 to work on a relative's farm. He stayed on the farm until age 18, attending the local schoolhouse and showing no real inclination toward the theater. His interest in entertainment was kindled by a traveling circus that came through town when he was a young man. Nonetheless, Keith did not set foot in a theater until the age of 21.

When he left the farm he moved to New York City and got a job with a dime museum, a low-budget sideshow form of entertainment. He moved on to work as a candy butcher in the circus, where he eventually met up with Albee. On at least three occasions he tried to start his own traveling variety show, but in each case went broke.

Keith died of heart failure in 1915, and was succeeded by his son, A. Paul Keith, who died of influenza just three years later. Albee assumed control of the empire in 1918 and continued to dominate the vaudeville industry.

LILLIAN RUSSELL

Lillian Russell, one of America's first entertainer celebrities, was actually buried with full military honors when she died in 1922. She had spent the last decade heavily immersed in politics, and immediately prior to her death, she had completed a fact-finding mission in Europe for President Warren Harding, who approved the military funeral. While politics consumed the latter part of her life, it was the stage that made her famous.

Born Helen Louise Leonard on December 4, 1861, in Clinton, Iowa, Russell grew up in Chicago and moved with her mother to New York in 1879 to pursue her musical studies more seriously. While performing in the chorus of a New York production of Gilbert and Sullivan's operetta *H.M.S. Pinafore*, she caught the attention of Tony Pastor, an early vaudeville pioneer. She assumed the stage name Lillian Russell, and began performing in Pastor's theater that year.

Russell was a sensation. Her singing voice was praised almost as much as her beauty. It was a full month before her mother knew she was performing in Pastor's theater, but once she became convinced that Pastor produced clean, family-friendly shows, she joined the audience and gave her approval to Russell's new found career.

Russell became a celebrity, and her every move was reported by the press. While this did wonders for her career, it also resulted in some scandal, not the least of which was caused by her four marriages or her rumored affair with flamboyant businessman "Diamond Jim" Brady, in whose company she was often seen from the time she arrived in New York until her death in 1922.

Brady showered Russell with gifts of diamonds and jewelry. Among the most ostentatious mementos he gave to her was a gold-colored bicycle that Russell could often be seen riding up Fifth Avenue while wearing her trademark shoulder-length white gloves.

For the next three decades Russell remained one of the foremost singers in the United States, starring frequently in operettas and on vaudeville. She performed with a variety of touring companies, including one that she headed. In 1888 she was earning upward of $20,000 a year headlining for the Casino Theater in New York. It was at the Casino that she performed her most famous role, Gabrielle Dalmont in *An American Beauty*, a title which became her soubriquet. At the turn of the twentieth century she was able to command over $3,000 a week to appear on the vaudeville stage.

Russell was a wealthy and generous woman. She headed a charity drive of actors who performed benefits for the victims of the Galveston flood in 1900 and made major donations to the actor's guild when they were on strike in 1919.

She began to wind down her career after marrying her fourth husband, prominent politician Alexander P. Moore in 1912. She devoted more of her time to furthering his political career and causes, including the sale of Liberty Bonds during WWI and successfully campaigning for Warren Harding during the 1920 presidential election.

Russell put on weight during her latter years, continued her dalliance with Jim Brady, and turned her attention to politics, yet she never fell out of favor with her adoring public. She was America's first true entertainment superstar.

PIERRE DE COUBERTIN

Pierre de Coubertin, a French educator, was born in Paris in 1863. He was the founder of the modern Olympic Games, serving as president of the International Olympic Committee from 1896 until 1925 and honorary president until his death in 1937.

He was born into an aristocratic Parisian family and raised in a highly cultured environment, traveling the world and dallying in sports throughout his young adult life. He was noble and idealistic. He refused comfortable positions in the military and politics and instead devoted his life to improving the French educational system, which he believed should include sports as a fundamental part of the curriculum.

De Coubertin was an active sportsman himself, participating in boxing, fencing, horseback riding, and rowing. It was this interest in sport, combined with the recent archeological finds in Olympia which aroused his interest in the ancient Olympic Games in the early 1890s. It led to a conviction on his part to resurrect the games.

He announced his intentions at an international congress held in Paris in 1894 but received little interest. Undeterred, he proceeded to organize the International Olympic Committee and scheduled the first modern games for Athens in 1896.

The games included only fourteen participating countries competing in track and field, fencing, weightlifting, shooting, tennis, bicycling, swimming, gymnastics, and wrestling. The venue was nearly moved to Budapest, Hungary, when the Greek government had trouble financing the games.

The first games were a success, but de Coubertin disappointed the Greeks when he announced that they would not host the next games, scheduled for 1900. He stressed the importance of changing host cities in an effort to involve more nations in what he saw as a noble effort to unite the world through sports. During WWI de Coubertin established the headquarters of the IOC in neutral Switzerland, where they remain to this day.

De Coubertin had a much higher standard for the Olympics than a mere sporting spectacle. He defined the purpose of the Olympic games on four principles: the pursuit of perfection, chivalry, egalitarianism, and truce among nations.

He died of a heart attack in Geneva, Switzerland, on September 2, 1937. He was laid to rest in Lausanne, though his heart was interred in a monument near the ruins of ancient Olympia. The International Committee for Fair Play established an award in his honor. The Pierre de Coubertin International Trophy for Fair Play has been given annually since 1964 in recognition of acts of good sportsmanship in athletics.

ELDRIDGE JOHNSON

Eldridge R. Johnson was born in Wilmington, Delaware, on February 18, 1867. Along with Thomas Edison, he is credited with the rise of the phonograph and recorded sound industry.

He graduated from the Dover Academy at age 15 and then began a five-year apprenticeship in a Philadelphia machine shop. At the end of his apprenticeship he took a position with the Scull Machine Shop in Camden, NJ. He bought the business in 1894 and renamed it the

Eldridge R. Johnson Manufacturing Company. As an employee at Scull, Johnson received the first of an eventual seventy-six patents he would earn during his lifetime.

In 1896 Johnson developed a spring-driven motor for a gramophone at the request of Emile Berliner. Johnson became intrigued by the gramophone and continued to work for Berliner. After perfecting the motor, he set about perfecting other parts of the machine, eventually remaking it as the Victrola, which would debut under his company logo a few years later. He also developed a new method of making recording masters using electroplated wax pressings. The recordings were superior to any disc on the market and became the foundation upon which his company would grow in the next century.

The original Berliner Gramaphone Company was forced out of business in 1900 through a series of legal maneuvers by the Columbia Company over a dispute about patent infringements. Emile Berliner retired from the industry a rich man.

With Berliner's withdrawal from the industry, Johnson and his attorney, Leon Douglas, formed a new company called the Consolidated Talking Machine Company. Their first action was to advertise the availability of their superior records. They took out ads in newspapers promising that anyone who owned a Berliner machine could get a free copy of the record simply by sending their name, address, and the serial number of the machine. The ad worked like a charm. Not only did people clamor for the free records, but they discovered that they truly were of a superior quality than what was on the market. They contacted Johnson's company wanting to buy more records. Sales took off, and Johnson's new company hit the ground running, producing both gramaphones and records.

Another court challenge arose, accusing Johnson of infringing on the same patents that had put Berliner out of business. This time, though, Johnson proved victorious. The Consolidated Talking Machine Company did, however, have to quit using the word gramophone to describe their record player.

Since he was the victor in the legal battle, Johnson renamed his company the Victor Talking Machine Company and his gramophones were renamed Victrolas. Victor would go on to become synonymous with the phonograph industry.

In the fall of 1900 Johnson bought the American rights to a painting called "His Masters Voice," which featured Nipper the dog listening intently to a gramophone. By the middle of the next year he was using it and the name "Victor" on his machines, records, and in his advertising. It would become one of the most recognizable trademarks in corporate history.

The Victor Talking Machine Company was wildly successful. Annual sales of Johnson's talking machines climbed from less than 10,000 the first year to nearly 100,000 in less than a decade and by 1917 topped the half million mark. The Victorla, became perhaps the most influential phonograph in the country. Its outstanding physical feature was the absence of the large horn that protruded, sometimes awkwardly, from the top of other talking machines. Instead, the horn turned down, underneath the mechanism and was enclosed in a cabinet. The Victrola was totally enclosed, resembling a fine piece of furniture as much as a technological innovation and the state-of-the-art home entertainment unit.

Despite the sub-par quality of its sound with the internal horn, Victrola had its greatest financial success in the years after its introduction. This had as much to do with other factors than the design of the machine. Johnson had shrewdly locked up the greatest singers to exclusive contracts and possessed superior advertising and marketing departments. He also held the patent on the tapered tone-arm, a technical breakthrough that was valuable and highly desired by every manufacturer.

Johnson recognized that the ultimate demand for the talking machines would be a function of the availability and quality of recordings to play on the machines, and he set out to perfect a process of mass producing quality recordings. Having accomplished that, he signed the greatest singing talent to exclusive contracts, and dominated the phonograph industry through control of the recordings. His Victrola was technically inferior to Edison's machine in many ways, but while Edison focused on perfecting the sound quality of the phonograph, Johnson secured a lock on the quality of the recordings to be played on it. This ultimately proved to be the undoing of Edison. While he is credited with the greatest technological breakthroughs, Johnson is credited with popularizing the invention.

Johnson sold his share of Victor in 1927 after a nearly decade-long slide due to competition from the radio industry. Johnson's share of the sale made him so rich he never had to work again. He spent the last eighteen years of his life engaged in various philanthropic causes and pursuing his hobbies of sailing and hunting. He bought a series of yachts, each more elaborate than the next, and used them to carry him to exotic hunting trips around the globe.

One of his eccentric passions was collecting memorabilia related to the Lewis Carroll book *Alice in Wonderland*. Johnson developed a fascination with the story and eagerly accumulated first editions of the book, ultimately crowning his collection when he acquired the original manuscript penned by Carroll. When he died on November 14, 1945, he was one of the richest men in the United States.

LEE DE FOREST

Lee de Forest graduated from Yale in 1899 at the age of 26 with a doctorate degree in mechanics and electricity. While at Yale, he designed numerous inventions, ranging from an ear cleaner to a steam condenser for engines. While none of his inventions were adopted, he remained undaunted. Convinced of his own genius, he believed that it was only a matter of time before the world would recognize his brilliance and reward him for his inventions. That day would eventually come, but his rewards would mostly be absorbed in a near lifelong battle in patent courts.

De Forest was born in Council Bluffs, Iowa, in 1873, the son of a Yale-educated preacher. As a young boy his family relocated to Alabama. The move was tough on the children, who were not welcomed by the blacks nor the native Southerners who did not take kindly to intruding Yankees, especially those who associated with blacks.

With few friends, de Forest turned toward tinkering to keep himself occupied. He designed and invented from an early age, showing an aptitude for mechanical engineering. de Forest's first job after graduation was with the Western Electric Company in Chicago. He was quickly promoted to a job in the company's research department, but alienated his boss by concentrating his work on wireless communication instead of the telephone. De Forest left Western Electric in 1900 for a job with the American Wireless Telegraph Company in nearby Milwaukee. This job did not last long either. de Forest designed a more efficient method of receiving signals, but chafed at the suggestion that his share of the proceeds from any future patents should be shared with his boss. He quit rather than divulge the invention.

Expanding upon ideas he read about in scientific journals, de Forest patented an improved method of receiving Marconi telegraph signals. His improvement tripled the speed with which signals could be received. It became his first in a long line of patents. As talented a scientist as de Forest was, he would never duplicate that success in business. Throughout his career he continuously found himself short of cash, involved in lawsuits, and erring in his judgment of humanity in general, as his four wives and poor choice of business partners suggested. His considerable ego would also prevent him from settling his numerous patent disagreements with others, resulting in long and costly court battles that drained much of the financial reward he would realize from his inventions.

De Forest would be accused many times over in his career of liberally borrowing from the work of others for his inventions. This was one reason he spent so much time and money fighting in patent courts. His most famous patent, the one that the radio industry was founded upon, was granted in the fall of 1906. The "audion tube" allowed wireless signals to be received from greater distances and with greater clarity than ever before. It marked a huge improvement on the Marconi invention and was directly responsible for the evolution of radio.

In 1915 de Forest stoked what was to become a lifelong rivalry with inventor Howard Armstrong when he wrote an article in an electrical journal stating that he had indeed invented the principle of oscillation in audion tubes before Armstrong. It initiated a patent suit, the first of what would become a lifelong series of legal battles and personal enmity between the two inventors. The legal fight over the oscillating audion would last nineteen years, consume thousands of hours of each inventor's time, cost millions of dollars in legal fees, and build a lifelong bitterness between the two men. Ultimately, de Forest would win the legal fight, though the scientific community never wavered in its recognition that Armstrong was the true inventor of the oscillating principle of de Forest's audion tube.

De Forest began regular radio broadcasts in the fall of 1916 from his factory in the Bronx. Owners of radio receiver sets were able to pick up his signal as far as 200 miles away. de Forest pursued his idealized vision of radio as a cultural dispensary, playing classical music and occasional lectures. In between, he advertised his radio components, emphasizing their superior quality. Thus was born the first regular broadcasts and the first regular advertisements. De Forest's ads were necessary to sell his equipment to finance his experiments. De Forest would not enjoy the financial stability of working for a large corporation or university until much later in his life. And then he did it only out of financial necessity. He preferred the freedom of being on his own. As his financial state would demonstrate, however, he was trying to be a successful inventor in the mold of a Thomas Edison or Henry Ford in an era when scientific invention was increasingly carried out under corporate umbrellas. RCA would become the model of this. A corporation which hired staffs of scientists, provided them a steady paycheck and a modern lab with plenty of assistants, and in return kept the profits from any resulting patents. It was becoming increasingly difficult for lone inventors to succeed. This was especially true when it came to patent fights. The corporate pocketbook was much deeper than the individual, making a court fight nearly impossible to win against the corporation.

After his audion tube invention and some further refinements which he patented and either sold or spent a lifetime defending in court, de Forest drifted out of the radio business and turned his attentions elsewhere. In a pattern that would become consistent over his lifetime, de Forest would sell his assets to raise capital for his latest project.

In 1923 he sold all his shares in the de Forest Company. He used the proceeds to finance his work on the Phonofilm, his new passion of recording sound on film to create "talking pictures." By 1925 he was dabbling in color film. Both of these ideas would prove to be the future of the movie industry, but de Forest was ahead of his time, and would not share in the riches when they finally became commercially successful.

In the midst of the depression, Armstrong and de Forest were recognized as the inventors who made the radio industry possible. It was generating revenues of nearly $2 billion annually and featured some of the most prominent companies in America: RCA, Zenith, Motorola, and Magnavox. Yet the inventors were largely broke. They had spent most of their money suing one another.

de Forest declared bankruptcy in 1934, listing his assets as $390 against liabilities of $103,000. He continued to have good ideas—for example, he conceived of the cathode ray tube, which became a key component of radar, but was never again to achieve great success as an inventor.

The eclipse of his inventing career dovetailed with the rise of his personal life. On October 3, 1930, at the age of 57, de Forest married for the fourth and final time. This one would last until his death. He married Marie Mosquini, an actress who would devote the rest of her life to taking care of de Forest. The marriage got off to a rocky start when it was discovered that de Forest had neglected to divorce his third wife before getting married. He did ultimately finalize his third divorce, and he and Marie settled into his only successful marriage.

De Forest spent the waning years of his life seeking fame and fortune. He lobbied intensely, though unsuccessfully, for the Nobel Prize in physics in the mid-1950s. He failed to interest the public in his autobiography, dabbled in several inventions that never caught on, proving once again, with his invention of a telephone answering machine, that his inventions were sometimes just too far ahead of their time.

De Forest died on June 30, 1961, four years after suffering a near fatal heart attack while on a cruise passing through the Panama Canal. His estate was worth $1,200. The industry his invention was responsible for was worth billions. Marie survived her husband by twenty-six years.

AL JOLSON

Al Jolson was born Asa Yoelson on May 26, 1888, in Lithuania. He was one of the first true superstars of the entertainment industry. His popularity extended from the vaudeville stage to the radio airwaves to the silver screen. Today he is perhaps best known for his ground-breaking and prophetic phrase "You ain't heard nothin' yet," the first spoken words in movie history. That line, from *The Jazz Singer* (1927) was Jolson's motion picture debut. It vaulted him to the top of the movie star system of the day, which he dominated much as he had the vaudeville circuit for the previous two decades.

The son of a rabbi, Jolson planned to become a cantor but instead turned to the stage. After his New York City debut in 1899 he worked in circuses, minstrel shows, and vaudeville. He first appeared on stage in blackface, an entertainment style in which white actors imitated African-Americans by coloring their face with cork, in 1909. The style brought him fame and fortune, though it is regarded today as a derogatory form of entertainment.

Jolson's career was typical of many famous entertainers in the early twentieth century. He honed his craft by working his way up the vaudeville ladder, from the small-time circuit to the big-time circuit, eventually translating his skills to Broadway, where he first appeared in 1911, the radio, and eventually the movies. This bottom-up career path allowed him to perfect his act in front of a variety of audiences, a skill which helped him adapt his routine to each new venue he encountered.

An accomplished singer and comedian, Jolson was a crowd favorite who easily adapted his skills to the rapidly changing entertainment media of the day. He hosted his own radio show beginning in 1932, made millions by endorsing songs (a practice known as plugging) and selling records, and became a famous movie star.

Jolson was not as popular with his fellow entertainers, many of whom considered him self-absorbed and egotistical, even by show business standards. He demanded, and was usually granted, star treatment. His tremendous ego served him well in his career progression, but he was not as narcissistic as his detractors claimed. He had a philanthropic streak, and generously donated his time to entertaining American troops both here and abroad during WWII.

His movie career peaked in 1946 with a musical based on his life: *The Jolson Story*. It was so successful that it begat a sequel, *Jolson Sings Again*, three years later. He was preparing to conquer the new entertainment frontier of television, mulling competing offers to star in his own show, when he died of a heart attack on October 23, 1950.

Jolson was one of the greatest entertainers of the first half century. He blazed the trail for media superstars, conquering every medium he entered, successfully cross-marketing himself and exploiting his fame through commercial endorsements.

DAVID SARNOFF

David Sarnoff is the personification of the classic American success story. He was born in 1891 in Minsk, Belarus. His family immigrated to America in 1900, and he worked his way up from a poor immigrant unable to speak a word of English to the president and CEO of one of the largest corporations in American history. At the time of his death he was a highly decorated war hero, recipient of numerous awards and honors and widely recognized as one of the greatest business minds in American history.

Sarnoff was an intense, shrewd, and driven young man with a sense of purpose and responsibility that would serve him well in his adult life. As a nine-year-old boy, he realized the importance of pitching in to help his family's financial situation in their newly adopted homeland. He began peddling newspapers on the streets of New York City and eventually devised a system of distributing them that he franchised to others, increasing his income and decreasing the amount of time he spent earning it. This is a pattern that would repeat itself throughout his life, an early indication of the sharp administrative and organizational skills that would eventually lead him to the top.

Sarnoff was primarily a self-educated man. He had a voracious appetite for knowledge and self-improvement and spent countless hours reading and studying. He did have some formal education in America at the Educational Alliance as a youth and later an intensive one-year course of studies in electrical engineering at the Pratt Institute in Brooklyn. He saved money from his many odd jobs and ploughed it into his education, including the purchase of books and a dummy telegraph key, which he used to teach himself Morse code for the job of telegraph operator that would eventually propel him to greatness.

As a young man he had grand ambitions and the drive and skills to accomplish them. He believed that the advantage in the wireless industry, in which he had cast his fortunes, would go to the man who understood both the business side and the technical side of the industry. To that end, he was determined to master both—and he did.

He began his career as a messenger boy for the Commercial Cable Company in 1906. The next year he took a job with the Marconi Wireless Company and within a year was promoted to a position as a wireless operator. Eventually he would own the company. In between, he gained fame as the telegraph operator who received the first news of the sinking of the *Titanic*. He stayed at his post for three days, relaying updates on the tragedy as the rest of the country hung on his every word.

Sarnoff stayed with the Marconi firm until it was absorbed by Radio Corporation of America (RCA) in 1921, at which time he was appointed general manager of RCA. He rose to president in 1930 and chief executive officer and chairman of the board in 1947. Under his leadership RCA became the premier company in the research, development, and promotion of the radio and television industries.

RCA's greatest achievements were not in the manufacture of radios and televisions, but the development of the technology which made them possible. Sarnoff was not the first person to develop a corporate research lab, but he perfected the idea. Though his labs were almost continually involved in patent litigation, they were crucial in the development of some of the key components of radio, television, and color television transmission and reception. One of Sarnoff's signature deals was to license RCA's patents to competitors who would then construct the radios and televisions, paying a percentage of the sale price to RCA. Sarnoff concentrated his firm's efforts on pushing the envelope of technology, financed by the construction and sale of sets by his competitors.

RCA became the leading firm in the communications industry by controlling the important patents. Some of them were developed in RCA's research lab, some were purchased from independent inventors or other labs, and some were "borrowed"—or outright stolen, as many would suggest—, and eventually taken over by RCA through the long drawn-out process of litigation. RCA, with its staff of lawyers, could afford to draw out patent litigation for years, especially if the opponent was a solo inventor. Ultimately, when the opposition ran out of funds, RCA would purchase the patent outright, then license it to others.

The federal government sued RCA for antitrust violations in 1930. The case dragged on for two years before a settlement was reached. While RCA nominally lost the case, Sarnoff was quite happy with the resulting settlement. It actually served RCA quite well, and solved a problem that Sarnoff saw developing. The settlement forced RCA to break up the monopolistic agreements they had with both GE and Westinghouse governing the manufacture of radios. Sarnoff was concentrating his efforts on the future of television, and the GE and Westinghouse contracts were a distraction to him. The settlement kept RCA out of federal court, severed the agreements with GE and Westinghouse, but left RCA in possession of its valuable patents and broadcast network. It had the additional benefit of shrinking the size of RCA's board, tightening Sarnoff's control of the membership.

Under Sarnoff's leadership RCA grew from a small participant in the electronics industry to the greatest corporation in America. Beside its pioneering work in the radio and television fields, RCA had a hand in the movie industry through its merger with Keith-Albee-Orpheum theaters. It also launched the National Broadcasting Corporation (NBC) to oversee the production and distribution of over-the-air entertainment. In addition, RCA pioneered car radios, striking a deal with General Motors to manufacture radios for their cars in 1931. He also merged with the Victor phonograph company, giving RCA control of the largest manufacturer in that industry. One of the outcomes of this merger was the combination radio-phonograph.

Sarnoff was a visionary who correctly predicted the importance of radio, television, war technology, and even the computer. His familiarity with wireless telegraphy gave him an up-close view of the industry, which he boldly predicted would change the face of America. In 1915 he proposed a radio receiving device that ultimately became the radio we know today. He foresaw the power of radio as an entertainment device for the American household far beyond that of a communication tool, which it was at the time.

His idea of entertainment, however, was not what ultimately developed. He was excited by the prospect of a radio in every home that would bring in classical music and lectures by famous persons, which would both entertain and educate. Sarnoff was correct in thinking the radio would become a centerpiece of American households as a source of entertainment. Very little of that entertainment would be classical music and lectures, however. And it would not be financed, as Sarnoff predicted, by radio manufacturers, who would underwrite broadcasts in order to sell more radio sets. Instead, Americans were entertained by comedy shows, soap operas, and popular music, all of which were financed by the sale of commercial air time.

While not happy with the direction of the entertainment at NBC, Sarnoff did not cry sour grapes. Instead, he turned NBC into a source of profit for RCA. It became a revenue generating arm of the company, totally committed to producing popular entertainment and selling commercial airtime. If "low brow" entertainment was what Americans demanded, then Sarnoff would provide it, and make a fortune in the process.

As early as 1964 Sarnoff was predicting the computer revolution. In a series of speeches that year he correctly predicted both the promise and pitfalls of the industry. He held out the promise that computers would revolutionize the communications and entertainment industries as no other technology had before. He also correctly predicted that the greatest impediment to the industry would be incompatible systems and uncoordinated development of the technology, including the writing of codes for programs that could not communicate with one another.

One of Sarnoff's few incorrect predictions centered on FM radio. He spent little time and effort on it because he believed that television would eventually cast radio into the dustbin of history. As a result, he concentrated his efforts on the future of television instead of what he considered a technological dead end.

He served his country in two world wars. During WWI his draft notice was deferred when the government declared his services in the wireless industry too important. He spent the war years shuttling between New York and Washington consulting with the navy and the army about the use and implementation of electronic communications in the theater of war. During WWII he was awarded the honorary title of brigadier general. This time his contributions, though of a similar nature as WWI, took him abroad, where he worked closely with General Dwight D. Eisenhower. In 1947 President Truman presented him with the Medal of Merit for his war service. The French government also recognized his achievements by awarding him the Cross of Commander of the French Legion of Honor that same year.

Sarnoff engaged in one of his bitterest battles over television, fighting the pesky Philo Farnsworth for the title of "Father of Television," and the rights to valuable patents which controlled the industry. Farnsworth was the only inventor to get the best of RCA and Sarnoff. He won his patent fight against RCA, propelled by the need for RCA to settle after their sensational demonstration of television at the 1939 World's Fair in New York. Unfortunately for RCA, the exhibition was created on the back of patents stolen from Farnsworth. For the only time in his career, Sarnoff had to agree to purchase the licensing rights to a patent from someone else. He licensed Farnsworth's patents for RCA's use. The Second World War interrupted the commercial debut of television, however, and it was not until after the war that the industry became the dominant form of household entertainment that Sarnoff had predicted more than a decade earlier.

The next frontier for Sarnoff to conquer was color television. In a by-now familiar pattern, RCA research labs worked diligently on the problem, made great progress, and found themselves involved in legal squabbles over patent rights. Once again RCA was the subject of an antitrust investigation by the federal government. Once again, Sarnoff settled to avoid a messy and potentially reputation-damaging federal court case. This time RCA agreed to pool all of its color television patents with its competitors' patents for anyone to use free of charge. It was just the boost that color television needed. Freed from the cost of licensing patents, manufacturers flooded the market with affordable color sets. With a huge potential audience of color sets on the horizon, networks were convinced of the profitability of converting their broadcasts to color.

Color television was the last accomplishment for David Sarnoff, who died on December 12, 1971. At the time of his death Sarnoff was lauded as one of the greatest executives in American business history. He was an acknowledged visionary, and while lionized as a thief by some, he was without equal in his pioneering of the electronic entertainment industry. The man who never formally attended high school or college had collected more than two dozen honorary degrees by the time of his death.

MARY PICKFORD

Mary Pickford (born Gladys Mary Smith) was the first true movie star and the first female executive in the industry. She began her career as an anonymous actress in silent films and ended it as one of the founding owners of United Artists, one of the top motion picture distribution companies in the world.

Pickford was born in Canada on April 9, 1892. Before her twentieth birthday she was acting for noted director D. W. Griffith. She was dubbed "America's Sweetheart" and "The Girl with the Curls" in the early days of the movie industry when actors were not given screen credits. Her magnetic stage presence won her legions of fans before they even knew who she was.

In 1919, at the height of her screen fame, she co-founded United Artists with Hollywood stars Charlie Chaplin, Douglas Fairbanks Sr. and director D. W. Griffith. United Artists went on to establish itself as one of the top film distribution companies in the world.

Pickford appeared in more than 180 films from 1909 until her final screen credit in 1933. Most of her movies were made during the silent picture era, about half of them short silent films. She made only four screen appearances after the arrival of talking pictures in 1927, though one of them, *Coquette* (1929) won her the Academy Award for best actress.

Pickford's career was highly unusual for a woman in the early twentieth century. She moved from acting to the business side of the movies with equal success. Before United Artists she had negotiated a contract that allowed her to produce her own films. She used her considerable audience appeal and resulting box-office-drawing power to negotiate film deals unique in the industry.

Pickford was instrumental in the creation of the star system that is commonplace today. She was one of the first to suggest that a studio capitalize on the popularity of its screen favorites by publicizing them. She suggested that Biograph, the company she worked for in 1908, use her name to market its films—of course she would have profited as well. When Biograph failed to act on her suggestion, she signed a contract with Carl Laemmle, who was only too happy to follow her advice, and reaped millions by exploiting the name of Mary Pickford to promote his movies. Mary did well by this arrangement herself. In 1916, at the height of her popularity and drawing power, she was earning more than $500,000 per year as both an actress and head of her own production company—the first woman producer in the business.

Mary Pickford's last screen appearance was in 1933, though she continued to produce films through United Artists until 1950. That year the company, nearly bankrupt, was turned over to outside management, which resuscitated it and returned it to its once powerful status. In 1956 Pickford sold her share of the company, severing her last formal ties to the industry that had brought her wealth and fame.

When she married actor Douglas Fairbanks Sr. in 1920, Mary Pickford may have been the most famous woman in the world. After exiting from the acting business she began to fade from the public eye. She became more reclusive as she aged, and was seldom seen again. At the time of her death, few even knew she had still been alive. She died in her sleep on May 27, 1979. Though she had faded from the film industry she maintained her sharp business skills throughout her life, leaving an estate estimated to be worth $50 million at her death, the bulk of which was designated for charity.

Pickford was one of the greatest actors in the history of filmdom, the first Hollywood superstar, and a pioneer in the economic structure of the industry. Tragically, she is largely unknown today because few copies of her films still survive and are seldom played. Part of this is due to Pickford herself, who believed that silent films were considered inferior to talkies, and that she would only be laughed at by future generations. As a result, she ordered the destruction of many of the copies of her films.

GEORGE HALAS

George Stanley "Papa Bear" Halas, one of the original franchise owners and a founder of the National Football League, was born February 2, 1895, in Chicago.

Halas was a sports enthusiast, playing multiple sports in both high school and college, at the University of Illinois and the Great Lakes Naval Training Station, where he was stationed during WWI. He was named MVP of the 1919 Rose Bowl game, leading Navy to a 17-0 victory over the U.S. Marine Corps.

Before he became involved with the NFL, he played professional baseball, earning a brief tour with the New York Yankees in 1919. An injury and the arrival of a new outfielder by the name of Babe Ruth ended the baseball career of Halas, much to the benefit of professional football.

After his abridged professional baseball career ended, Halas accepted a position with a starch manufacturing company in Decatur, Illinois. He filled multiple roles, including sales representative, player on the company baseball team, and player-coach of the company football team. It was in this latter position that he represented the company's owner, A. E. Staley, at the 1920 meeting in Canton, Ohio, that formed the NFL. Halas was awarded one of the inaugural franchises, the Decatur Staley's, which were moved to Chicago and renamed the Bears after one financially unsuccessful season in Decatur.

For the next decade, Halas *was* the Bears, acting as head coach, general manager, team president, head of ticket sales, part owner, and star player. It was as general manager that he made the move considered to be pivotal to the eventual success of the fledgling league. In 1925 he signed All American football star Red Grange to a contract. The signing gave the league an immediate and much needed boost in stature and image. Prior to the arrival of Grange, the NFL was regarded as little more than a refuge for "ne'er do well roughnecks."

In 1930 Halas retired as a player and as coach, for the first of what would eventually be four retirements. He remained in the front office, eventually becoming sole owner in 1932. He resumed the head coach role in 1933, retired again when he returned to active military service from 1943 to 1945, and returned to the sidelines for another decade before retiring for a third time in 1956. In 1958 he began his final tour of duty as coach of the Bears, retiring from coaching permanently in 1967. During his various stints as coach, the Bears were one of the most successful franchises in league history, winning eight titles in his forty years as coach. Halas was an innovative coach, designing the universally copied T-formation in the late 1930s. This formation was credited for the still record 73-0 victory over the Washington Redskins in the 1940 Championship game.

Halas was also a pioneer off the field. He was the first owner to broadcast NFL games on radio and television, and it was his idea to share television revenues equally among all league teams, arguing that the league would only be as strong as its weakest member. His foresight in the sharing of league revenues is widely regarded as among the wisest business decisions in all professional sports.

Halas was not always a trendsetter, however. He refused to sign any black players, aiding in the league's unwritten segregation policy in the 1930s. He eventually relented, however, as much for business reasons as moral ones, when he drafted George Taliaferro in 1949. Even though he never played for the Bears, the drafting of Taliaferro was significant as it marked the first African-American drafted since 1933. In 1953 Halas added Willie Thrower to the Bears' roster. Thrower became the first black quarterback in NFL history.

Halas succumbed to cancer on October 31, 1983, at the age of 88. He remained active in the operation of the Bears from their inauguration as the Staleys in 1920 until his death. He was honored on numerous occasions by the NFL, and has been cited by ESPN as one of the ten most influential personalities in sports history, as well as the U.S. Postal Service, which honored him as a legendary football coach on a 1997 postage stamp.

WILLIAM S. PALEY

William S. Paley was the first president of Columbia Broadcasting System and the creator of the network system of affiliated television and radio stations that dominates the industry to this day. The affiliate system, as it was first created by NBC, was a subscription system in which local stations paid a fee to the network and received programming in return. Paley turned that system on its head. He paid local stations, which then agreed to air the network programming. Paley correctly figured that the he could reap more advertising revenue with the promise of the larger nationwide audiences his system garnered.

Paley was born in Chicago on September 28, 1901. His middle initial S stood for nothing. He added it later in life in order to give himself a more distinguished sounding name for business purposes.

Samuel Paley, Bill's father, bought the struggling Columbia Phonographic Broadcasting System in 1927 to use it as an advertising medium for the family cigar business. The next year it was reorganized as the Columbia Broadcasting System (CBS) and Bill took over as president. He had no radio experience but possessed a gift for recognizing entertainment that appealed to the average listener. He was a master at programming and CBS dominated the ratings under his leadership. He frequently raided rival NBC, bidding away their top stars with better financial offers.

Another innovation of Paley's was the network newscast. He created the CBS news division in the waning years of the 1930s as war built in Europe. He recognized the public's desire for information about the war and profited from an outstanding news department that carried over to television. The CBS news division dominated broadcast journalism during his lifetime.

While he promoted an independent news division, it was not out of duty, but for profits. He saw its value on the bottom line, and ruffled some feathers in the division with some of his later decisions. He was accused of sacrificing truth for politics, for example, when he curtailed the airing of a news special on Watergate at the behest of a Nixon aide. He also objected to some of the stories covered by news programs such as *60 Minutes* and *See It Now*, which on occasion rankled some sponsors.

Paley remained president of CBS until 1947, when he was elevated to chairman of the board, a position he held for the rest of his life. The last decade of his career was largely spent trying to handpick a successor. He hired and fired two replacements while CBS fell from the top of the ratings ladder, before succumbing to death.

Before CBS, Paley worked in the family's highly successful business, Congress Cigar Company. He earned a business degree from the University of Pennsylvania before becoming vice president of the company.

During WWII he served as the deputy chief of psychological warfare, working under General Dwight Eisenhower in Europe, ultimately rising to the rank of colonel. After the war he turned his attention to transferring his radio network model to the new television industry. He duplicated the radio model and turned CBS television into the industry leader.

Paley was active in civic affairs and served as the trustee of numerous boards, including the Museum of Modern Art (MOMA) for more than half a century. He was a major contributor to both the MOMA and the Museum of Television and Radio from the founding of each museum until his death on October 26, 1990.

PHILO FARNSWORTH

Philo Farnsworth may be the most famous obscure inventor in American history. Like Thomas Edison and Henry Ford, his invention is so commonplace that it seldom receives a second thought. Unlike Edison and Ford though, Farnsworth is hardly a household name, despite being credited with inventing the television.

Farnsworth was born August 19, 1906, in Utah, but grew up on a farm in Idaho after the family moved there when he was young. The farm had an electrical generator which fascinated Philo. He studied the repairman who made frequent visits to repair it, asking him questions, and learning about electricity from him. Ultimately he was able to repair the generator himself, without any advanced education in electronics. His formal education ended with one year of college. His father died that year, making it impossible for him to continue his education.

Like his contemporary, Lee de Forest, Farnsworth was enamored with science and spent most of his free time poring over scientific magazines and journals. Also like de Forest, he spent most of his earnings in court on patent lawsuits.

His breakthrough idea for television came to him as a teenager while he was on horseback plowing a field. He noticed the rows of parallel lines he was plowing, when it hit him: television would be possible by transmitting rows of scanned images. This was the breakthrough that would set the quest to invent television on the successful path it ultimately took. Others were working on a mechanical method for transmitting images that would occupy countless dollars and hours of research, but Farnsworth knew it to be impractical from the beginning. He correctly perceived electricity as the key to television.

When he first revealed his idea for television, his father urged him to keep it secret—not so that his idea would not be stolen, but because he thought it so preposterous that people would think Philo was crazy. By the time he died (in the same year as his nemesis David Sarnoff), there were more homes in the world with television sets than indoor plumbing.

Farnsworth connected with two businessmen who had faith in his idea for electronic television. The three formed a corporation, and in 1926 Farnsworth moved to California and set up his first real laboratory, becoming a full-time inventor, a job title he would hold for the rest of his life. The initial capital investment was a mere $6,000, an investment which would ultimately fund the critical discoveries that would yield commercial television. Unfortunately for the investors, the rewards would be reaped largely by RCA, which would dominate the television industry in the same way it did the radio industry: by controlling patents.

Farnsworth was the embodiment of the lone genius. He spent most of his life in research labs, perfecting television initially, then later working on fusion. Especially early in his career, he spent this time in ramshackle laboratories, working with a small staff, the size of which fluctuated according to his financial conditions, which waxed and waned according to how close he was to developing a commercially successful television.

While Farnsworth won the court battles that acknowledged him as the inventor of television, by the time he won his patents were on the verge of expiring, and he lost the financial windfall they entailed.

On January 7, 1927, Farnsworth filed his first patent application for a television system. Exactly nine months later, he conducted experiment number twelve at his Green Street lab in San Francisco, and the first documented television transmission took place. It would hardly have won any ratings wars, since it was a picture of a triangle broadcast from one end of his lab to the other, but it was exciting nonetheless, for it was the true beginning of an industry that would change the world. It would take two decades, a world war, and a monumental court battle before television would become the commercial success we know today.

On September 1, 1928, Farnsworth and his backers held a press conference and successfully demonstrated his television. Farnsworth showed the press a clip of a Mary Pickford movie that he transmitted over his television system with great results. The resulting publicity proclaimed him a genius and gave his financial backers the confidence they needed to continue to back him.

The publicity over his progress made Farnsworth rich by inflating the value of his corporation's stock, of which he held 20 percent. Farnsworth sold some of his shares and generously shared some more with his family members, making them all very well off.

Farnsworth's first break in his attempt to commercialize television came when he struck a deal with Philco, the world's largest radio manufacturer, in 1931. Philco licensed several of Farnsworth's patents with the intention of manufacturing televisions. While this was not a financially lucrative deal for Farnsworth, it provided the outlet for commercialization that he sought. And if it worked, it would turn into a financial bonanza. Farnsworth moved his main laboratory east to Philadelphia, home of Philco. RCA had its main laboratory directly across the river in Camden, NJ, and the two companies raced to perfect television. Each set up an experimental television station and broadcast parts of their research over the air. The partnership with Philco broke off in 1933, when RCA threatened to revoke Philco's licenses to produce radios. At the time, commercial television was still a distant prospect, one that Philco could no longer afford to entertain.

Things started to look up for Farnsworth when the patent courts officially acknowledged him as the inventor of television in 1935. In March of 1939 he issued 600,000 shares of stock in Farnsworth Television & Radio Corporation to an enthusiastic public. This came on the heels of Farnsworth's purchase of the Indiana-based radio manufacturing firm Capehart Company. The purchase provided Farnsworth with a new home for his lab and a source of income from the current sales of radios and record players.

Farnsworth saw his financial fortunes evaporate in 1947 with the expiration of his original television patents. With the expiration of his patents, the end of Farnsworth's television career was near. His company was in financial straits. Perpetual use of his remaining patents was sold to television manufacturers for $3 million, just enough to pay off the company's debts, and the company was then sold to International Telephone and Telegraph Corporation in 1949 for a mere

$1.4 million. ITT had no interest in the television industry, they were only interested in Philo Farnsworth. Part of the deal required Farnsworth to stay on as vice president of research, designing various electronic components for ITT's other interests.

Farnsworth wearied of his new position, and instead turned his interests to an attempt to harness a cheap, safe source of power: nuclear fusion. His efforts would absorb the rest of his life, but never prove successful. ITT eventually lost patience with Farnsworth's lack of success, cut off his funding in 1966, and put him on medical retirement. Farnsworth then returned to Utah, where he died on March 11, 1971.

Farnsworth's contributions to television were honored in 1990 when his statue was unveiled as one of Utah's two allotted honorees in the U.S. Capitol's National Statuary Hall. The bronze statue of Philo T. Farnsworth holding a television tube reads "Father of Television."

BABE DIDRIKSON ZAHARIAS

Mildred "Babe" Didriksen (later changed to Didrikson) was born in Port Arthur, Texas, in 1911 to Norwegian immigrant parents. She succumbed to cancer in 1956. She is widely regarded as the greatest female athlete of all time. At an early age she demonstrated her tremendous athletic skills, excelling at every sport she attempted: basketball, baseball, tennis, lacrosse, bowling, and cycling, to name just a few. Her nickname, "Babe," allegedly stemmed from her prodigious baseball skills. Her greatest fame, however, was achieved in track and golf.

She dropped out of high school to take a job as a stenographer with the Casualty Insurance Company in Dallas, a sideline which allowed her to train and compete in athletics. She achieved her first fame as a basketball player for the company team, leading it to a national championship in 1931 and earning All-American honors three years in a row, from 1930 to 1932.

Perhaps the highlight of her athletic career came in 1932 when she thoroughly dominated the track and field scene. At the National Amateur Athletic Union track and field championships she won five events outright, setting world records in four of them, and tied for first in another. Her 30-point performance vaulted her team, sponsored by the insurance company, to the championship. Babe was the only member of the team. The University of Illinois, with twenty-two members, finished in second place with 22 points. A mere two weeks later she posted record performances in capturing two gold medals (javelin and 80-meter hurdles) at the Olympic Games in Los Angeles. She tied for first in a third event, the high jump, but was awarded a silver medal after the judges determined that her jumping style was illegal. The only thing that kept her from winning more medals was an Olympic prohibition on women participating in more than three events. To cap off the year, she was voted Woman Athlete of the Year by the Associated Press. She would go on to earn that distinction again in 1945, 1946, 1947, 1950, and 1954.

She used her Olympic achievements to vault her into a professional career beginning in 1932. She toured the nation exhibiting her remarkable athletic skills on vaudeville, as a barnstorming basketball player, and in sporting exhibitions where she would challenge both women and men alike in a variety of sports.

In 1938 she married professional wrestler George Zaharias and changed her name to Didrikson Zaharias. Domestic life had no impact on her athletic abilities, it only served as a transition to conquer another sport. George Zaharias devoted his time to managing Babe's career, which focused primarily on golf for the rest of her life. She won several professional tournaments before abstaining for three years, from 1940 to 1943, in order to regain her amateur status. She spent the war years perfecting her golf swing through a series of exhibitions to help sell war bonds.

Didrikson Zaharias mastered golf as thoroughly as she had track and field. She won more than eighty tournaments in a career which began in 1935. In her final two years as an amateur Didrikson Zaharias won the two top amateur titles: the U.S. Golf Association Amateur Championship in 1946 and the British amateur title the following year—the first American to win that tournament. These were just two of the seventeen consecutive titles she won in that span—a mark never equaled by any golfer, male or female. She became the first woman to play in a professional men's tournament when she appeared in the Los Angeles Open in 1945. After returning to the professional ranks she became a founding member of the Ladies Professional Golf Association in 1948. She is credited with its early survival and eventual success. She won thirty-three tournaments on the tour, including the U.S. Open in 1948, 1950, and 1954.

In 1953 Didrikson Zaharias was diagnosed with cancer. She underwent radical surgery in April, and amazed the sporting world by entering a professional golf tournament three months later. She did not win the tournament, but improved enough over the course of the summer to be cited as the comeback player of the year and won her third and final U.S. Open the following year. In 1955 doctors discovered that her cancer had returned. She died in Galveston, Texas, on September 27, 1956.

JACKIE ROBINSON

Jackie Robinson became the first African American to play in Major League Baseball (MLB) in the twentieth century when he joined the Brooklyn Dodgers for the 1947 season. Prior to the arrival of Robinson, no African American had played on a white baseball team in more than half a century. Robinson was not only a great player, which was validated by his election to the Baseball Hall of Fame in 1962, but a civil rights pioneer as well.

Robinson was born on January 31, 1919, in Cairo, Georgia, but moved to California as a boy. He was an outstanding athlete in every sport he attempted. He was the first athlete to letter in four varsity sports at UCLA. He was variously described during his years at UCLA as the greatest football player, basketball player, and runner in the country. He also won collegiate titles in swimming and tennis and played professional football in Hawaii.

Robinson's brother Mack won a silver medal in the long jump at the 1936 Olympics, finishing behind Jesse Owens. Jackie won the NCAA long-jump championship in 1940 and missed a chance at Olympic glory when the games were cancelled due to WWII.

Branch Rickey, General Manager of the Brooklyn Dodgers, carefully chose Robinson as much for his temperament as his athletic skills. Rickey offered him the opportunity to break the unofficial color barrier that had barred black players from white baseball since the nineteenth century. He primed Robinson for the abuse he was likely to face when he took the field and warned him that he could not fight back, either physically or verbally. He had to let his baseball skills do the talking.

Robinson was the right man for the job. He had stared down discrimination before and emerged a victor. Robinson enlisted in the army during WWII and was assigned to the segregated U.S. 761st Tank Battalion. He was initially denied entry into officer training school. After protesting the ruling he was eventually granted entrance and graduated as a second lieutenant. While in training at Fort Hood, Texas, he refused an order to go to the back of the bus, some twenty years before Rosa Parks would launch the civil rights movement with the same defiance. Robinson was court-martialed and as a result never saw active duty. He was tried for insubordination in a military court, won his case, and in 1944 received an honorable discharge, acquitted of all charges.

Having played several years in the Negro Leagues, Robinson began an outstanding MLB career as a twenty-eight-year-old rookie, and won the Rookie of the Year award in 1947. He would go on to win the Most Valuable Player award two years later, and lead the Dodgers to the World Series championship in 1955.

Before integrating the major leagues, Robinson spent the 1946 season at the Dodgers' top farm club in Montreal, becoming the first black player in the International League in fifty-seven years. He helped lead the team to a championship while leading the league in batting.

When he arrived in Brooklyn his most immediate problem was his own team. His manager, Leo Durocher, had to quell a planned strike by his own players, several of whom objected to playing with a black man. While traveling with the team, Robinson frequently was forced to stay at segregated hotels and dine in different restaurants. Partly in response to this type of discriminatory treatment, the Dodgers built their own lodging and dining facilities at their Dodgertown spring training complex in Florida.

During his rookie season Robinson was subjected to merciless taunting and derisive comments, but never fought back or responded in public. During his second season, however, with the silence restriction removed, Robinson began to speak out and achieved renown far beyond baseball as a civil rights spokesman. In 1949 he testified before Congress in the House Un-American Activities Committee to rebut Paul Robeson's contention that American blacks would not fight against the Soviet Union because of the racist treatment they received at home. Robinson later regretted that he had made the appearance, feeling that he had been used. It would not be his only public regret. During the 1960 presidential election he publicly endorsed Richard Nixon, an endorsement that he later wrote he was sorry he had made.

The Dodgers sold Robinson's contract to the San Francisco Giants after the 1956 season, but rather than report to a new team, he retired. He expressed a desire to become the first black manager, but was never given the chance. In fact, it wasn't until 1974 that this racial barrier was broken in MLB.

After baseball, Robinson accepted a position as vice president for the Chock Full O' Nuts corporation and served on the board of the NAACP. He devoted much of his post-retirement time to making public appearances for civil rights causes.

Robinson's final years were hard on him. He lost his eyesight to diabetes, suffered from heart problems, also related to diabetes, and in 1971 lost his oldest son in an automobile accident. Robinson died on October 24, 1972. His eulogy was delivered by the Reverend Jesse Jackson.

Honors were heaped on Jackie Robinson after his death. In 1982 he became the first professional baseball player to be honored on a postage stamp by the U.S. Postal Service. Major League Baseball honored Robinson in 1997 on the fortieth anniversary of his landmark season by renaming the Rookie of the Year Award after him. Ten years later they designated April 15 each year as "Jackie Robinson Day" in all MLB ballparks. In addition, his number 42 jersey was retired by every MLB team. In 2003 he was posthumously awarded the Congressional Gold Medal, the highest award bestowed by Congress.

TED TURNER

Robert Edward "Ted" Turner III is one of the pioneers of cable television in America. He began with one local station in Atlanta in 1970 and built it into one of the largest and most powerful media empires in the world. On the side he also purchased two professional sports teams, became the largest private landholder in the country, and opened a chain of restaurants specializing in fresh bison meat.

Turner was born on November 19, 1938, in Cincinnati, Ohio. His family moved to Savannah, Georgia, when he was nine. He graduated from Brown University, a mediocre student but an excellent yachtsman, competing in the Olympic trials in 1964 and skippering the winning yacht in the America's Cup championship in 1977.

Turner got his start in business at age 24 when he took over the family billboard company after his father's death. He added the Atlanta television station a few years later and began to move into electronic media.

CNN, which is now a television staple, was a radical idea when Turner debuted it in 1980. Prior to that he pioneered the concept of the "superstation" in 1970 when he convinced distant cable companies with excess capacity to carry his Atlanta station, WTCG (which Turner dubbed "watch this channel grow"). The real interest in his station was that it had the television rights to Atlanta Braves baseball games. WTGC was eventually renamed WTBS, from which Turner's entire broadcast system, TBS, took its name.

Turner's broadcasting empire comprises several television stations, among them CNN, Headline News, TBS, TNT, TCM, Turner South, and the Cartoon Network. In 1986 he purchased MGM studios for $1.5 billion. He sold off the studio lot and trademark logos, keeping the film library, which he exploited to launch his Turner Classic Movies channel (TCM). In 1995 Turner merged his cable empire with Time Warner, becoming vice chairman of the media conglomerate. Five years later America Online (AOL) was added to the stable. Turner resigned his position with the company in 2003.

Satellite transmission of television programming was another area pioneered by Ted Turner. He was one of the first to use it, beginning in the late 1970s. By 1980 satellite was the standard by which cable television was distributed. Today most television signals and an increasing number of radio signals are transmitted via satellite.

Beginning in 1976 he used his money to fuel his sports interest by purchasing the Braves and the NBA Atlanta Hawks. In 1986 he started the Goodwill Games in Moscow as an effort to ease tensions during the cold war. When the cold war thawed, the emphasis of the games was shifted to youth initiatives. The games were held every four years in different cities, much like the Olympics. They were disbanded after the 2001 games held in Brisbane, Australia. The games were a nonprofit venture and succeeded in raising millions for charity during their sixteen year history.

Turner has been a generous, if somewhat controversial, individual. He made a billion-dollar pledge to the United Nations, created the Turner Tomorrow Fellowship program to honor outstanding works of fiction that offered solutions to global problems, and created politically slanted children's shows, such as Captain Planet. He also made headlines with his marriage to Jane Fonda in 1991. Unfortunately, it did not fare as well as his media empire, ending in divorce in 2001.

BILL GATES

William Henry Gates dropped out of Harvard at age 19. Far from regretting it, he has gone on to found one of the largest and best known corporations in the world and become one of the richest men in the world. Gates, chairman and chief software architect of Microsoft, oversees a company that generates tens of billions of dollars of revenue annually and employs over 61,000 workers in plants located in more than 100 countries.

Gates is also well known as a philanthropist. He and his wife, Melinda, established the Bill and Melinda Gates Foundation, the largest charity in the world. Its goal is to help fight poverty and improve health care around the world. He has also established a scholarship fund in the amount of $1 billion to finance college scholarships for minority students. His charity work and astute business skills earned him the title of Knight Commander of the Most Excellent Order of the British Empire from Queen Elizabeth.

Gates was born in Seattle, Washington, on October 28, 1955. He showed an early aptitude for computers, writing his first program code at the age of 13. While at Harvard he developed a version of the BASIC programming language. He left Harvard after his junior year to found Microsoft with his boyhood friend Paul Allen. They began developing software for PCs in an effort to simplify their use and lower their cost. They ultimately developed an operating system, which became the highly successful Windows that would grow to dominate the industry, running 80 percent of the world's computers. Its popularity is tied to the success of other Microsoft products, such as word processing and data management programs which were designed to run on the Windows operating system.

Gates proved to be correct in his belief that the desktop computer was the wave of the future. He started Microsoft in the belief that it would become a common business tool, and there was a future in the business of developing software for those computers.

Gates is intent on innovation. He ploughs billions of dollars each year back into research and development in his company, primarily in the area of software development.

Not all has gone smoothly for Gates. In 1998 the federal government filed an antitrust lawsuit against Microsoft accusing him of monopolizing the personal computer industry. The company was accused of exercising monopoly control over PC operating systems and using its power to the detriment of consumers. Microsoft settled with the Justice Department in 2001.

Besides running Microsoft, Gates has authored two books. In 1995, *The Road Ahead* spent seven weeks as the number one seller on the New York Times list. His next book, *Business @ the Speed of Light*, written in 1999, has been translated into twenty-five languages. Gates has donated all the proceeds of both books to charity.

On New Year's Day 1994 he married Melinda French. They have three children and continue to reside in the Seattle area. Besides his position with Microsoft, Gates is a member of the board of directors of Berkshire Hathaway and a founder of Corbis, one of the largest repositories of visual images in the world.

Suggestions for Further Reading

Aitken, Hugh. *Syntony and Spark: The Origins of Radio*. Princeton, NJ: Princeton University Press, 1985.

Allen, Jeanne Thomas. "The Decay of the Motion Picture Patents Company," *Cinema Journal*, 10, Spring 1971, 34–40.

Altherr, Thomas L., ed. *Sports in North America: A Documentary History*. Gulf Breeze, FL: Academic International Press, 1997.

Attali, Jacques. *Noise: The Political Economy of Music*. Minneapolis, MN: University of Minnesota Press, 1985.

Auletta, Ken. *Media Man: Ted Turner's Improbable Empire*. New York: W. W. Norton, 2004.

Balio, Tino, ed. *The American Film Industry*. Madison, WI: University of Wisconsin Press, 1966.

Balio, Tino. *United Artists: The Company Built by the Stars*. Madison, WI: University of Wisconsin Press, 1976.

Balio, Tino, ed. *Hollywood in the Age of Television*. Boston, MA: Unwin Hyman, 1990.

Balio, Tino. *Grand Design: Hollywood as a Modern Business Enterprise 1930–1939*. New York: Charles Scribner's Sons, 1993.

Bankes, Christina, ed. *Chronicle of the Olympics 1896–1996*. New York: DK Publishing, 1996.

Barnouw, Eric. *A Tower in Babel: A History of Broadcasting to 1933*. New York: Oxford University Press, 1966.

Barnouw, Eric. *The Golden Web: A History of Broadcasting from 1933 to 1953*. New York: Oxford University Press, 1968.

Barnouw, Eric. *The Image Empire: A History of Broadcasting from 1953*. New York: Oxford University Press, 1970.

Batten, Frank. *The Weather Channel: The Improbable Rise of a Media Phenomenon*. Boston, MA: Harvard Business School Press, 2002.

Baumol, William J. and William G. Bowen. *Performing Arts: The Economic Dilemma*. New York: Twentieth Century Fund, 1966.

Bernheim, Alfred L. *The Business of the Theater: An Economic History of the American Theater, 1750–1932*. New York: Benjamin Bloom, 1964.

Bibb, Porter. *Ted Turner: It Ain't as Easy as It Looks: The Amazing Story of CNN*. Virgin Books, 1996.

Bilby, Kenneth. *The General: David Sarnoff and the Rise of the Communications Industry*. Harper & Row, 1986.

Block, A. *Out-Foxed: The Inside Story of America's Fourth Television Network*. New York: St. Martin's Press, 1990.

Boyer, Peter J. *Who Killed CBS? The Undoing of America's Number One News Network*. New York: Random House, 1988.

Browne, Nick, ed. *American Television: New Directions in History and Theory*. Chur, Switzerland: Harwood Academic Publishers, 1994.

Burk, Robert F. *Never Just a Game: Players, Owners, and American Baseball to 1920*. Chapel Hill, NC: University of North Carolina Press, 1994.

Burk, Robert F. *Much More Than a Game: Players, Owners, and American Baseball since 1921*. Chapel Hill, NC: University of North Carolina Press, 2001.

Caffin, Caroline. *Vaudeville*. New York: Mitchell Kennerley, 1914.

Cairncross, F. *The Death of Distance: How the Communications Revolution Will Change Our Lives*. Boston, MA: Harvard Business School Press, 1997.

Carpenter, Paul S. *Music, an Art and a Business*. Norman: University of Oklahoma Press, 1950.

Caves, Richard E. *Creative Industries: Contracts between Art and Commerce*.

Chapple, Steven and Reebee Garofalo. *Rock and Roll Is Here to Pay: The History and Politics of the Music Industry*. Chicago, IL: Nelson Hall, 1977.

Coase, Ronald. "The Economics of Broadcasting and Government Policy," *American Economic Review*, 56, May 1966.

Comstock, George. *The Evolution of American Television*. Newbury Park, UK: Sage Publications, 1989.

Conant, Michael. *Antitrust in the Motion Picture Industry*. Berkeley, CA: University of California Press, 1960.

Cooke, Andrew. *The Economics of Leisure and Sport*. London: Routledge, 1994.

Corio, Ann and Joseph DiNona. *This Was Burlesque*. New York: Grosset & Dunlap, 1968.

Corry, Catherine S. *The Phonograph Record Industry: An Economic Survey*. Washington, D.C.: Library of Congress Legislative Reference Service, 1965.

Csida, Joseph and June Bundy Csida. *American Entertainment: A Unique History of Popular Show Business*. New York: Watson-Guptill, 1978.

Curtis, James. *W. C. Fields, A Biography*. New York: Alfre A. Knopf, 2003.

Custen, George F. *Twentieth Century's Fox: Darryl F. Zanuck and the Culture of Hollywood*. New York: Basic Books, 1997.

Davis, Clive, with William Willwerth. *Clive: Inside the Record Business*. New York: Morrow, 1975.

Davis, Jeff. *Papa Bear: The Life and Legacy of George Halas.* New York: McGraw-Hill, 2005.

Day, J. *The Vanishing Vision: The Inside Story of Public Television.* Berkeley, CA: University of California Press, 1996.

De Long, Thomas A. *The Mighty Music Box: The Golden Age of Musical Radio.* Los Angeles: Amber Crest Books, 1980.

DeForest, Lee. *Father of Radio: The Autobiography of Lee DeForest.* Chicago, IL: Wilcox & Follet, 1950.

Denisoff, R. Sere. *Solid Gold: The Popular Record Industry.* New Brunswick, NJ: Transaction Books, 1975.

Dick, Bernard F. *Engulfed: The Death of Paramount Pictures and the Birth of Corporate Hollywood.* Lexington, KY: The University Press of Kentucky, 2001.

DiMeglio, John E. *Vaudeville U.S.A.* Bowling Green, OH: Bowling Green University Popular Press, 1973.

Douglas, George H. *The Early Days of Radio Broadcasting.* Jefferson, NC: McFarland Pub., 1987.

Douglas, Susan J. *Inventing American Broadcasting 1899–1922.* Baltimore, MD: Johns Hopkins University Press, 1987.

Dulles, Foster Rhea. *A History of Recreation: America Learns to Play.* New York: Appleton-Century-Crafts, 1965.

Dupagne, M. and P. Seel. *High-Definition Television: A Global Perspective.* Ames, IA: Iowa State University Press, 1998.

Edgerton, Gary R. and Peter C. Rollins, eds. *Television Histories.* Lexington, KY: University Press of Kentucky, 2001.

Edrman, Andrew L. *Blue Vaudeville: Sex, Morals and the Mass Marketing of Amusement, 1895–1915.* Jefferson, NC: McFarland and Co., Inc., 2004.

Eliot, Marc. *Rockonomics.* New York: Franklin Watts, 1989.

Epstein, Edward Jay. *The Big Picture.* New York: Random House, 2005.

Erickson, Don. *Armstrong's Fight for FM Broadcasting: One Man vs. Big Business and Bureaucracy.* University, AL: University of Alabama Press, 1973.

Eyman, Scott. *The Speed of Sound: Hollywood and the Talkie Revolution, 1926–1930.* Baltimore, MD: Johns Hopkins University Press, 1997.

Farnsworth, Marjorie. *The Ziegfeld Follies.* New York: G. P. Putnam's Sons, 1956.

Fulton, A. R. *Motion Pictures: The Development of an Art from Silent Pictures to the Age of Television.* Norman, OK: University of Oklahoma Press, 1960.

Gelatt, Roland. *The Fabulous Phonograph, 1877–1977.* New York: Macmillan, 1977.

Gelernter, David. *1939: The Lost World of the Fair.* New York: Avon Books, 1995.

George-Graves, Nadine. *The Royalty of Negro Vaudeville.* New York: St. Martin's Press, 2000.

Gilbert, Douglas. *American Vaudeville: Its Life and Times.* New York: McGraw-Hill, 1940.

Glick, Ira and Sidney Levy. *Living with Television*. Chicago: Aldine Pub. Co., 1962.

Godenson, L. and M. Wolf. *Beating the Odds: The Untold Story behind the Rise of ABC*. New York: Scribner's and Sons, 1991.

Goldberg, Isaac. *Tin Pan Alley: A Chronicle of American Popular Music*. New York: Frederick Ungar, 1970.

Gomery, Douglas. "Problems in Film History: How Fox Innovated Sound," *Quarterly Review of Film Studies*, August 1976.

Gomery, J. Douglas. "Writing the History of the American Film Industry: Warner Brothers and Sound," *Screen*, 17(1), 1976.

Gomery, Douglas. "Rethinking U.S. Film History: The Depression Decade and Monopoly Control," *Film and History*, 10(2), 1980.

Green, Abel and Joe Laurie, Jr. *Show Biz: From Vaude to Video*. Garden City, NY: Permabooks, 1953.

Halberstam, David. *The Powers That Be*. New York: Alfred A. Knopf, 1979.

Haupert, Michael. "Economic History of Sports," in *The Oxford Encyclopedia of Economic History*, edited by Joel Mokyr New York: Oxford University Press, 2003.

Haupert, Michael. "The Economic History of Major League Baseball," in *EH.Net Encyclopedia*, edited by Robert Whaples. August 27, 2003. http://eh.net/encyclopedia/article/haupert.mlb.

Heilbrun, James and Charles M. Gray. *The Economics of Art and Culture*. New York: Cambridge University Press, 2001.

Hilliard, Robert L. and Michael C. Keith. *The Broadcast Century*. Boston, MA: Focal Press, 1992.

Hughes, Jonathan R. T. *The Vital Few*. New York: Oxford University Press, 1986.

Isaacs, Edith J. R. *The Negro in the American Theater*. New York: Theater Arts, Inc., 1947.

Keating, S. *Cutthroat: High Stakes and Killer Moves on the Electronic Frontier*. Boulder, CO: Honson Books, 1999.

Kotler, P. and J. M. Scheff. *Standing Room Only*. HBR Press, 1997.

Laurie, Joe. *Vaudeville: From the Honky Tonks to the Palace*. New York: Henry Holt & Co., 1953.

Leavitt, M. B. *Fifty Years in Theatrical Management*. New York: Broadway Publishing Co., 1912.

Levine, Faye. *The Culture Barons: An Analysis of Power and Money in the Arts*. New York: Crowell, 1976.

Lewis, Tom. *Empire of the Air: The Men Who Made Radio*. New York: Harper Collins, 1991.

Lowe, Janet. *Ted Turner Speaks: Insights from the World's Greatest Maverick*. New York: Wiley, 1999.

Lyons, Eugene. *David Sarnoff*. New York: Harper and Row, 1966.

Matlaw, Myron, ed. *American Popular Entertainment: Papers and Proceedings of the Conference on the History of American Popular Entertainment*. Westport, CT: Greenwood Press, 1977.

McChesney, R. W. *Telecommunications, Mass Media, and Democracy: The Battle for the Control of U.S. Broadcasting, 1928–1935.* New York: Oxford University Press, 1993.

McClellan, Keith. *The Sunday Game: At the Dawn of Professional Football.* Akron, OH: The University of Akron Press, 1998.

McLean, Albert F., Jr. *American Vaudeville as Ritual.* Lexington, KY: University of Kentucky Press, 1965.

Millard, Andre. *America on Record: A History of Recorded Sound.* New York: Cambridge University Press, 1995.

Miller, I. "Models for Determining the Economic Value of Cable Television Systems," *Journal of Media Economics*, 10(2), 1997.

Morell, Parker. *Lillian Russell: The Era of Plush.* New York: Random House, 1940.

Moul, Charles C., ed. *A Concise Handbook of Movie Industry Economics.* New York: Cambridge University Press, 2005.

Poggi, Jack. *Theater in America: The Impact of Economic Forces, 1870–1967.* Ithaca, NY: Cornell University Press, 1968.

Pratt, George. "No Magic, No Mystery, No Sleight of Hand," *Image*, 8, December 1959, 192–211.

Read, Oliver and Walter L. Welch. *From Tin Foil to Stereo: Evolution of the Phonograph.* Indianapolis, IN: Howard W. Sams & Company, 1959 and 1976.

Riess, Steven A. *The American Sporting Experience: A Historical Anthology of Sport in America.* Champaign, IL: Leisure Press, 1984.

Riess, Steven A. *City Games: The Evolution of American Urban Society and the Rise of Sports.* Urbana, IL: University of Illinois Press, 1989.

Robinson, John P. and Geoffrey Godbey. *Time for Life: The Surprising Ways Americans Use Their Time.* University Park, PA: Pennsylvania State University Press, 1997.

Rubin, Rachel and Jeffrey Melnick, eds. *American Popular Music.* Amherst, MA: University of Massachusetts Press, 2001.

Sammons, Jeffrey T. *Beyond the Ring: The Role of Boxing in American Society.* Urbana, IL: University of Illinois Press, 1988.

Sanjek, Russel. *Pennies from Heaven: The American Popular Music Business in the Twentieth Century.* New York: Da Capo Press, 1996.

Schenone, Laura. *A Thousand Years over a Hot Stove.* New York: W. W. Norton & Company, 2003.

Schicke, C. A. *Revoultion in Sound: A Biography of the Recording Industry.* Boston, MA: Little, Brown and Company, 1974.

Schwartz, Evan I. *The Last Lone Inventor.* New York: Harper Collins, 2002.

Scott, Allen J. *On Hollywood: The Place, The Industry.* Princeton, NJ: Princeton University Press, 2005.

Sedgewick, John. "Product Differentiation at the Movies: Hollywood, 1946 to 1965," *Journal of Economic History*, 62(3), Fall 2002.

Smith, Bill. *TheVaudevillians.* New York: Macmillan Publishing Co., 1976.

Smith, Sally Bedell. *In All His Glory: The Life and Times of William S. Palye and the Birth of Modern Broadcasting.* New York: Simon and Schuster, 1990.

Snyder, Robert W. *The Voice of the City.* Chicago, IL: Ivan R. Dee, 2000.

Sobel, Robert. *RCA.* New York: Stein and Day, 1984.

Spitzer, Marian. *The Palace.* New York: Atheneum, 1969.

Stein, Charles W., ed. *American Vaudeville as Seen by its Contemporaries.* New York: Alfred A. Knopf, 1984.

Taubman, Howard. *The Making of the American Theater.* New York: Coward-McCann, Inc., 1965.

Toll, Robert. *On with the Show! The First Century of Show Business in America.* New York: Oxford University Press, 1976.

Towse, Ruth, ed. *Cultural Economics: The Arts, the Heritage and the Media Industries*, Vol. 1, Cheltenham, UK: Edward Elgar, 1997.

Tygiel, Jules. *Baseball's Great Experiment: Jackie Robinson and His Legacy.* New York:Vintage Books, 1983.

Udelson, J. H. *The Great Television Race: A History of the American Television Industry, 1925–1941.* Tuscaloosa, AL: University of Alabama, 1982.

Vogel, Harold L. *Entertainment Industry Economics*, 5th edn. New York: Cambridge.

Whitfield, Eileen. *Pickford: The Woman Who Made Hollywood.* New York: Faber and Faber, Inc., 2000.

Wilk, Max. *Memory Lane, 1890–1925: The Golden Age in American Popular Music.* New York: Ballantine, 1973.

Wilk, Max. *The Golden Age of Television.* New York: Delacorte Press, 1976.

Zimbalist, Andrew. *Baseball and Billions.* New York: Basic Books, 1992.

Index

About the Author

MICHAEL HAUPERT is Professor of Economics at the University of Wisconsin—LaCrosse.